Teacher's Anno

HOUGHTON MIFFLIN math CENTRAL

My Math Activity Book

Level K

HOUGHTON MIFFLIN

Boston • Atlanta • Dallas • Denver • Geneva, Illinois • Palo Alto • Princeton

Dear Math Central Teacher,

The *Math Central* activity workbook provides children with the opportunity to step up to the next development level — from the concrete or pictorial level to the pictorial or symbolic level. The pages target the skill listed in the focus of the activity. Frequently, questions are asked that require children to explain their thinking or to write problems of their own.

Some workbook pages are to be used with the ongoing Calendar Time Elements. Other workbook pages are used after the children have had opportunities to experience the Investigations and Partner Games. **Each of these pages is intended to be used only after a student has developed a strong understanding of the skill or concept.**

At the end of each month there is a review page to evaluate children's understandings. Four times a year, a spot check is included on this page. Spot Checks review previously learned skills and provide a way for you to see that those skills are maintained.

You will find numerals on pages 167 through 172 for the children to practice writing. These numerals may be used at any time throughout the year, and we give you permission to copy these particular pages to use as often as you find necessary for each child.

Remember that communication is the heart of *Math Central.* Whether it's the questions posed on the workbook pages or the questions you ask while observing the children, questioning is an extremely important tool in evaluating the depth of their understanding of the concepts being constructed in each month.

COVER CREDITS
© Larry Lefever/Grant Heilman Photography (background garden)
© Ray Juno/The Stock Market (background sky)
Allan Landau Photography (front figure, screen inset)
Image Copyright © 1996 PhotoDisc, Inc. (inset)

Printed in U.S.A.

ISBN: 0-395-92070-1

123456789-PO-04 03 02 01 00 99 98

CONTENTS

Name ____________________

Color Recognition

Children color the frogs green. Then they color the monkeys brown.

August/September: Use when children are familiar with the *Counting Tape*.

Color Matching

Children color one pair of matching boots red. Then they color another pair blue and the other pair yellow.

Name ____________________

Before, Between, and After

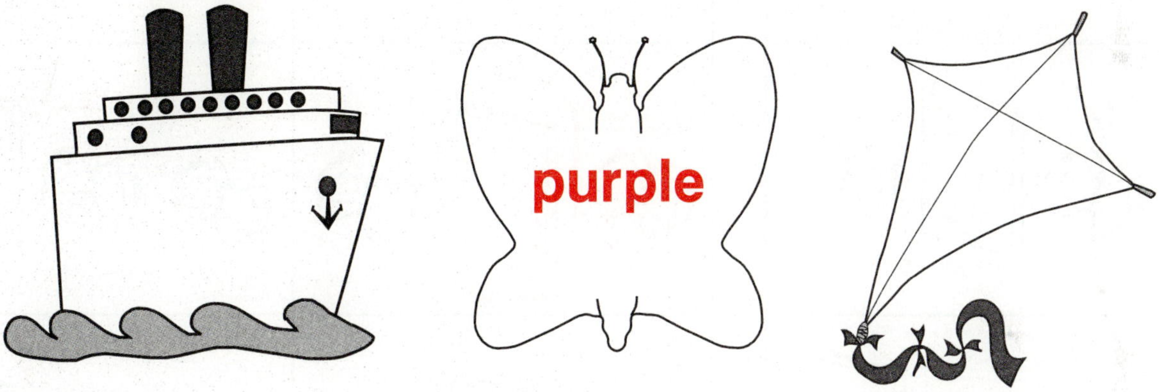

Turtle: Children color the apple red. Then they color the object **before** the apple brown. **Frog:** Children color the object **between** the ship and the kite purple. **Fish:** Children color the flower yellow. Then they color the object **after** the flower green.

Same Position

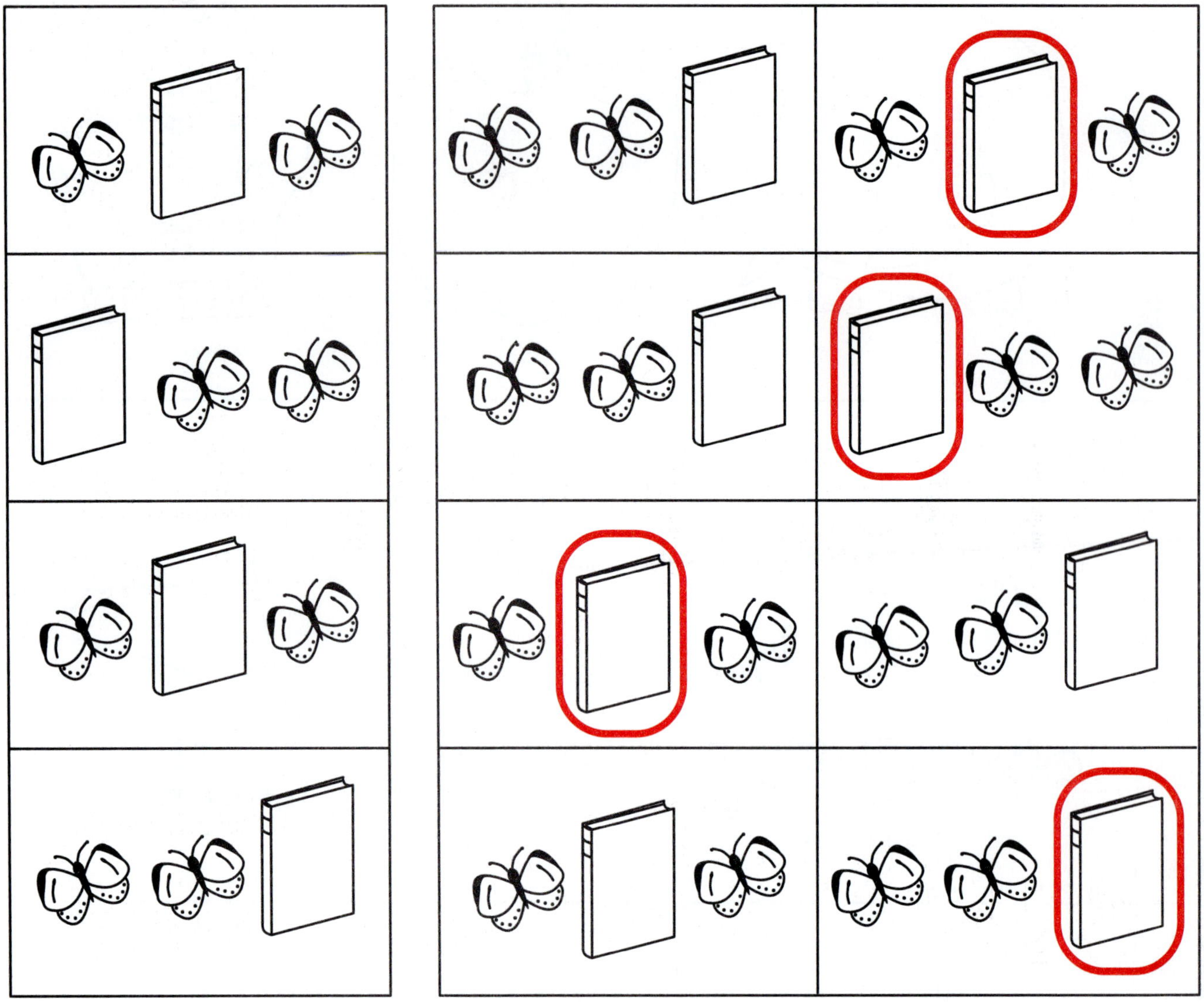

Discuss whether each book comes **before, between,** or **after.** Then children circle the picture of the book that is in the same position as the book in the first picture in each row.

Name ______________________________

Same Number

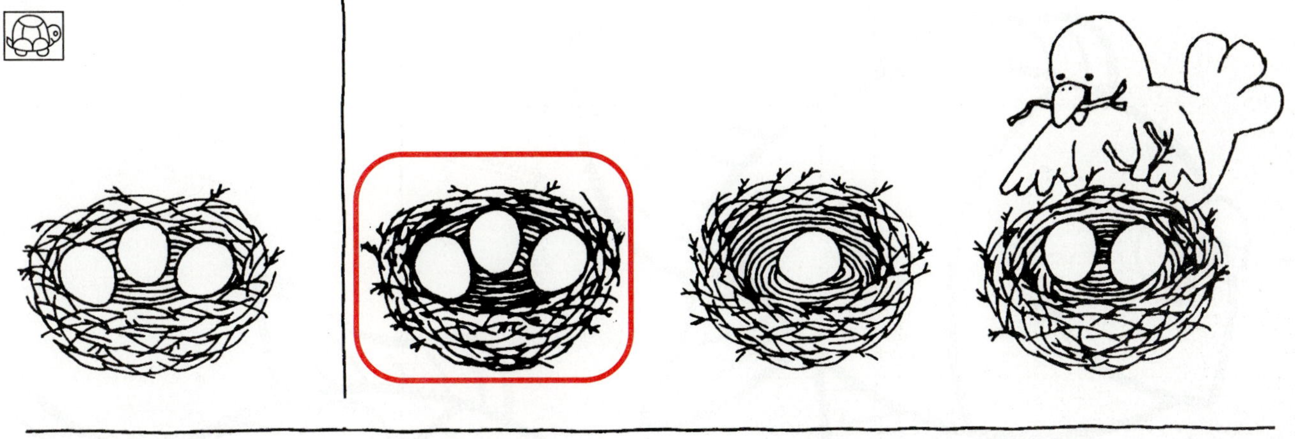

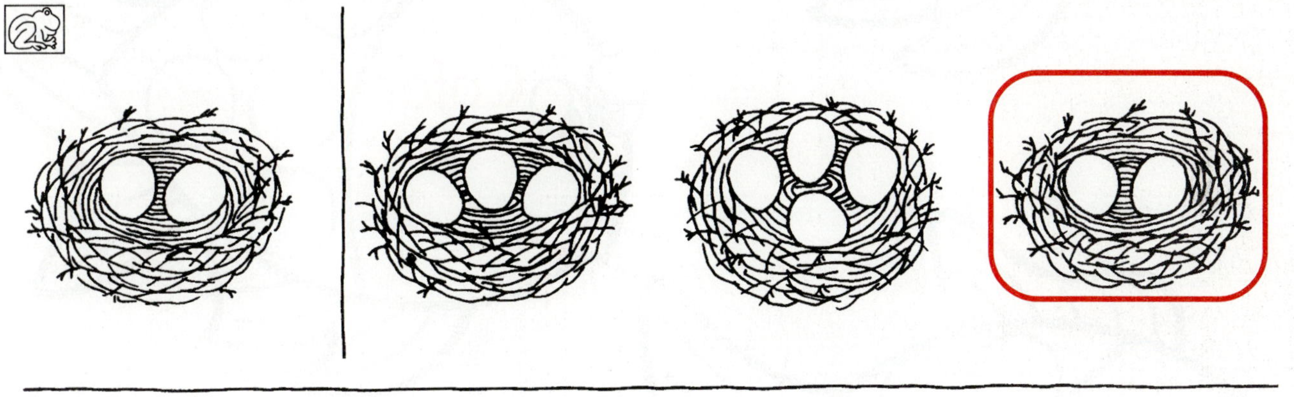

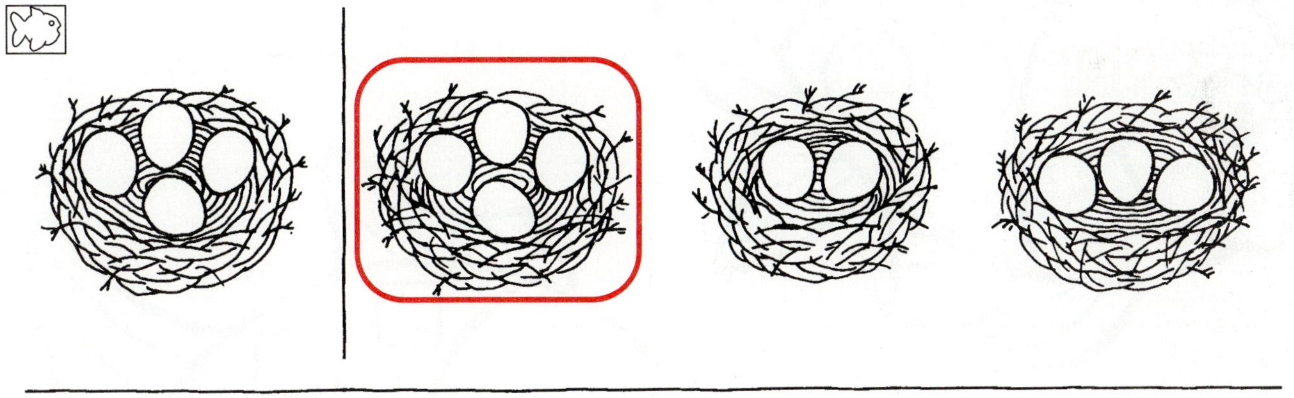

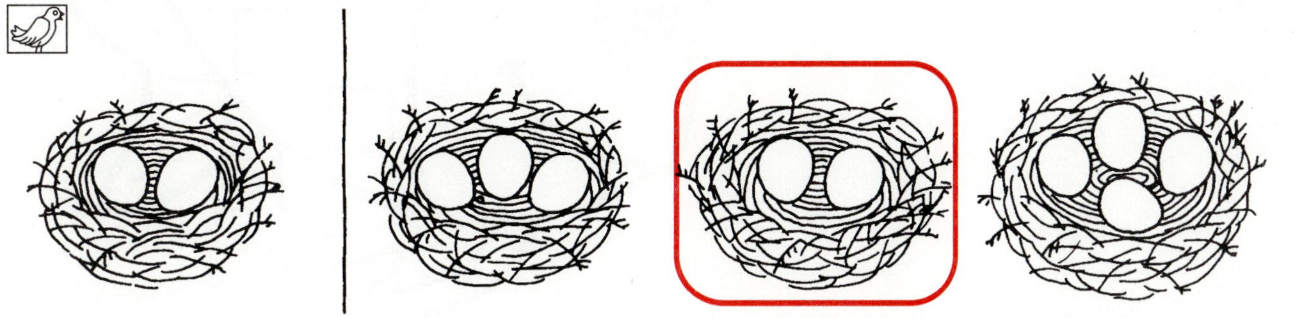

Children circle the nest that has the same number of eggs as the nest in the first picture in each row.

Sort the Shapes

Children color the two fish that are the same. Then they explain their reasoning.

Name ______________________________

Match and Color

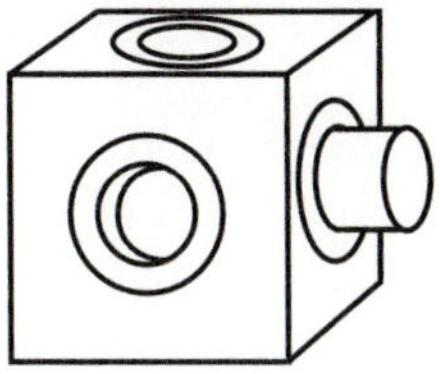

Colors will vary.

1

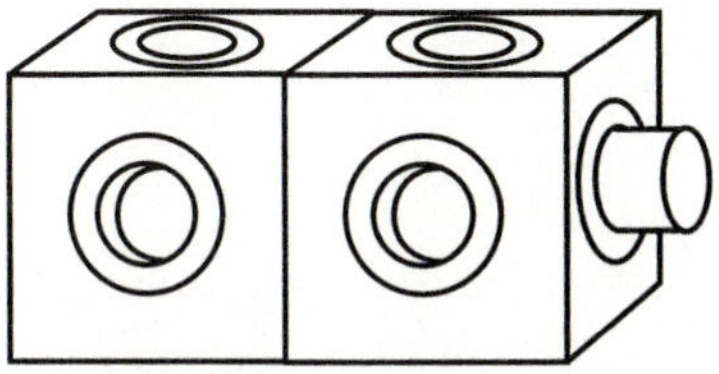

2

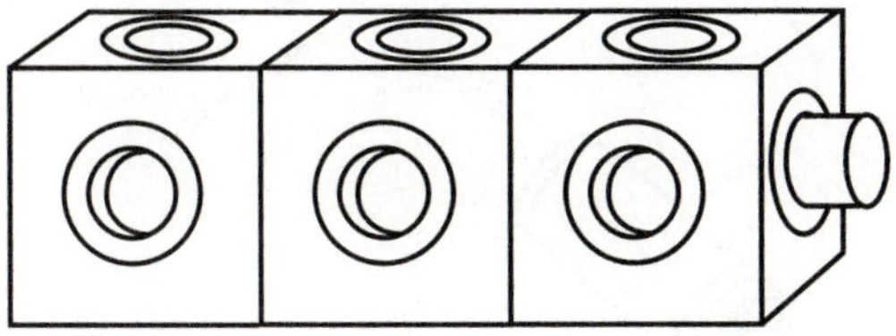

3

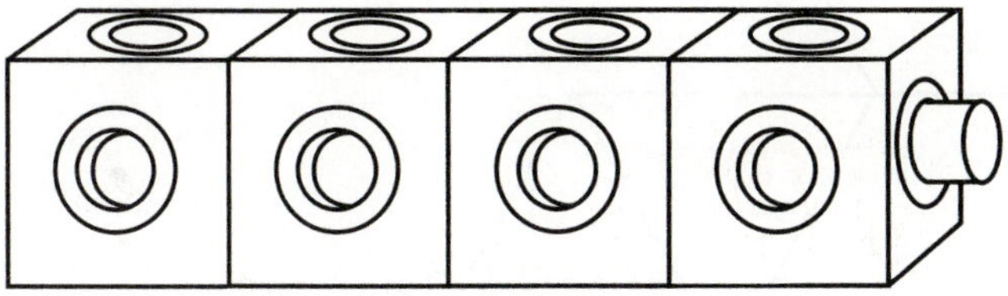

4

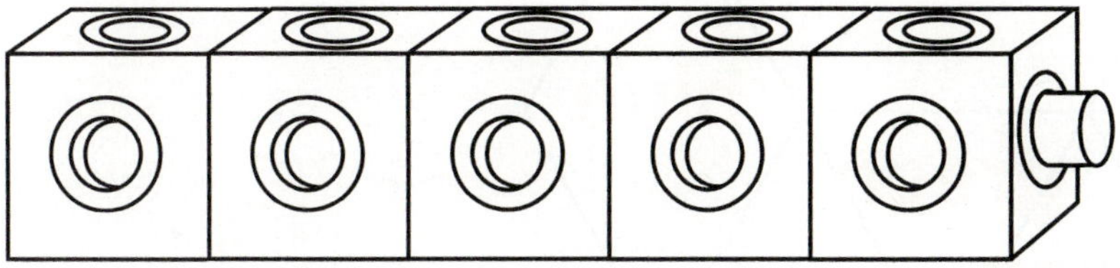

5

Children make cube trains to match. Then children color their trains and trace the corresponding number.

August/September: Use when children are familiar with *Connecting Cubes.*

Pattern Block Designs

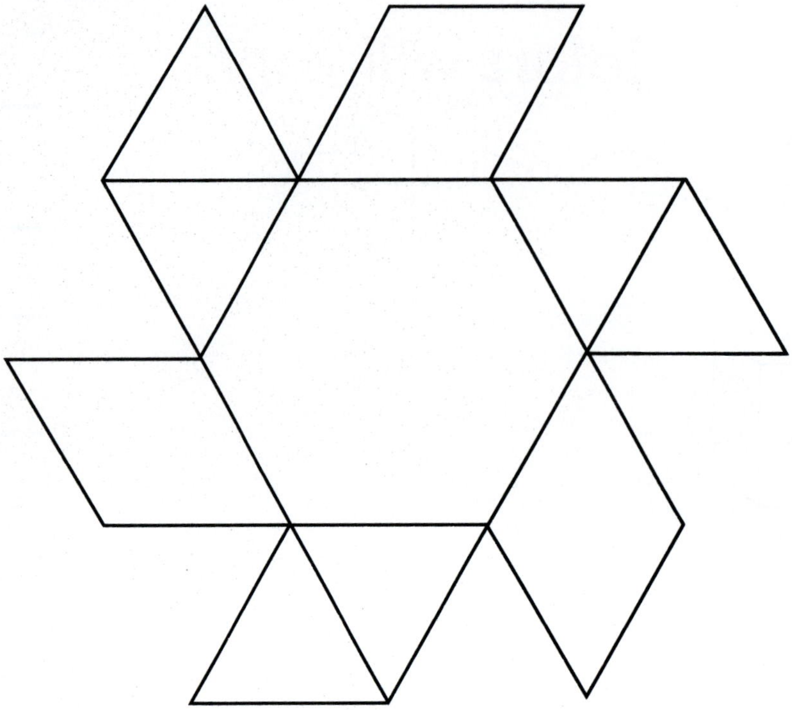

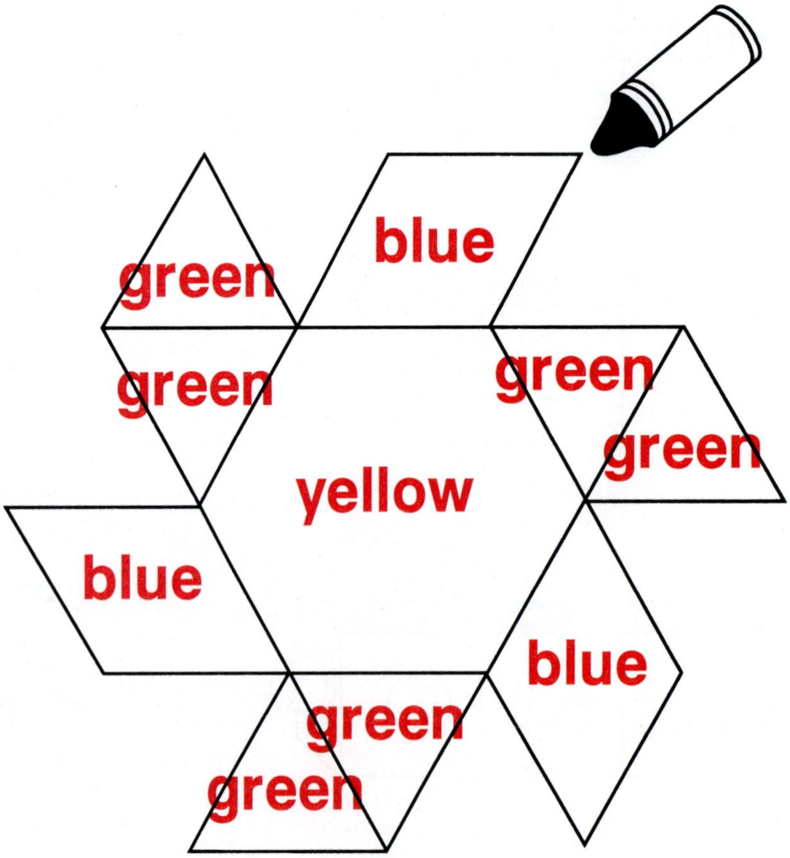

Children place corresponding pattern blocks on the top design and then color the bottom design to match. They tell why they put the blocks where they did.

Name ______________________________

Bead Patterns

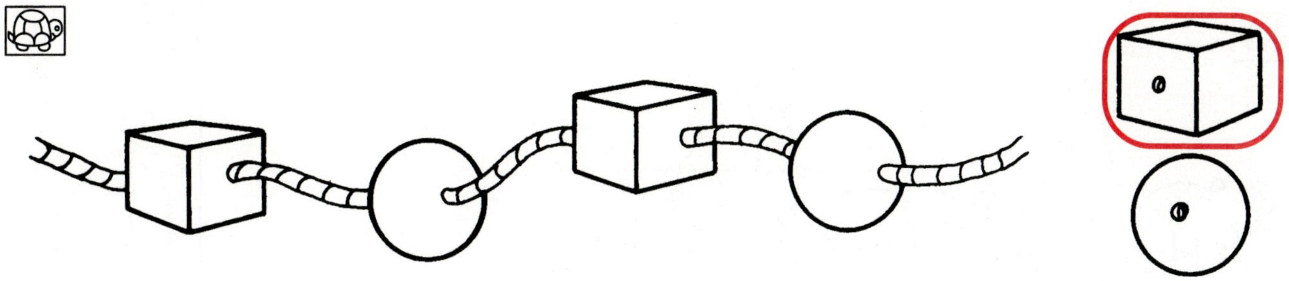

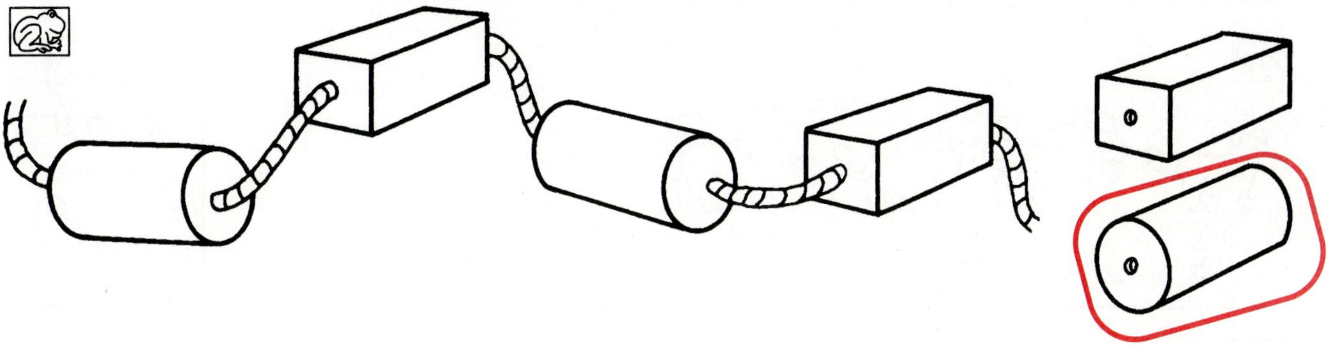

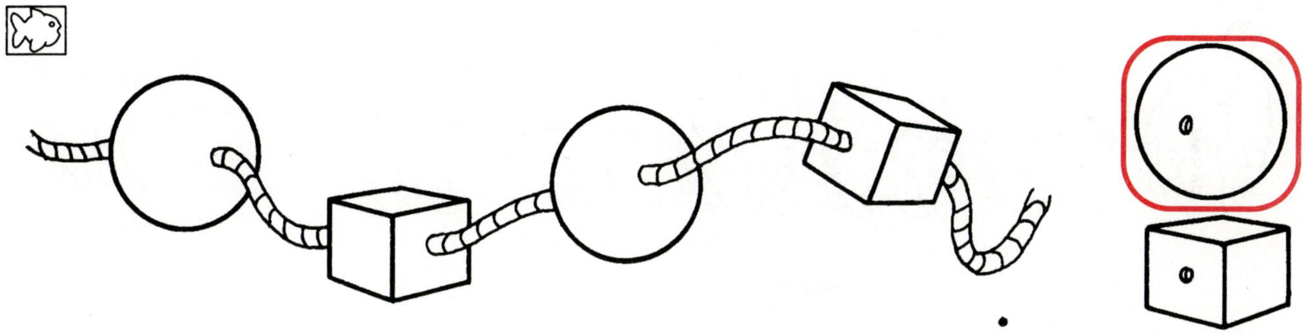

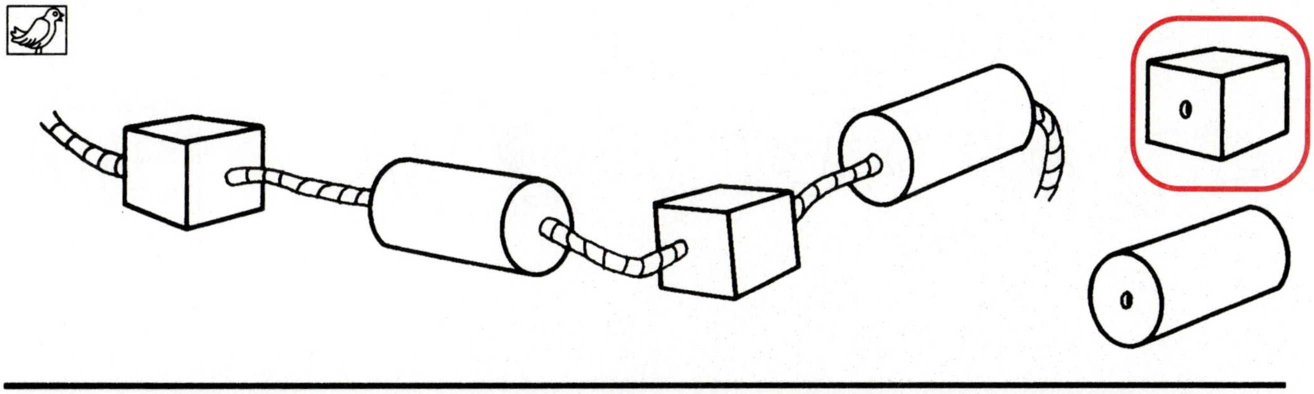

Together, name the beads in order and then have children circle the bead that comes next in each row.

August/September: Use when children are familiar with *Connecting Cubes*.

Animal Patterns

Together, name the animals in order and then have children circle the animal that comes next in each row.

Name ______________________________

Fill in the Dots

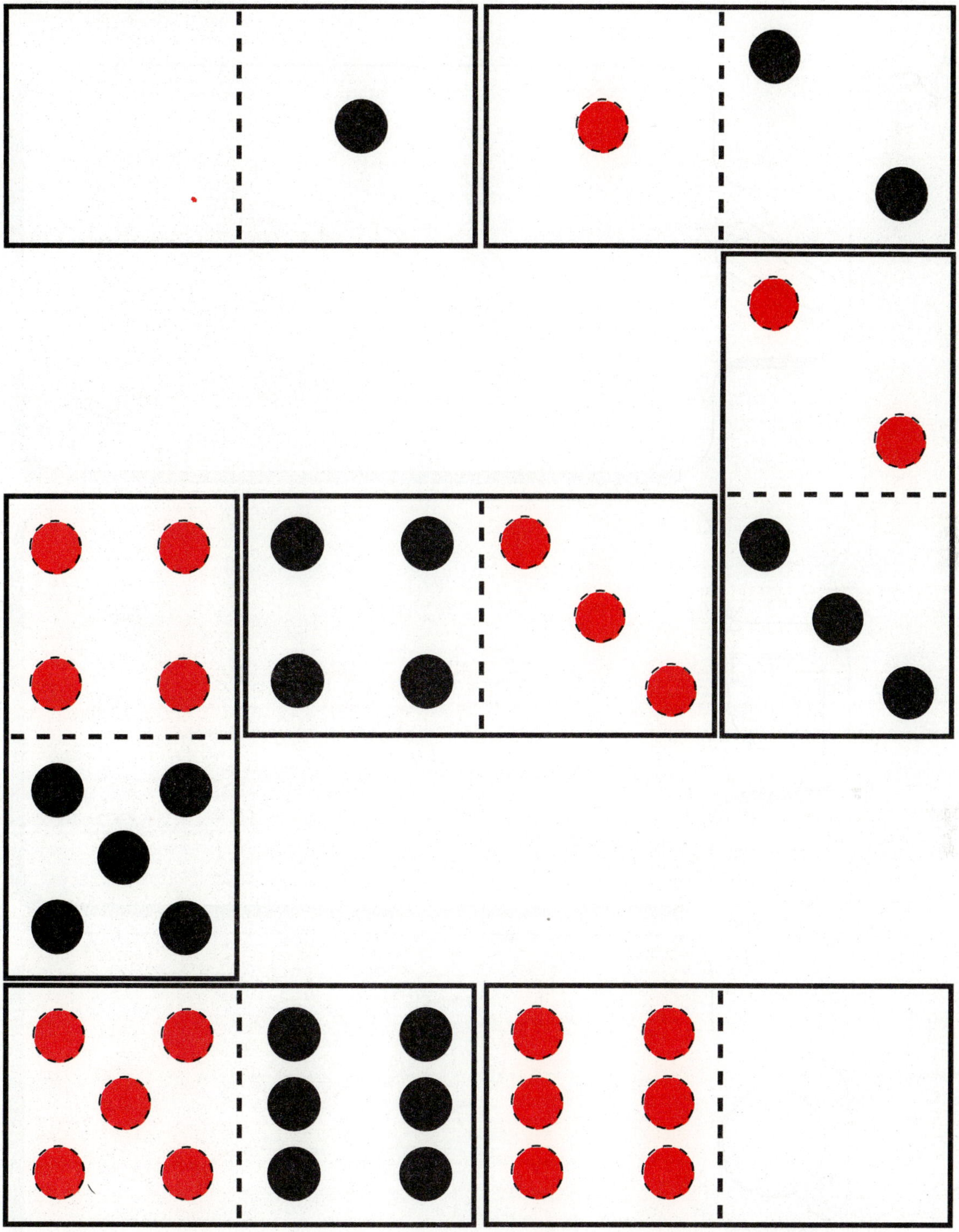

Children color the dots on the dominoes. When completed, ask children to name each domino half and point to its matching domino half.

August/September: Use when children are familiar with *Dominoes.*

Sort the Objects

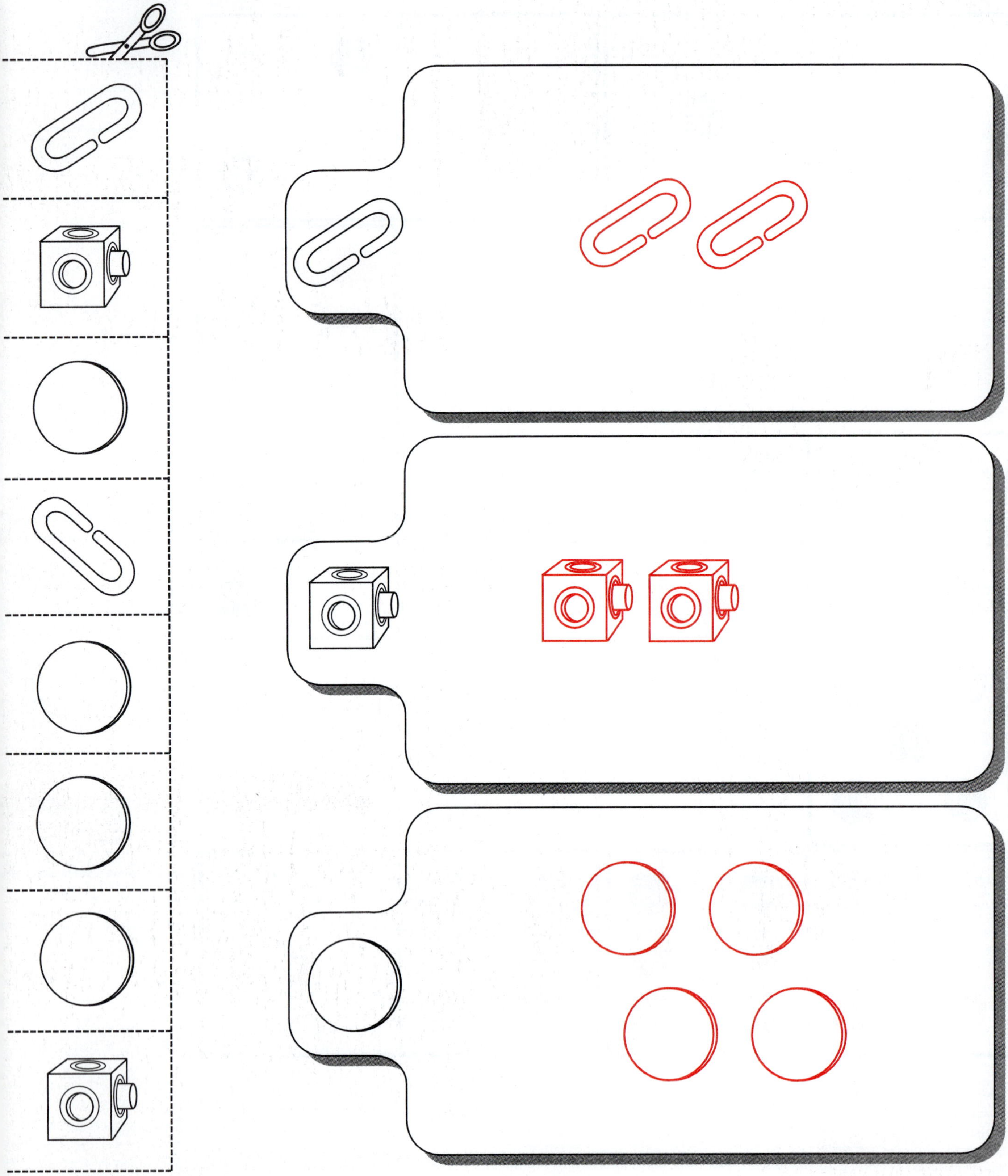

Children cut out the objects, sort them, and then paste them in the appropriate space. Children can also use real clips, cubes, and counters for this activity.

Name ______________________________

One-to-One

Answers will vary, but children should draw a hat on each head.

Turtle: Children draw lines to match each hat to a head. **Frog:** Children draw a hat on each head. Children can put a counter on each hat and then slide each counter down to the appropriate head.

Review/Test

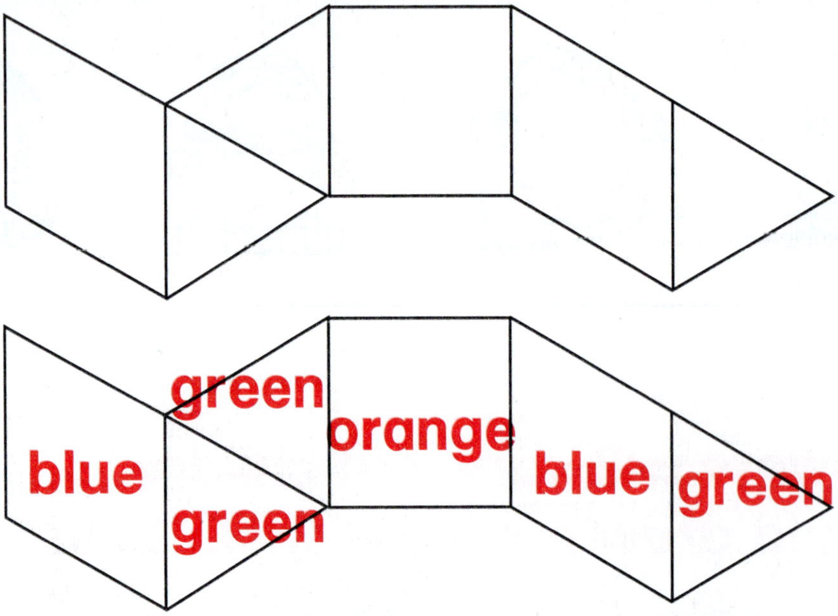

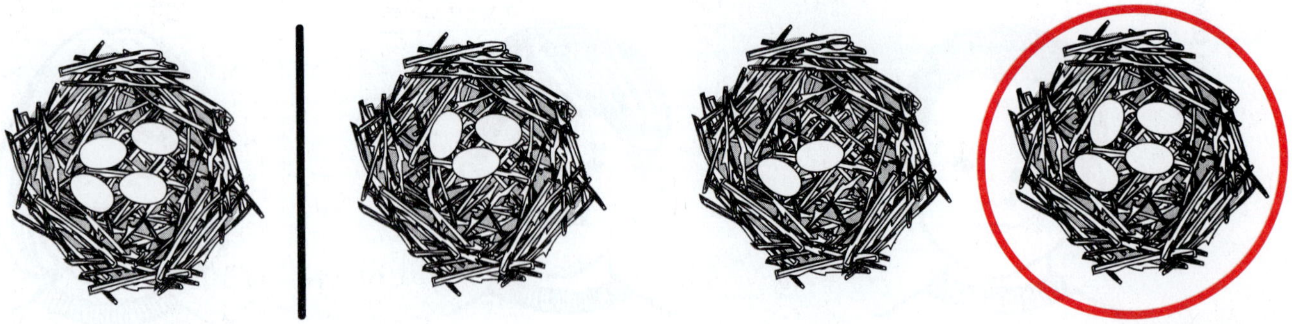

Turtle: Children color the object **after** the flower blue; the object **before** the flower orange. **Frog:** Children place corresponding pattern blocks on the top design. Children color the bottom design to match. **Fish:** Children circle the nest that has the same number of eggs as the nest in the first picture.

Remember!
- Understand
- Plan
- Try it
- **Look back**

October

Sunday	Monday	Tuesday	Wednesday	Thursday	Friday	Saturday
				1	2	3
4	5	6	7	8	9	10
11	12	13	14	15	16	17
18	19	20	21	22	23	24
25	26	27	28	29	30	31

➤ **Look back** Children check the pattern on the calendar and the shapes they drew. They decide if their answers make sense. Possible answer: The other days show three squares, then one circle, so my answer makes sense.

4

FOLD

Name ______________________

My Problem Solving Book

Strategy: Look for a Pattern

Remember!
- **Understand**
- Plan
- Try it
- Look back

October

Sunday	Monday	Tuesday	Wednesday	Thursday	Friday	Saturday
				1	2	3
4	5	6	7	8	9	10
11	12	13	14	15	16	17
18	19	20	21	22	23	24
25	26	27	28	29	30	31

➤ **Understand** Children talk about what they need to find to continue the pattern on the calendar. Ask, "What comes next?"

1

Remember!
- Understand
- **Plan**
- Try it
- Look back

October

Sunday	Monday	Tuesday	Wednesday	Thursday	Friday	Saturday
				1	2	3
4	5	6	7	8	9	10
11	12	13	14	15	16	17
18	19	20	21	22	23	24
25	26	27	28	29	30	31

➤ **Plan** Children explain how they can tell what shape comes next.

❷

Remember!
- Understand
- Plan
- **Try it**
- Look back

Possible answer: I see three squares, then a circle. So after the last three squares, there should be another circle.

➤ **Try it** Children decide what shape should come next and draw it.

❸

Name ____________________

Place in Line

Children color hats according to the directions for each row. **Turtle:** Color the first musician's hat blue. **Frog:** Color the third musician's hat orange. **Fish:** Color the fourth musician's hat red. **Bird:** Color the second musician's hat green.

October: Use when children are familiar with the *Calendar.*

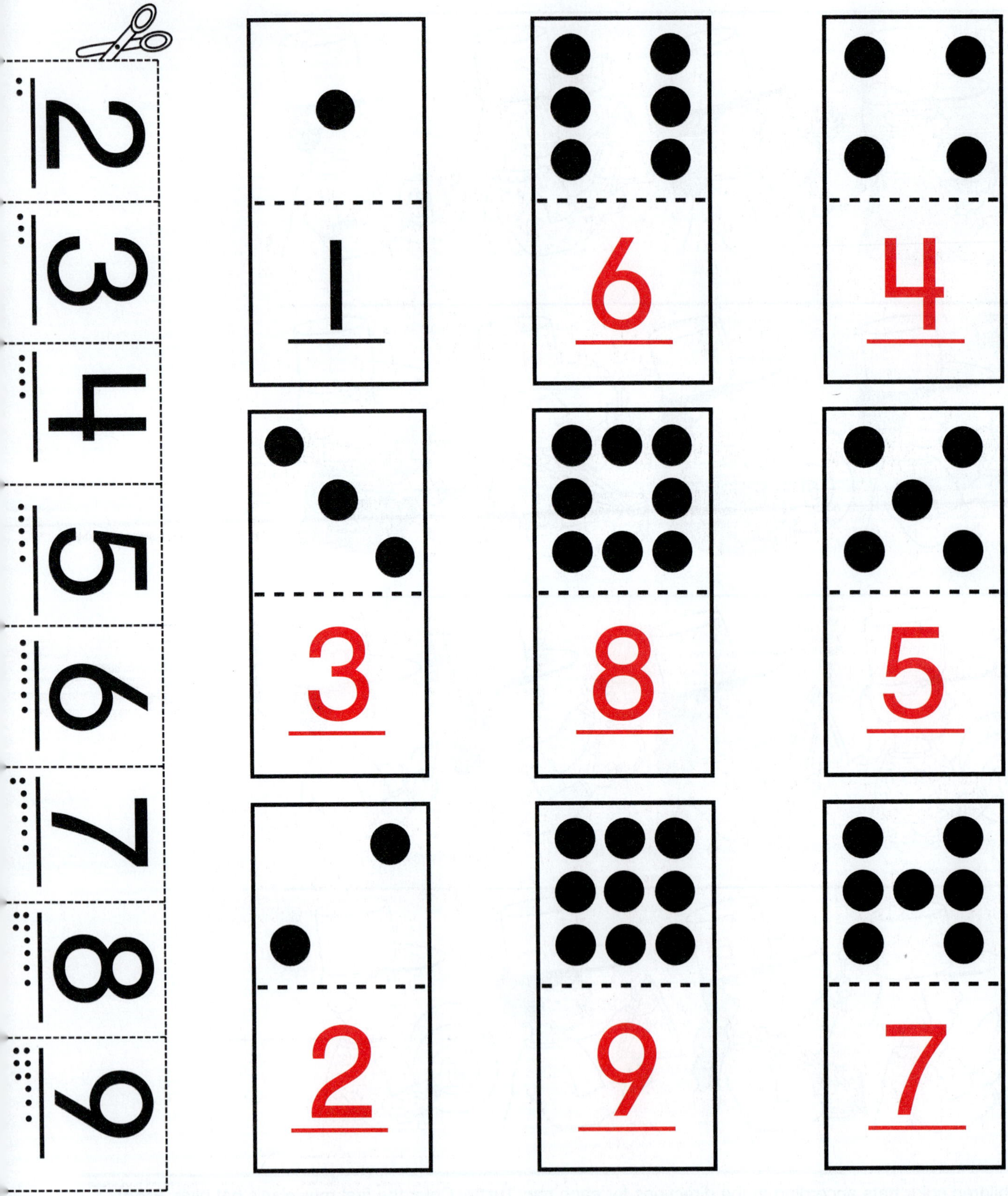

Children cut out numeral dot cards and paste each one under the dots on the domino that shows that number.

Name ______________________________

Graph the Presents

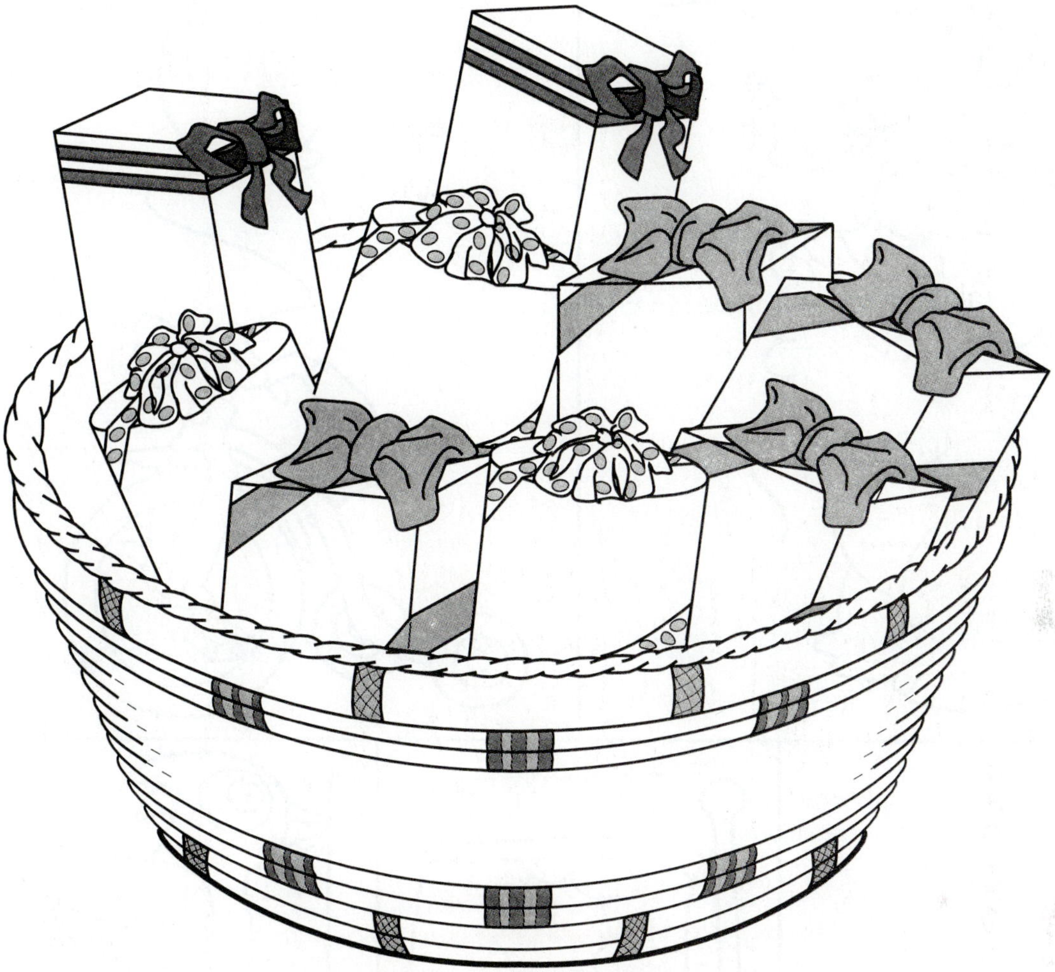

How Many Presents?

Children color the appropriate box in the graph for each present. You may want children to cross out the presents in the basket as they record them on the graph.

October: Use when children are familiar with the *Graph.*

Which Is Above?

Children color the object or animal in each picture that is **above.**

Name ______________________________

Which Is Below?

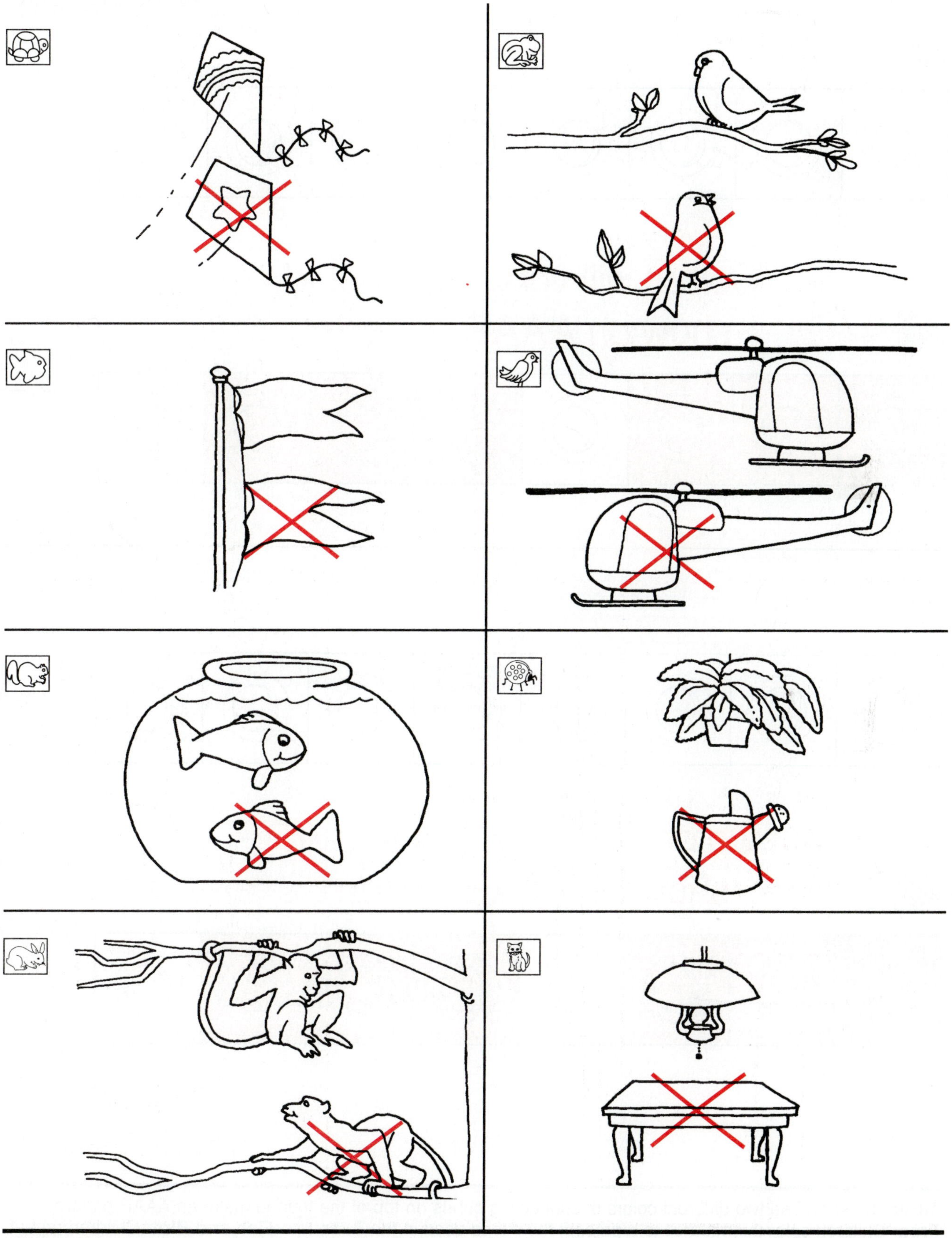

Children mark an X on the object or animal in each picture that is **below.** Then they describe the relative positions of the objects.

October: Use when children are familiar with *What Is It?*

Pattern Trains

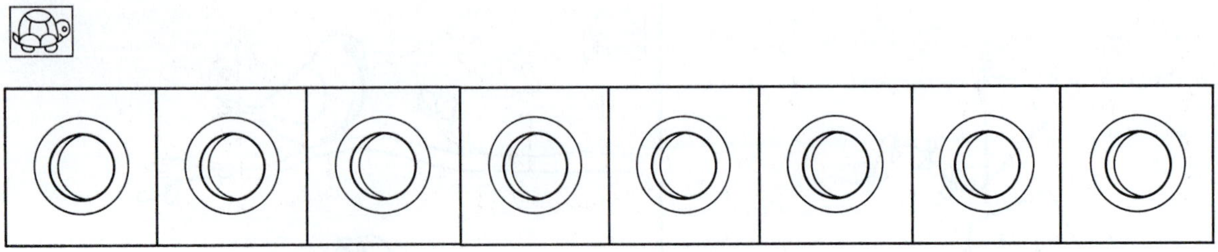

Colors will vary, but should show an AAAB pattern.

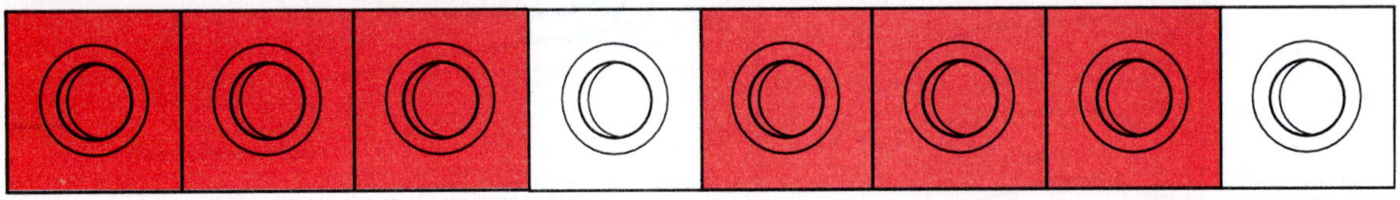

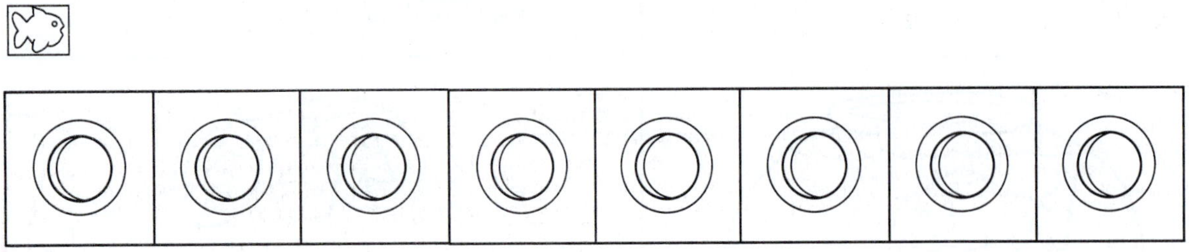

Colors will vary, but should show an AAAB pattern.

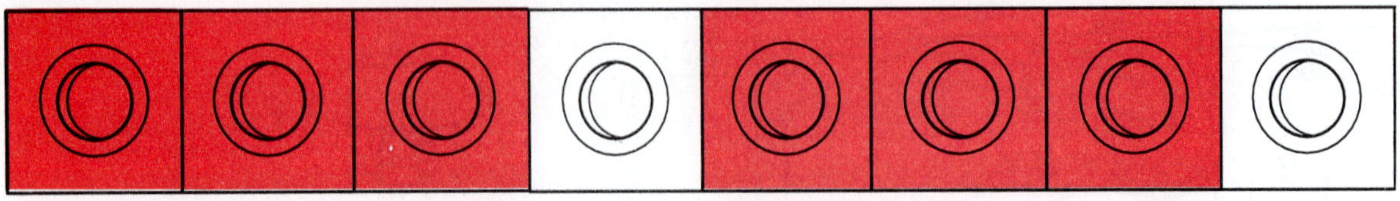

Turtle: Children use two different colors of connecting cubes on top of the train to make an AAAB pattern. **Frog:** Children color the squares to represent the cubes used in the Turtle row. **Fish and Bird:** Children repeat the steps above using two different colors of cubes.

Name ____

Groups to 4

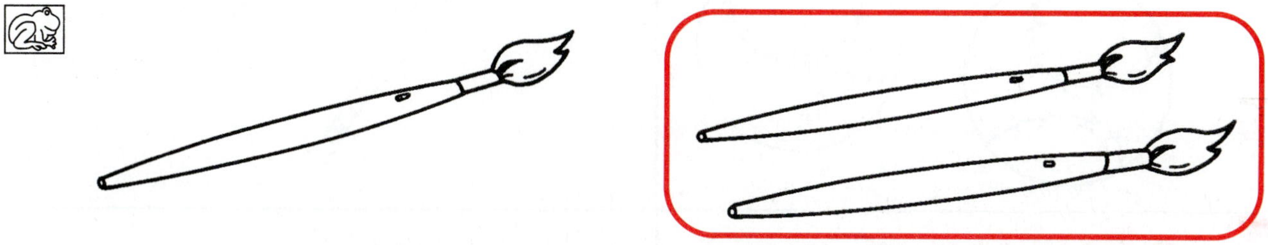

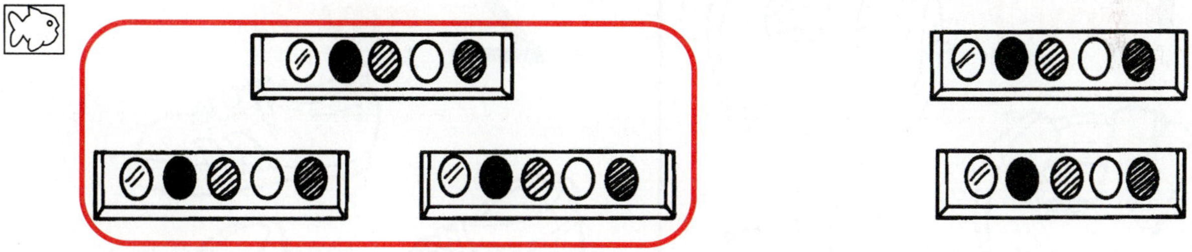

Turtle: Children circle a group of 1. **Frog:** Children circle a group of 2. **Fish:** Children circle a group of 3. **Bird and Squirrel:** Children circle a group of 4. Children may model the situations using counters or other objects.

October: Use when children are familiar with *Collect Ten.*

Color the Number Groups

2

Color any 2.

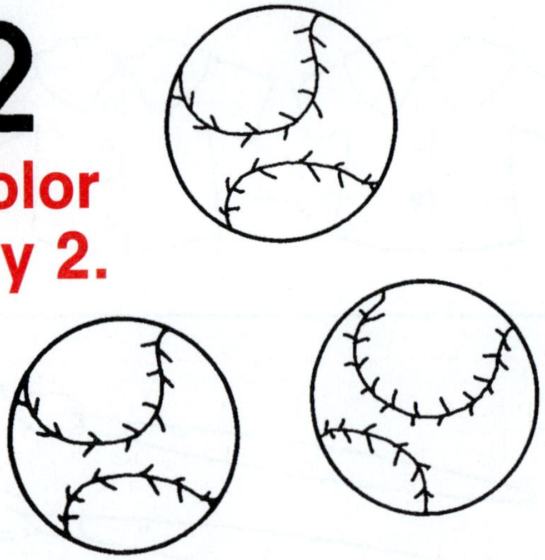

3

Color all 3.

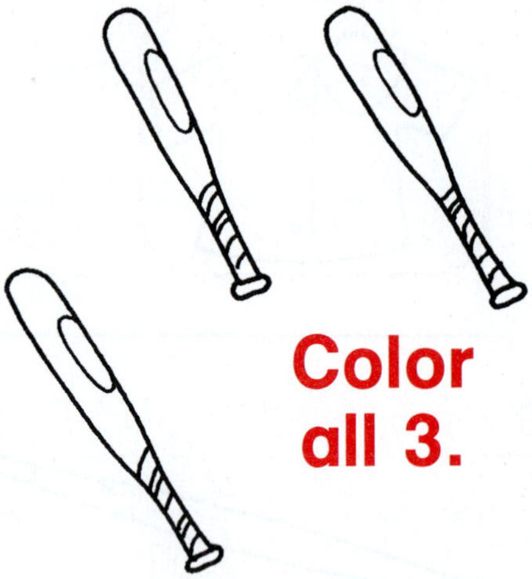

1 Color any 1.

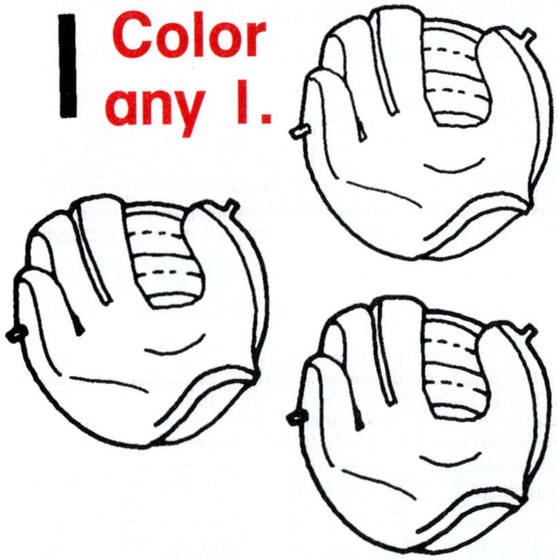

2 Color any 2.

Color all 3. 3

2 Color any 2.

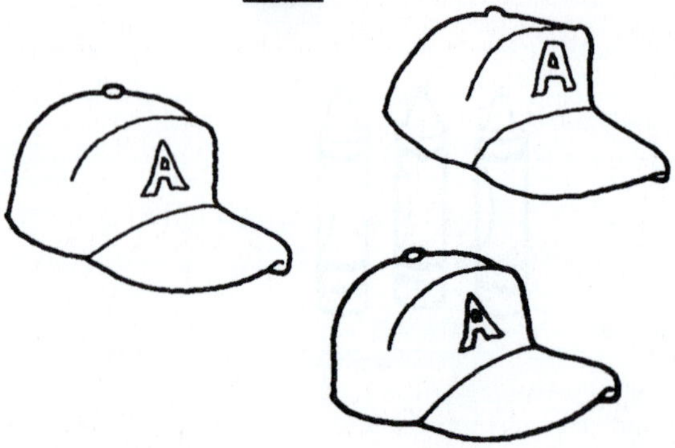

Children look at the number, count out that many counters, and place them on the appropriate number of objects. They remove the counters, one at a time, and color the objects.

Name ______________________________

Groups to 5

1
2
3
4
5

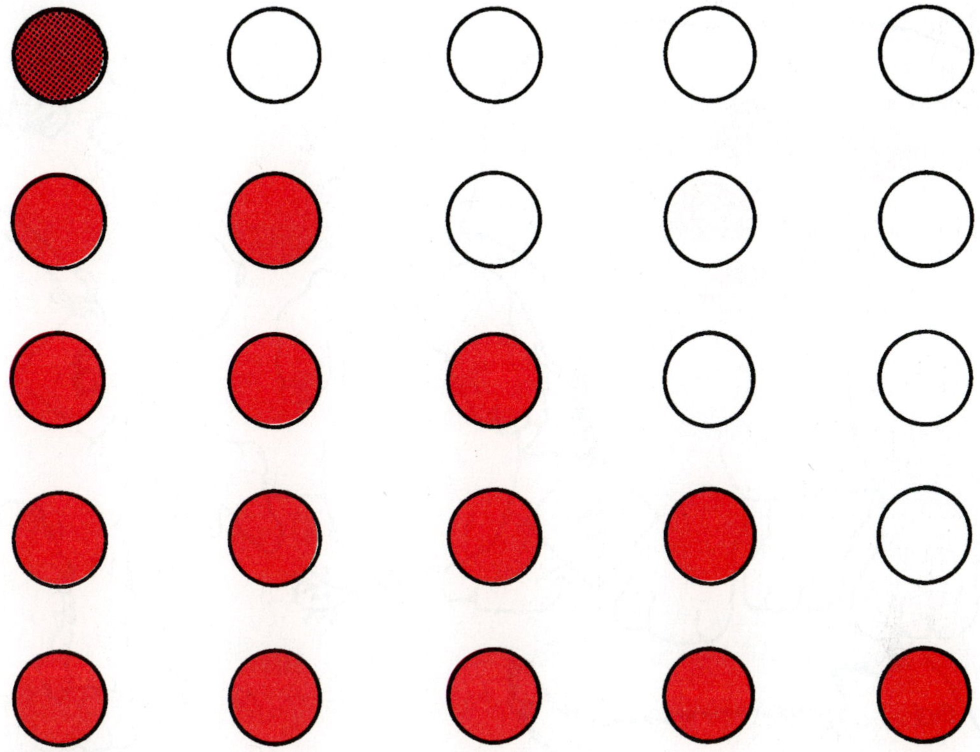

1
2
3
4
5

Children color as many objects in each row as indicated by the number at the beginning of the row. They can place counters on each picture to help them count.

October: Use when children are familiar with *Quick As You Can.*

Show the Numbers

Children place as many counters on each dog as indicated by the number on the dog's tag. They remove the counters and color that many spots.

Name ____________________

On the Left

Children color the object or animal that is on the **left** in each picture.

October: Use when children are familiar with *Left-Right Tug.*

Left or Right?

left

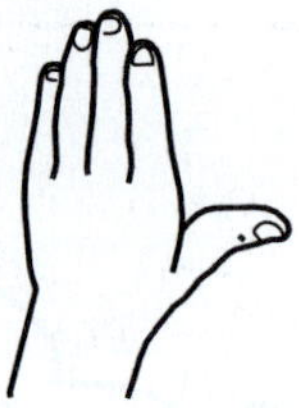

right

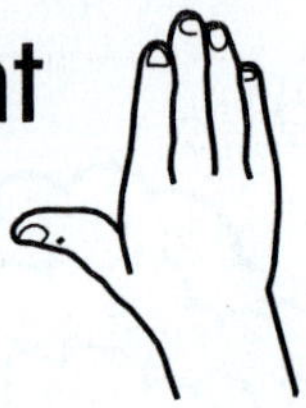

Have children identify the cutouts. Children cut and paste vehicles that go in the water on the left and vehicles that go in the air on the right.

Name ______________________________

Sorting Left and Right

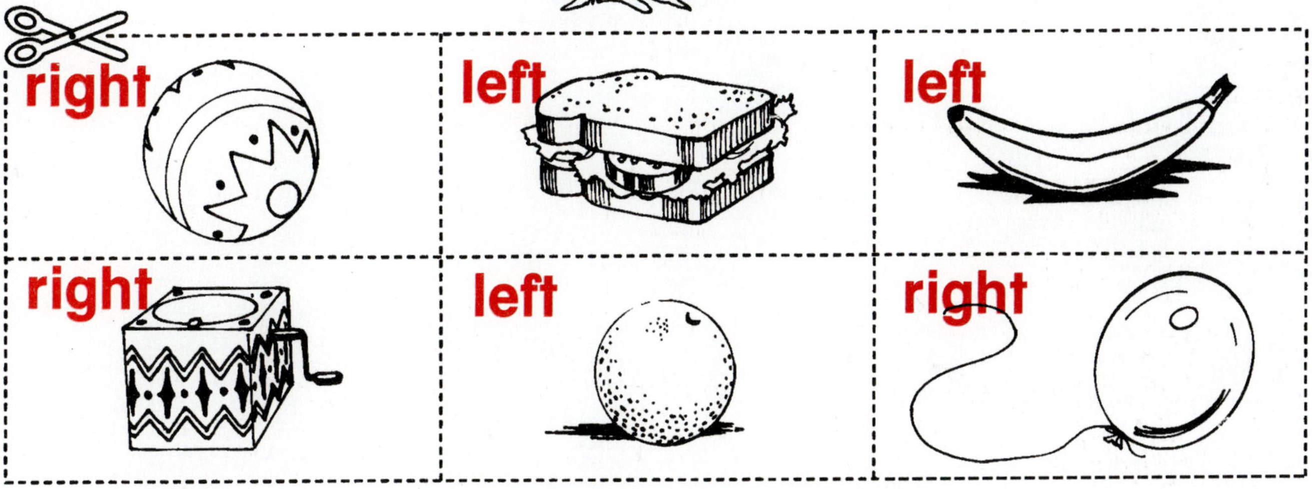

Have children identify the cutouts. Children cut and paste pictures of food on the left side of the tree and pictures of toys on the right side of the tree.

October: Use when children are familiar with *Left-Right Tug.*

Name ______________________________

One-to-One Match

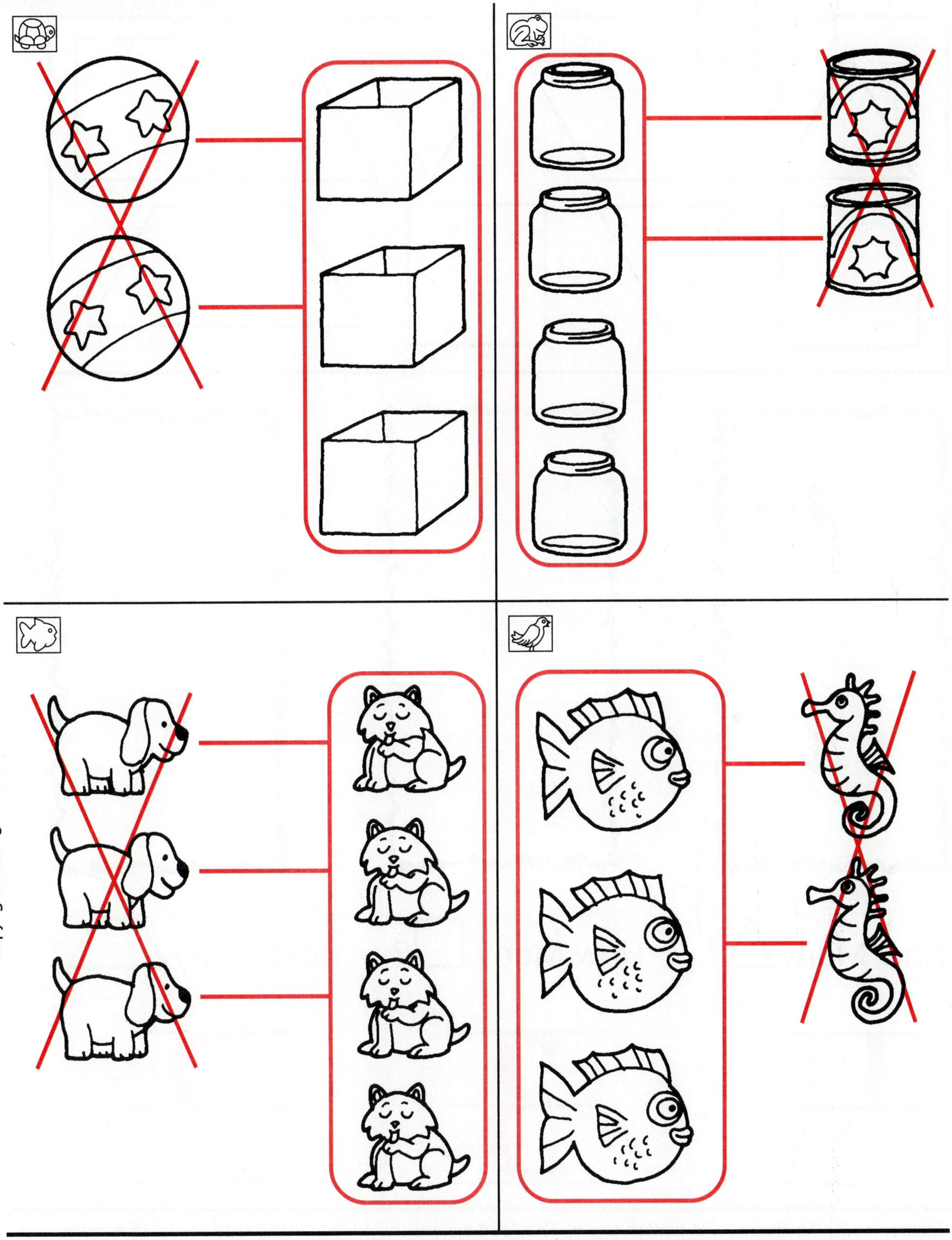

In each box, children draw lines to match the objects or animals. They circle the group that has **more.** They put an X on the group that has **fewer.** Then they explain their reasoning.

October: Use when children are familiar with *Matchups.*

Sort the Blocks

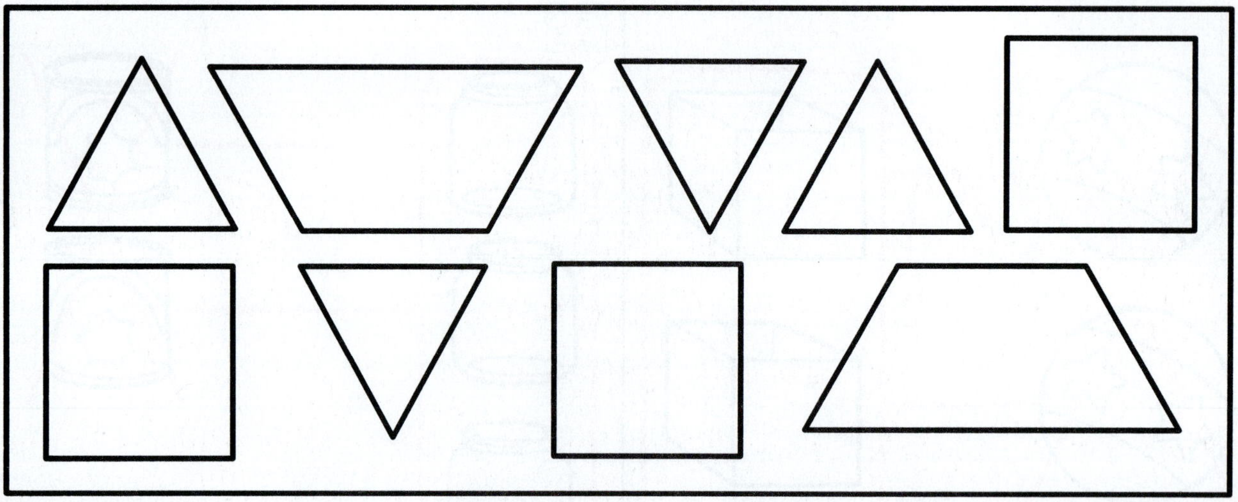

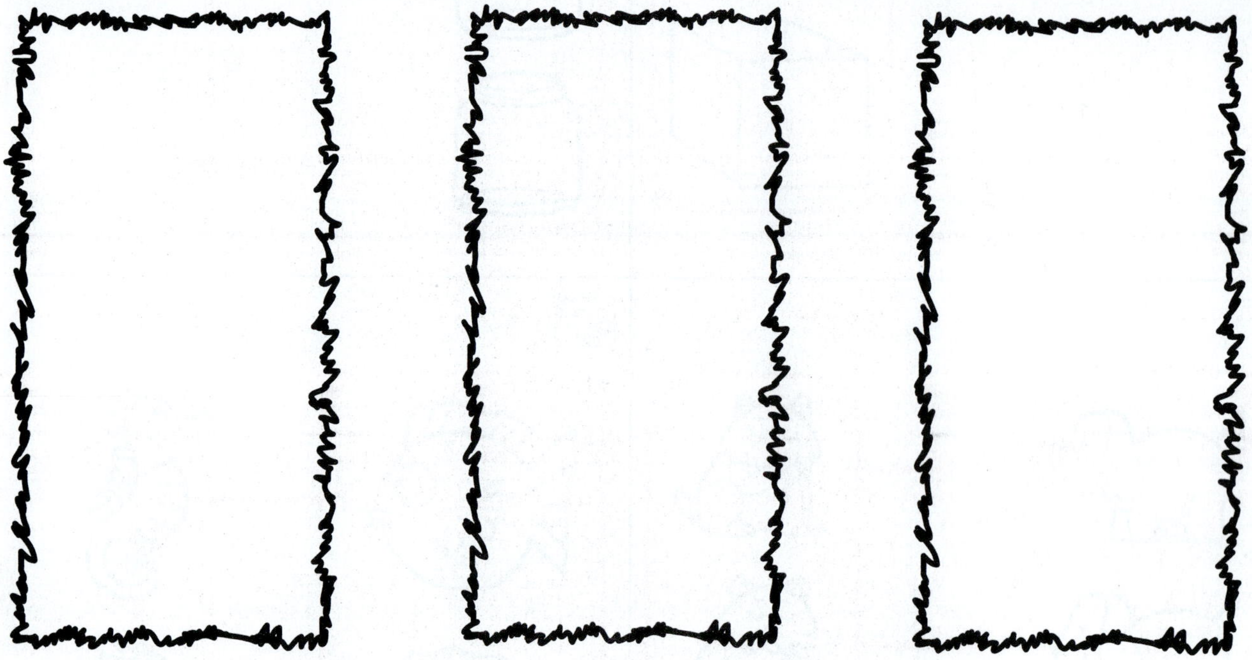

How Many △? 4

How Many □? 3

How Many ⏢? 2

Children cover the shapes with pattern blocks. They sort the shapes on the sorting mats, count how many, and write the number. Have children explain how they grouped the blocks.

Name ____________________

Which Is the Same?

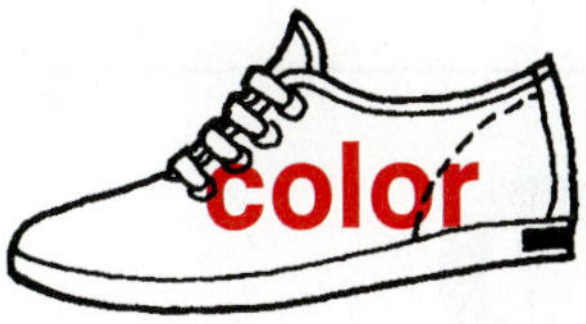

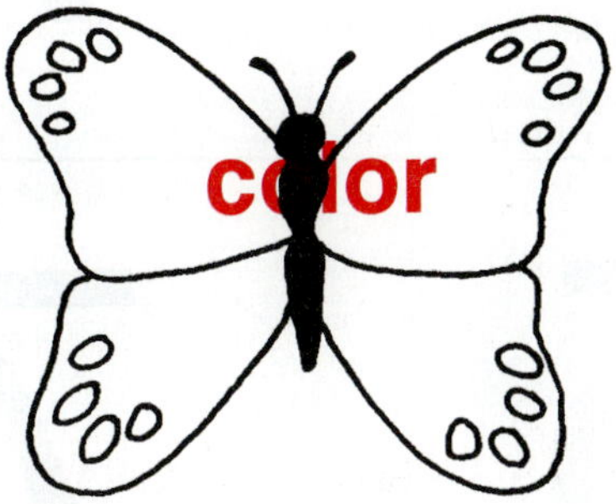

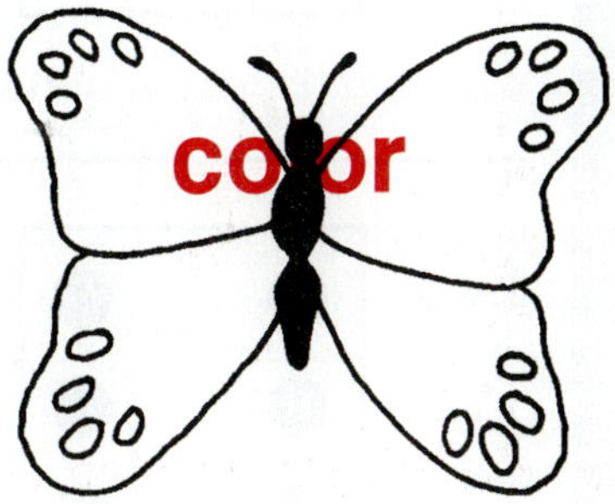

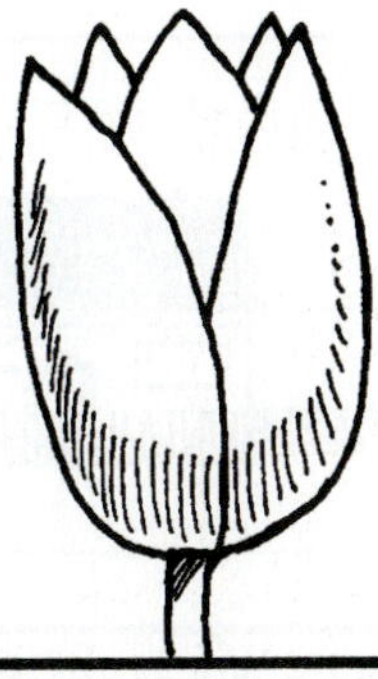

Children color the pictures that are the same in each row.

October: Use when children are familiar with the *Classroom Project.*

Review/Test

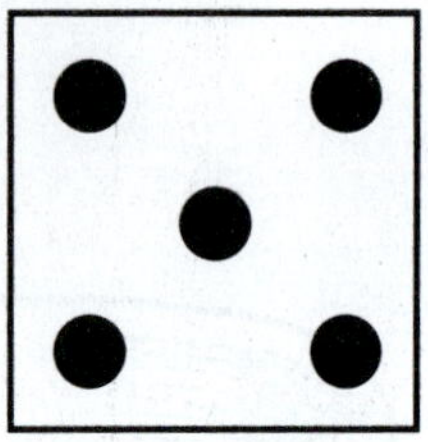

4 6 5

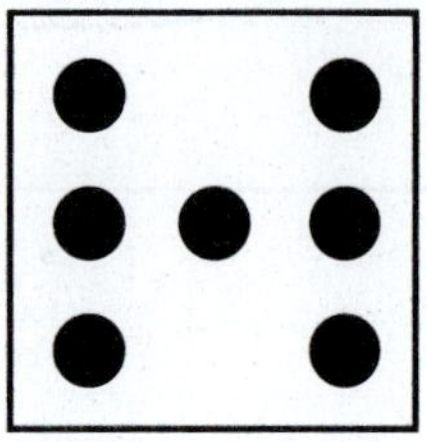

7 8 6

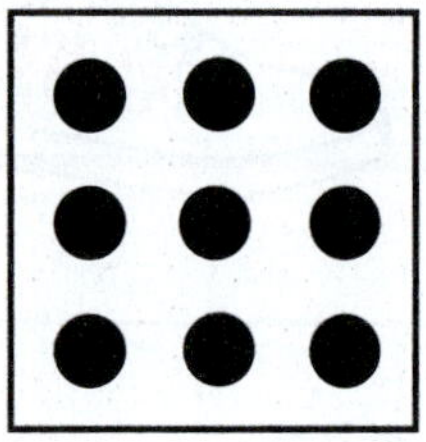

8 9 7

6 5 7

Turtle, Frog, Fish, and Bird: Children circle the number represented by the domino in each row.
Squirrel: Children color the left train blue and the right train red.

Name ______________________

My Problem Solving Book

Strategy: Act It Out

Remember!
- Understand
- Plan
- Try it
- Look back

➤ **Understand** Read the following story: Three children are playing soccer. One more child comes to play with them. How many children are there in all? Children tell what is happening. Ask, "What do you need to find out?"

1

Remember!
- Understand
- Plan
- Try it
- Look back

____

Answers will vary.

____

➤ **Look back** Children draw their own stories and write how many in all. Ask, "How can you check your answer? Why does it make sense?"

4

FOLD

Remember!

- Understand
- **Plan**
- Try it
- Look back

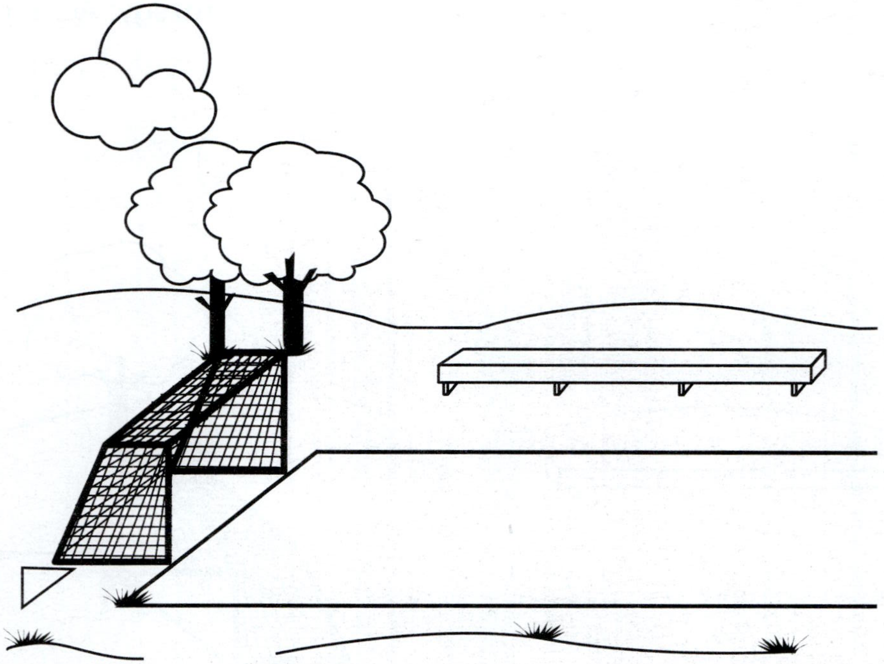

4

➤ **Plan** Children explain how they can find the answer. Possible answer: I show three children, and one more. Then I count to find how many in all.

❷

Remember!

- Understand
- Plan
- **Try it**
- Look back

➤ **Try it** Children act out the story with people counters. They write how many in all. Three children and one more makes four children.

❸

Name ______________________________

Odd and Even

2	4	6	8	10
12	14	16	18	20
22	24	26	28	30
32	34	36	38	40
42	44	46	48	50

Boxes shaded below should be red.
All other boxes should be blue.

1	2	3	4	5	6	7	8	9	10
11	12	13	14	15	16	17	18	19	20
21	22	23	24	25	26	27	28	29	30
31	32	33	34	35	36	37	38	39	40
41	42	43	44	45	46	47	48	49	50

Turtle: Children use the numbers to skip-count by 2. **Frog:** Children color the even numbers blue. Then they color the odd numbers red. They can talk about the patterns they see.

Identifying 5

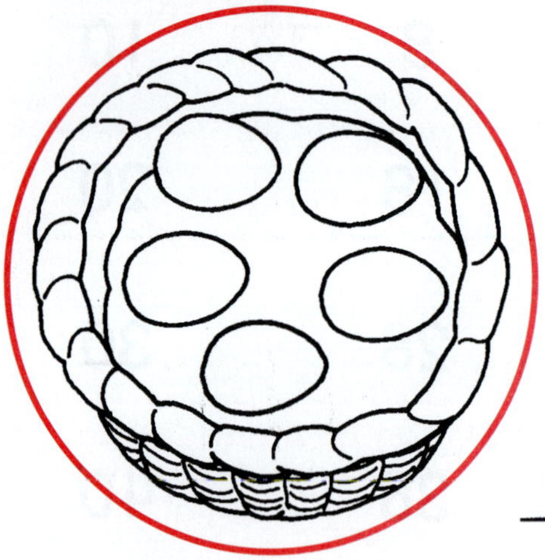

5

5

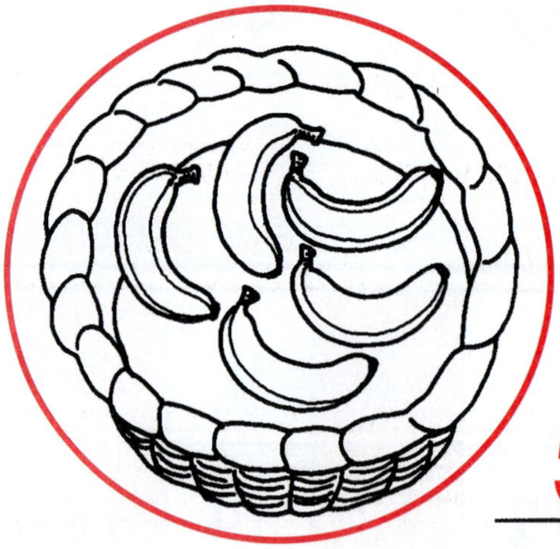

5

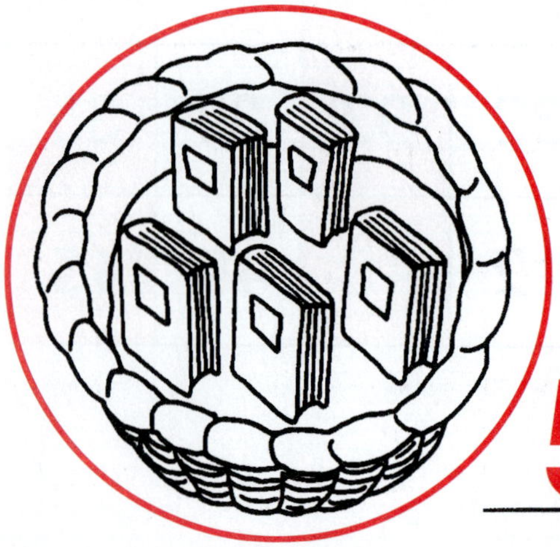

5

Children circle the pictures that show 5. Then they write the numeral 5 next to each picture that shows 5 objects or animals.

Name ______________________________

Writing 0–5

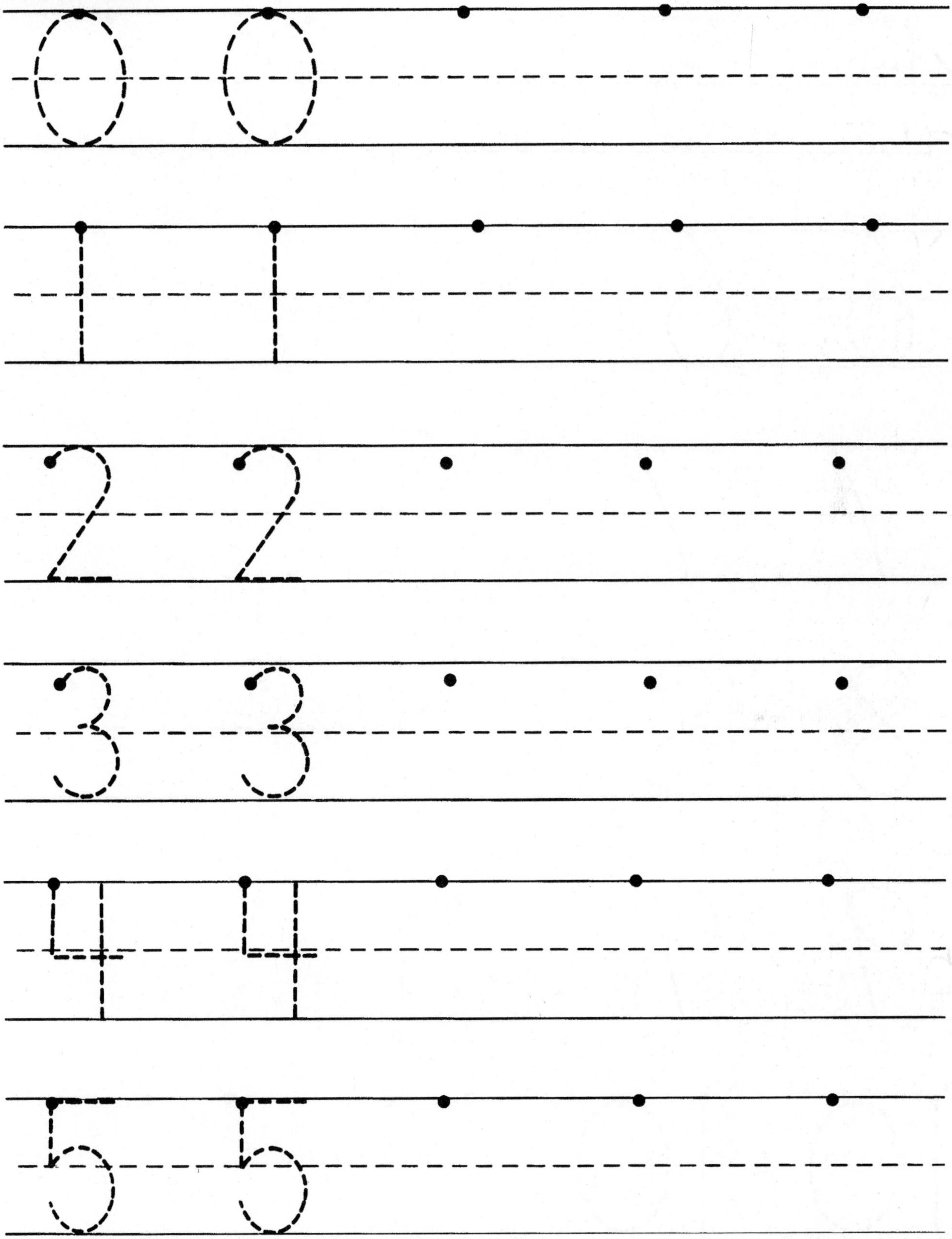

Children trace the two numbers at the beginning of each row and then write the number three more times.

November: Use after the *Counting Tape and Clip Collection.*

Writing 5–10

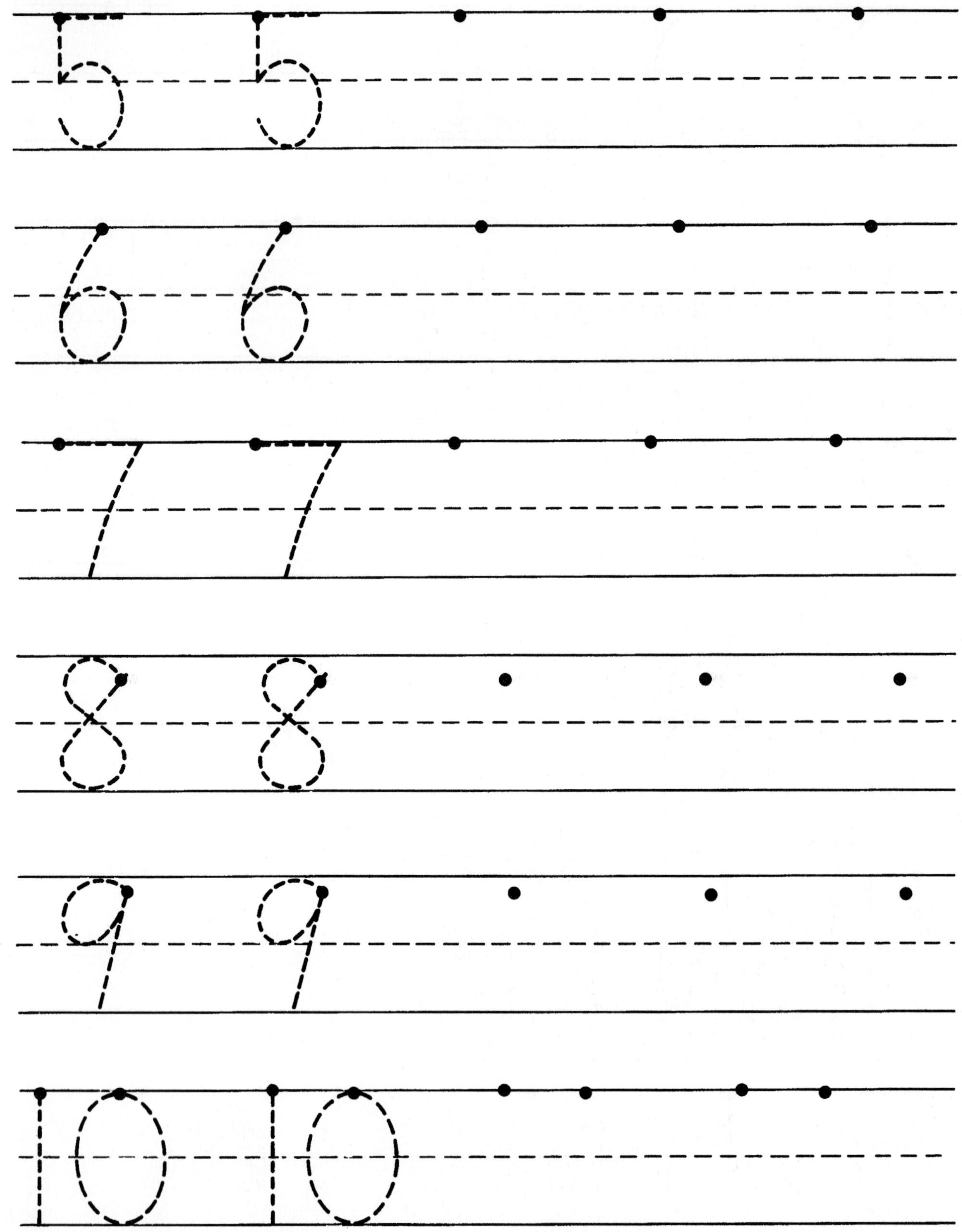

Children trace the two numbers at the beginning of each row and then write the number.

Name ______________________________

What to Wear

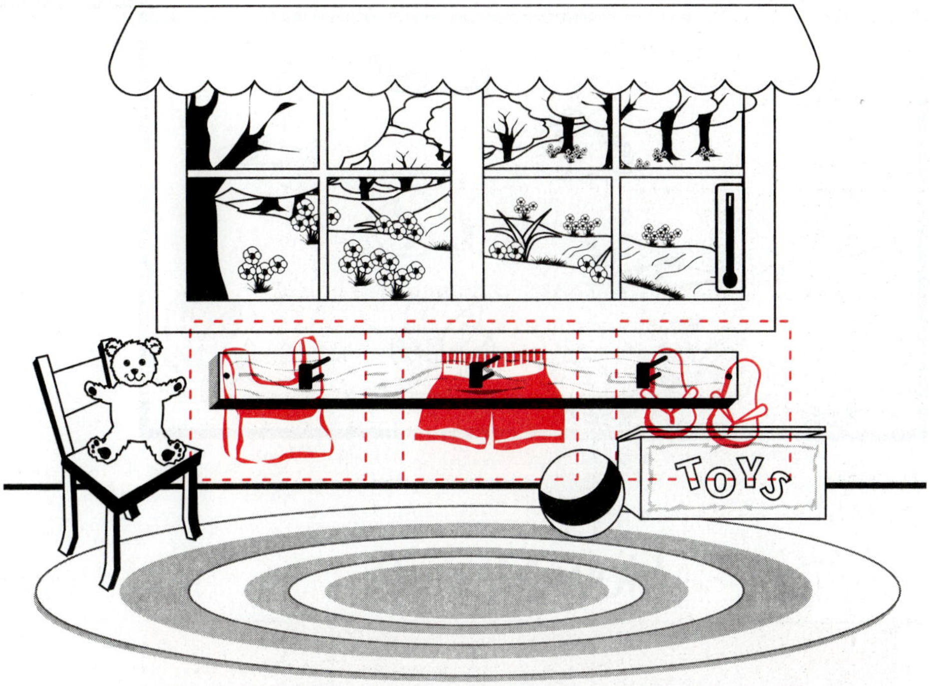

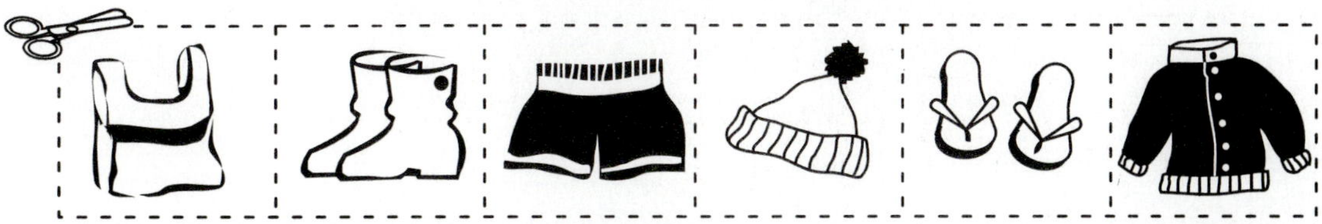

Children cut out the items of clothing and paste them on the clothes rack for the appropriate season. When they have finished, children can explain their choices.

November: Use when children are familiar with the *Graph*.

Aquarium Graph

How Many?

Children look at the aquarium and then color a box in the graph to represent each item. Children may cross out each item as they record it in the graph. Discuss **most, fewest,** and **same.**

Name ______________________________

Complete the Patterns

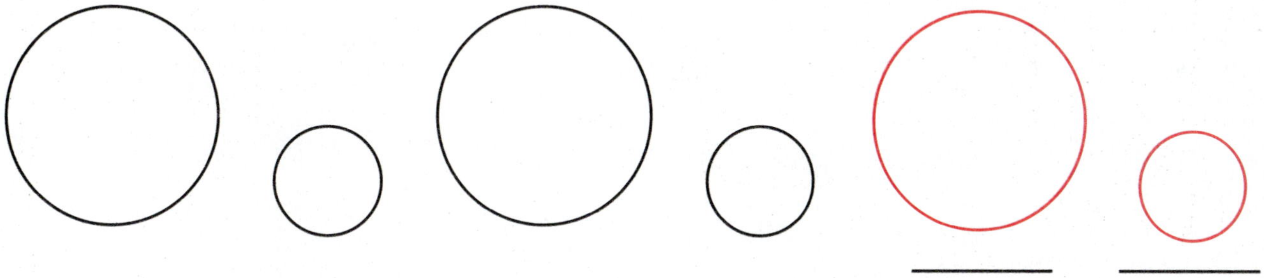

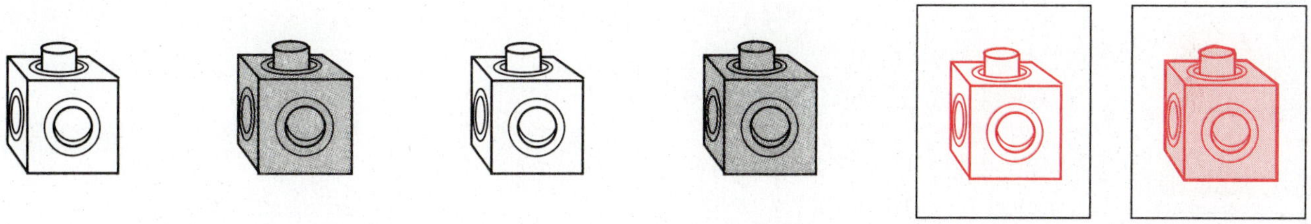

Answers will vary, but should show an ABAB pattern.

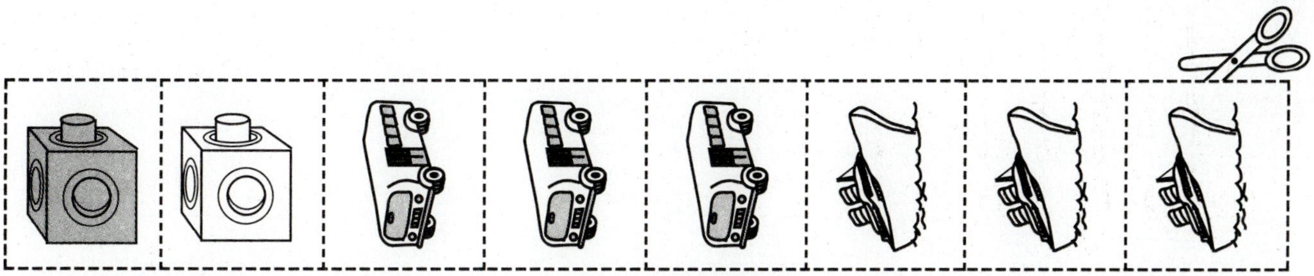

Turtle: Children say the pattern and then complete it. **Frog:** Children cut and paste cubes to complete the pattern. **Fish:** Children cut and paste buses and boats to make their own ABAB pattern.

November: Use when children are familiar with *Make Your Own Patterns.*

Name ______________________________

Count the Cubes

Children build towers with connecting cubes to match the towers pictured. Then they cut out numerals and paste them beside the corresponding cube towers.

November: Use when children are familiar with *Match My Stack.*

Long or Short?

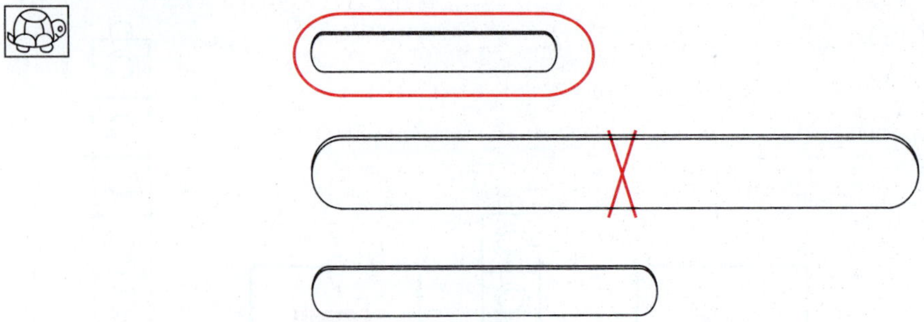

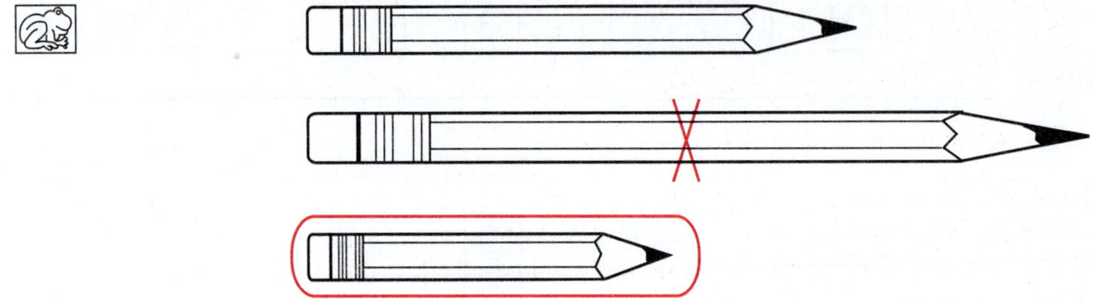

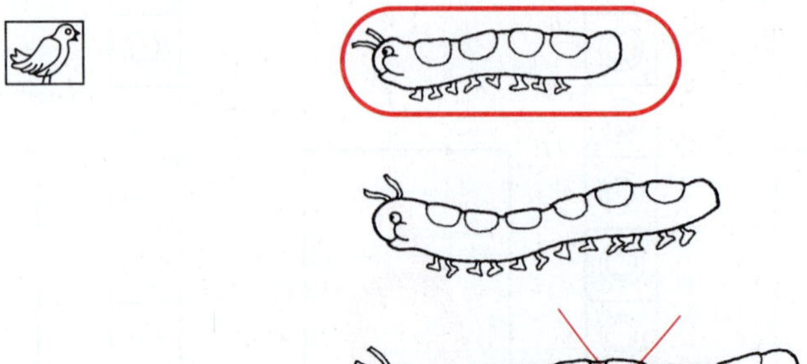

In each section, children circle the **shortest** item and put an X on the **longest** item.

Name ______________________________

Which Is Shorter?

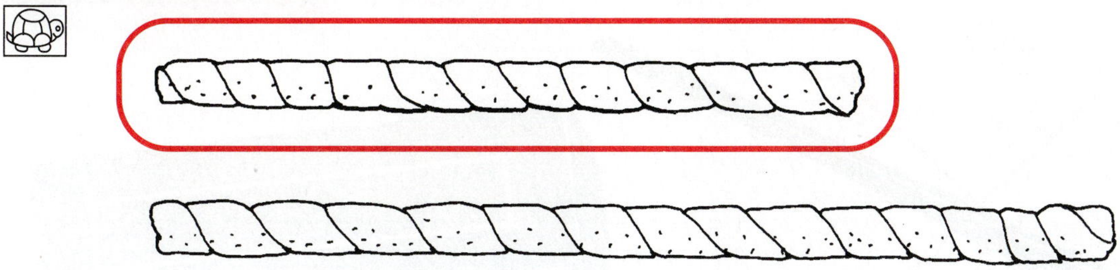

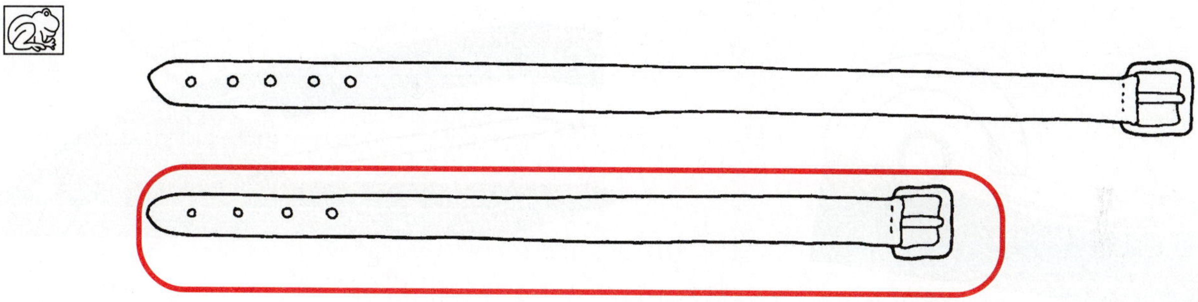

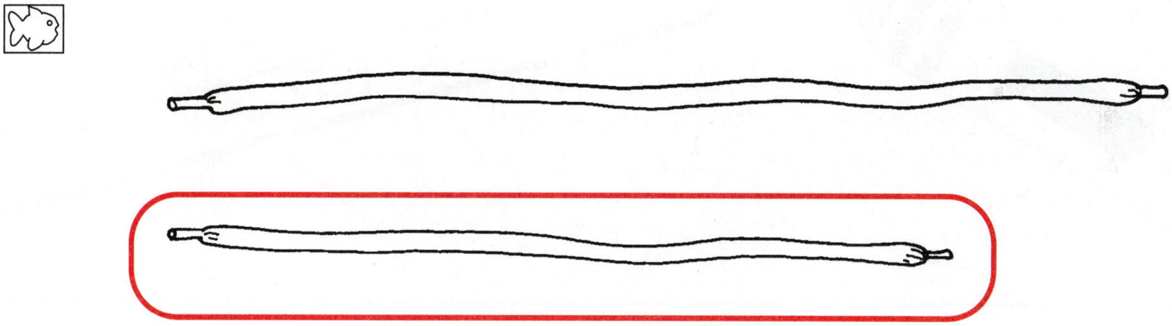

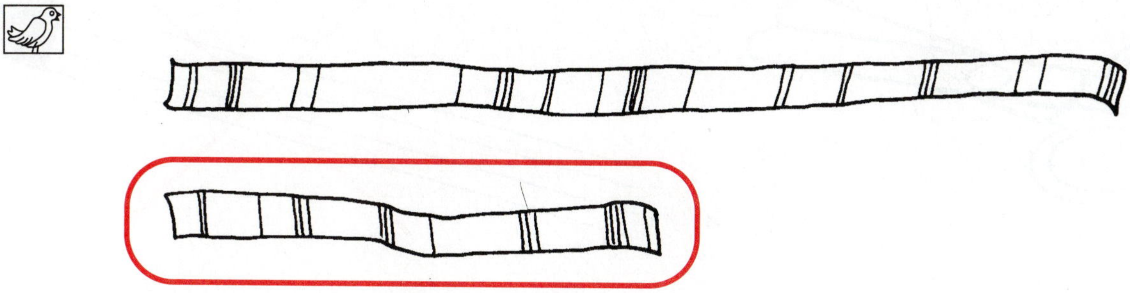

In each section, children circle the **shorter** item.

November: Use when children are familiar with *Length Comparing.*

Which Is Longer?

Answers may vary, depending on objects available.

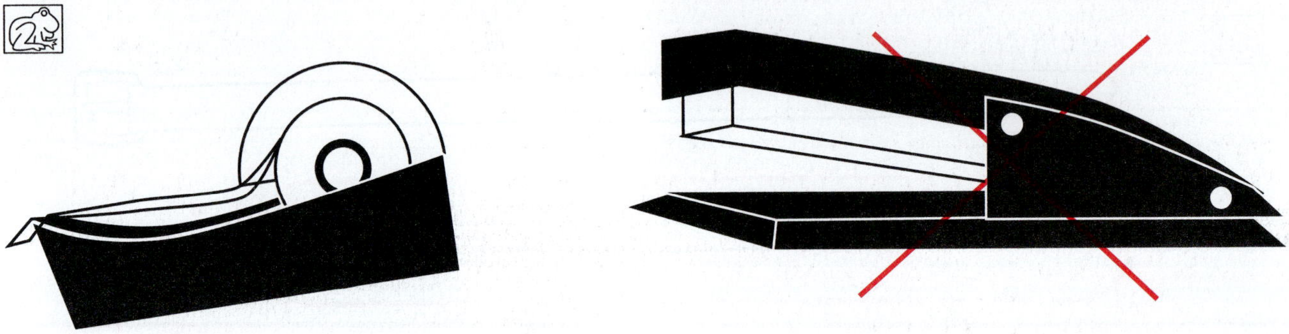

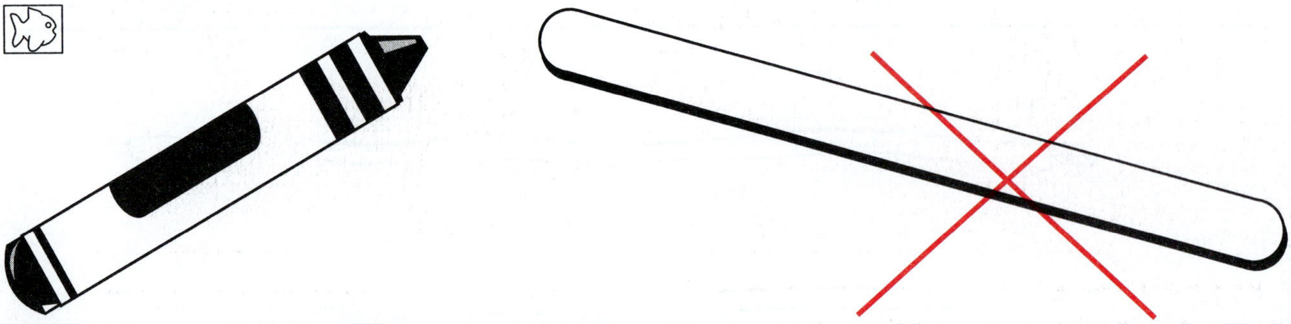

In each section, children find and compare the lengths of the real objects shown in the pictures. They decide which is longer and mark it with an X. When they are finished, have children explain what they did.

Name ____________________

What Is Missing? 

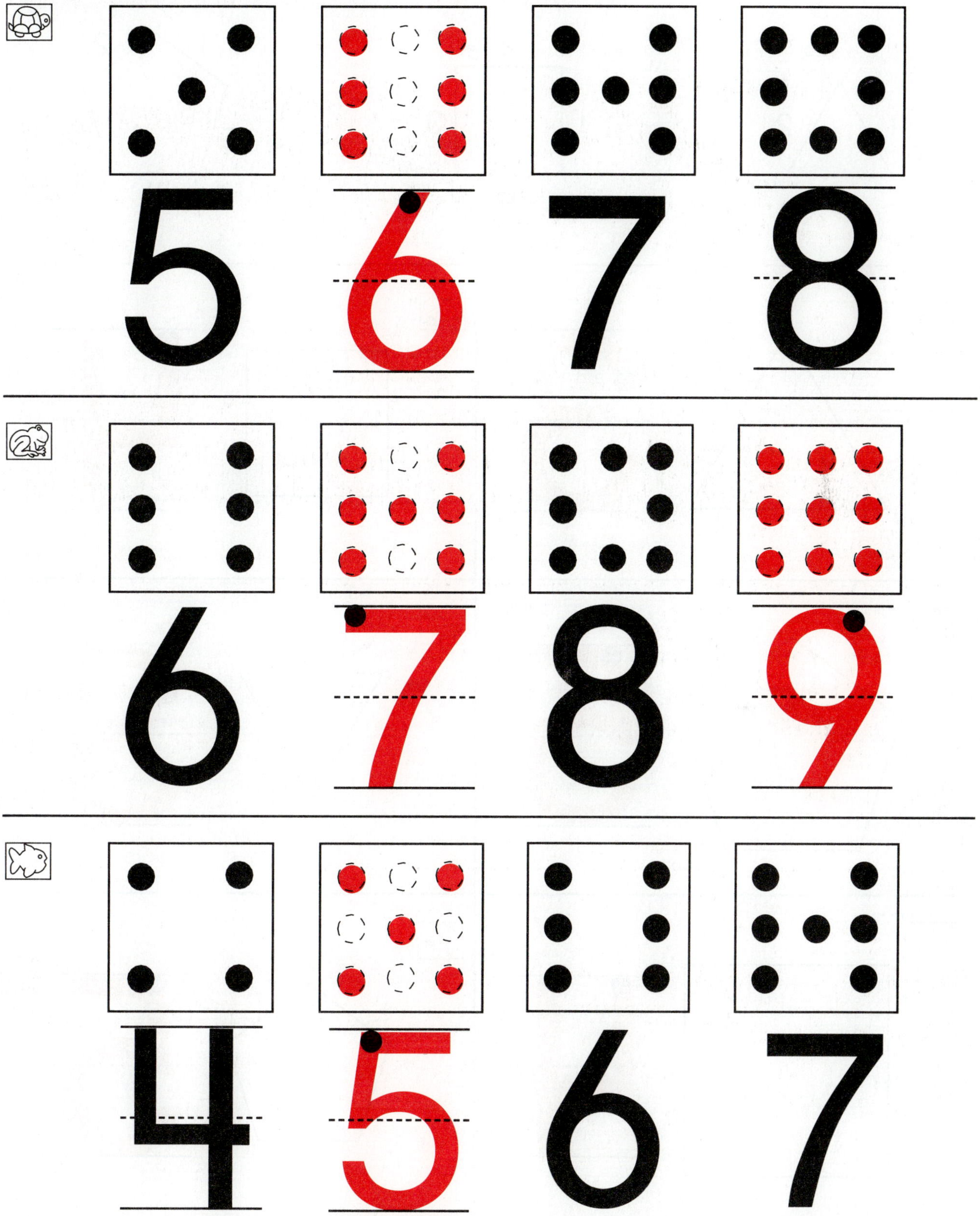

Using the domino icons as models, children shade in the correct number and placement of dots in each unshaded domino and then write the numeral.

November: Use when children are familiar with *Counting Tape to Ten.*

How Many Sides?

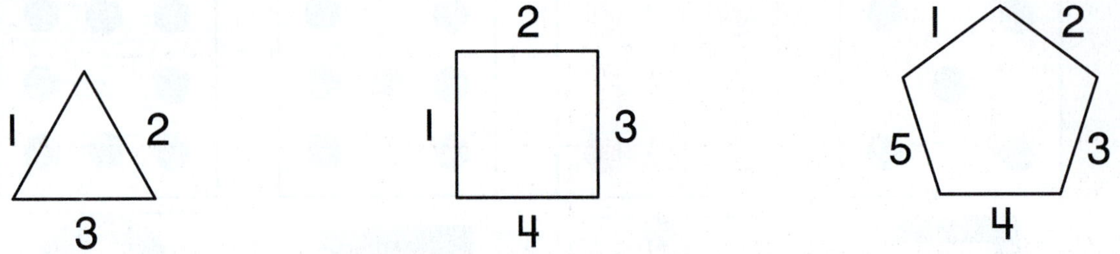

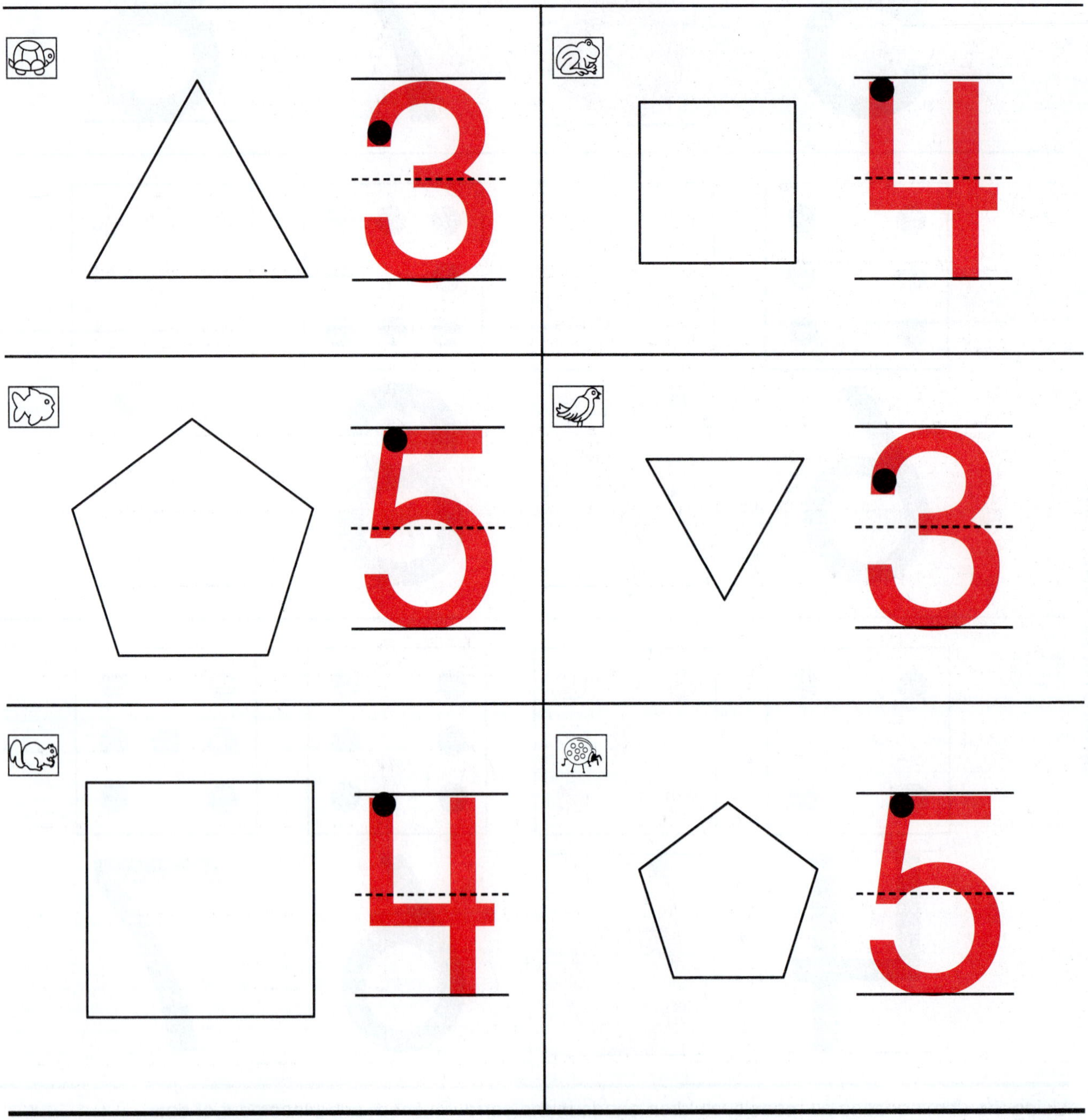

In each row, children state the number of sides for each shape and then record that numeral next to the shape.

Name ______________________________

Reviewing 0–5

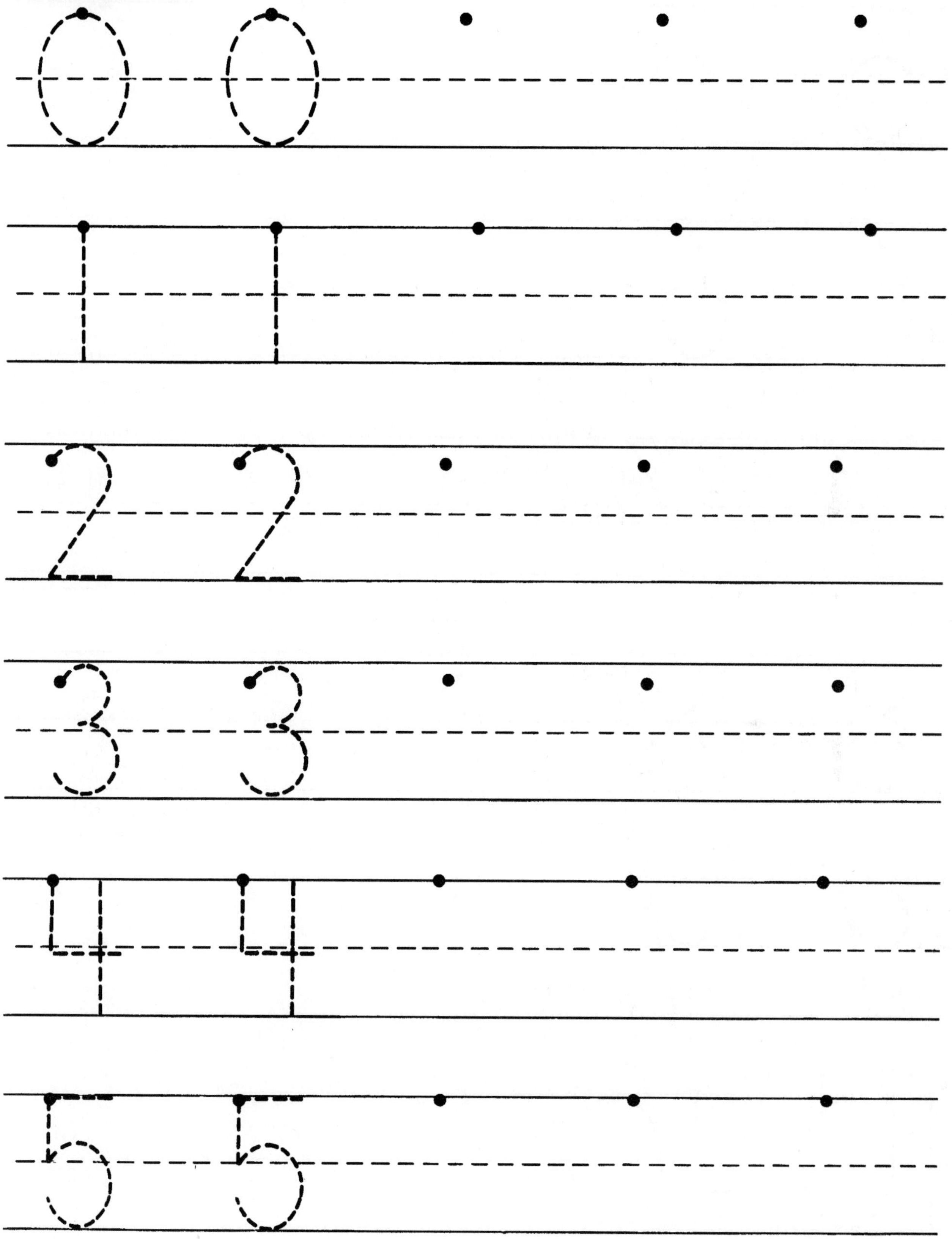

Children trace the two numbers at the beginning of each row and then write the number three more times.

November: Use when children are familiar with *Days in School Game.*

Reviewing 5–10

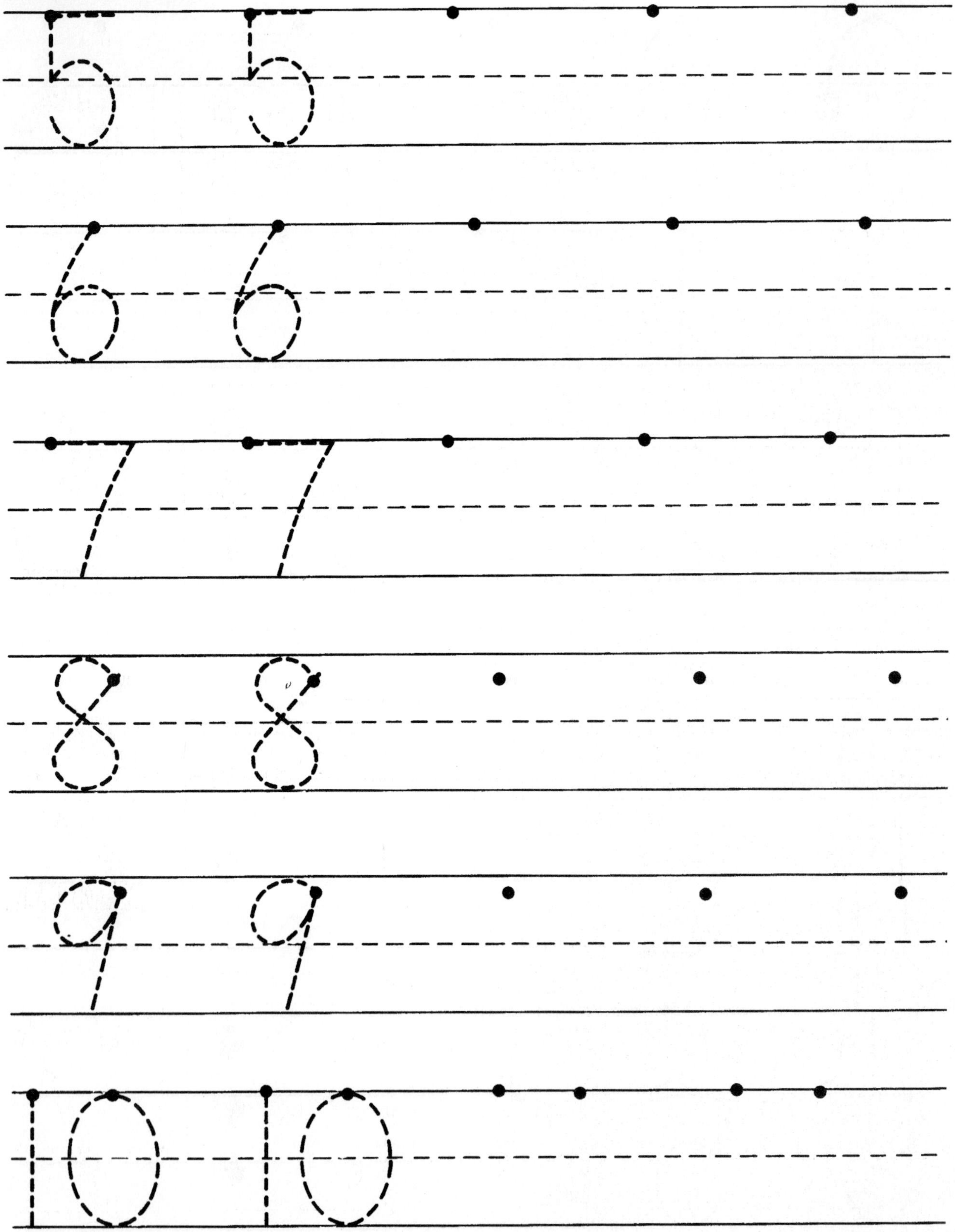

Children trace the two numbers at the beginning of each row and then write the number.

Name ______________________________

Count the Dots

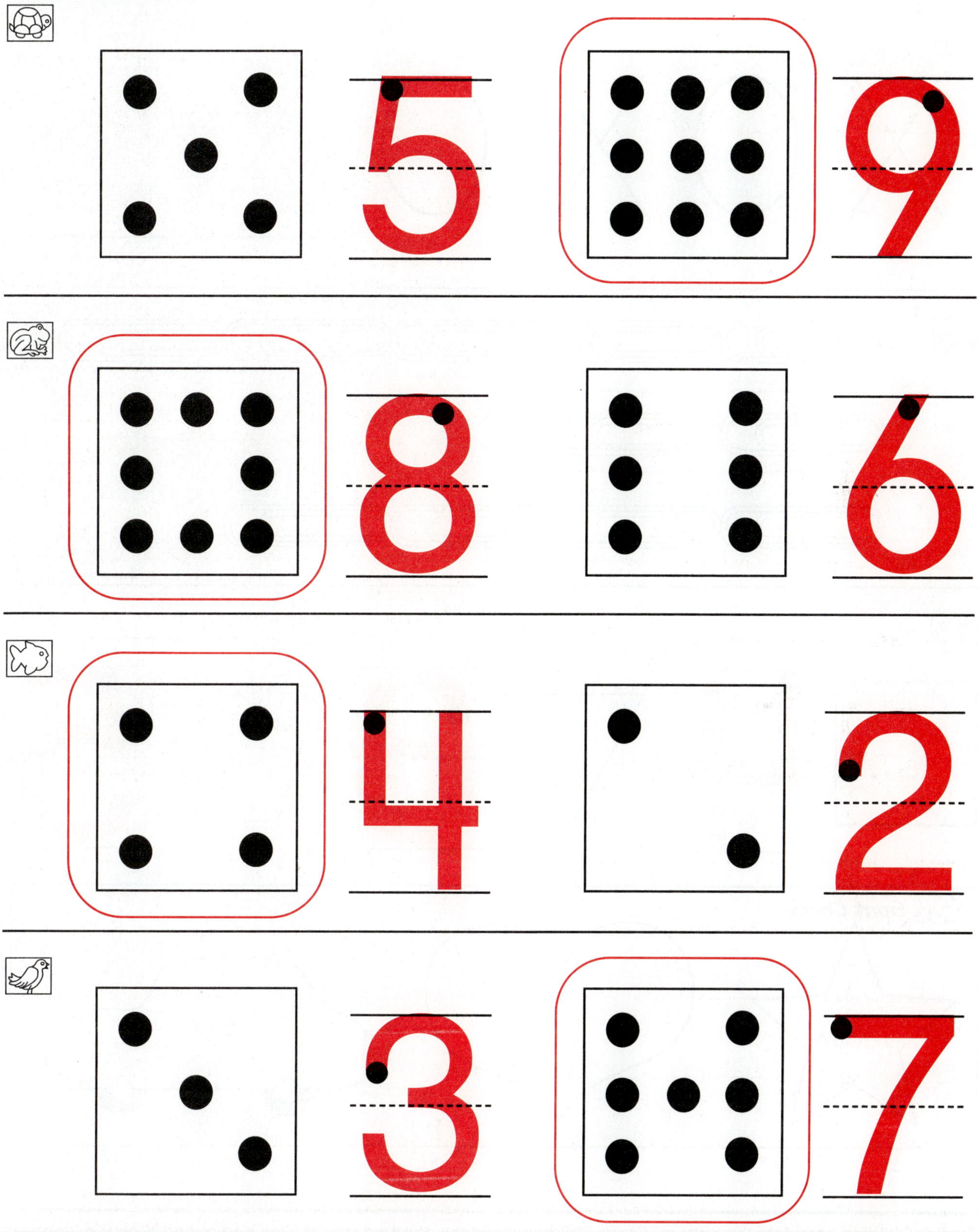

Children write the corresponding numeral beside each domino. Next, they circle the domino with more dots in each of the rows.

November: Use when children are familiar with *Domino Comparing*.

Review/Test

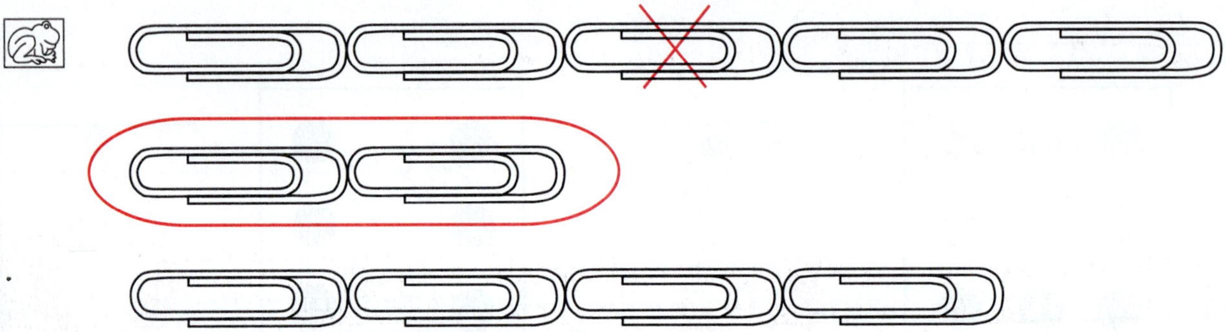

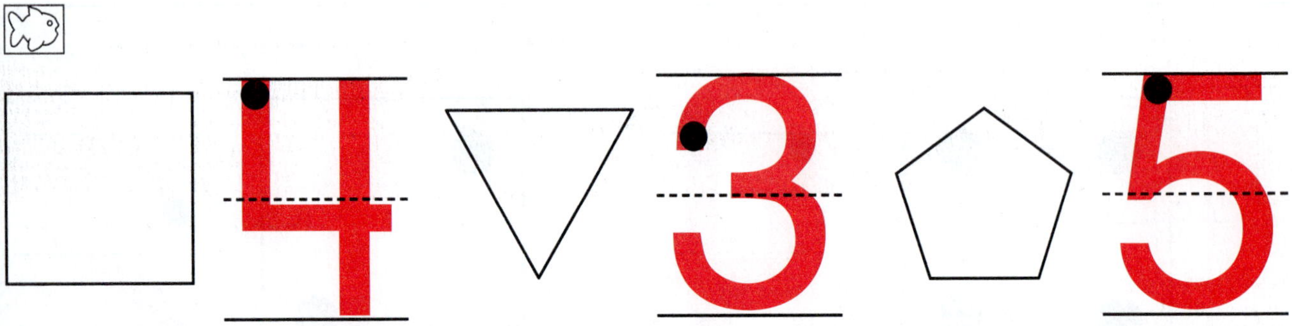

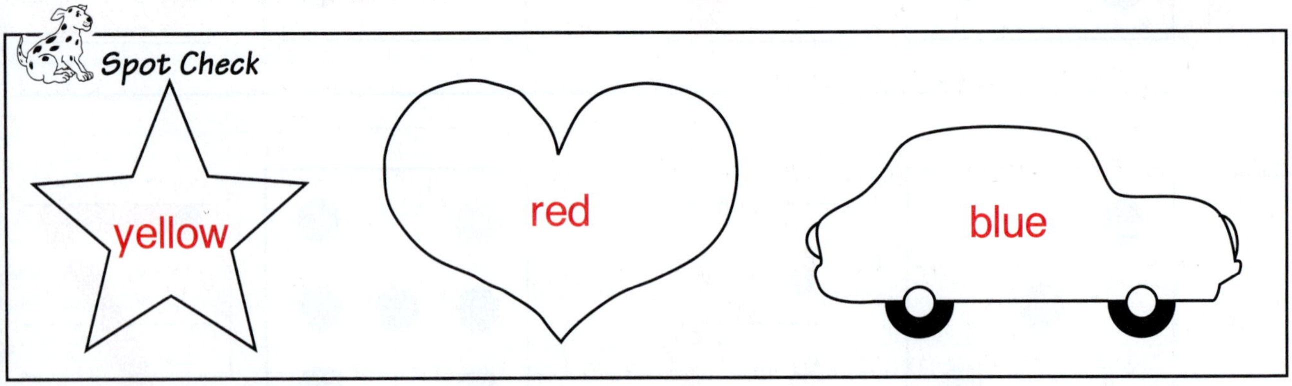

Turtle: Children complete the pattern. **Frog:** Children circle the shortest row of clips and put an X on the longest row of clips. **Fish:** Children record the number of sides for each shape. **Spot Check:** Children color the heart red. Then they color the object **before** the heart yellow and the object **after** the heart blue.

Name ____________________

Writing 10–15

10 10

11 11

12 12

13 13

14 14

15 15

Children trace the two numbers at the beginning of each row and then write the number.

December: Use when children are familiar with the *Daily Depositor.*

Writing 15–20

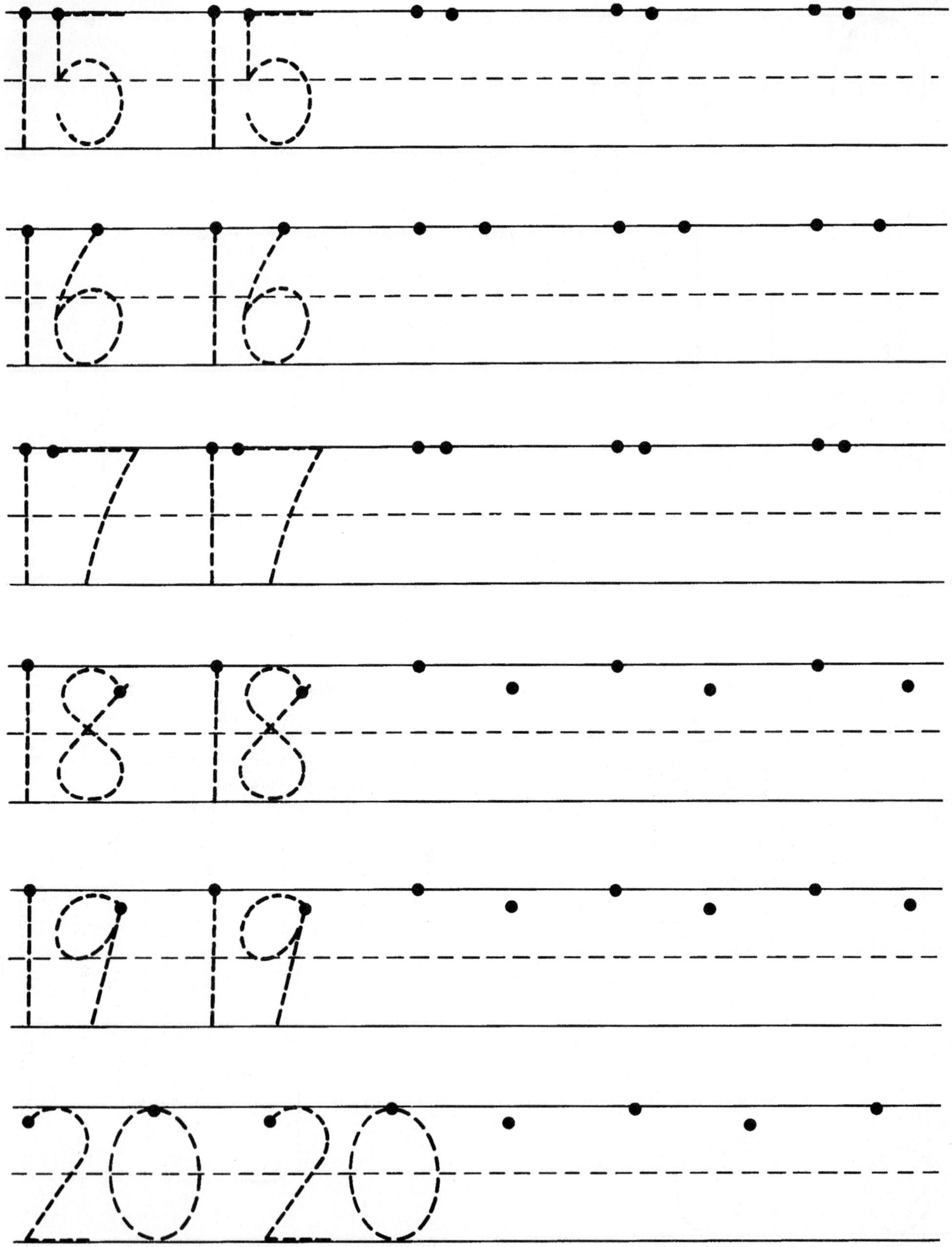

Children trace the two numbers at the beginning of each row and then write the number.

Name ______________________________

My Problem Solving Book

Strategy: Draw a Picture

Remember!
- Understand
- Plan
- Try it
- Look back

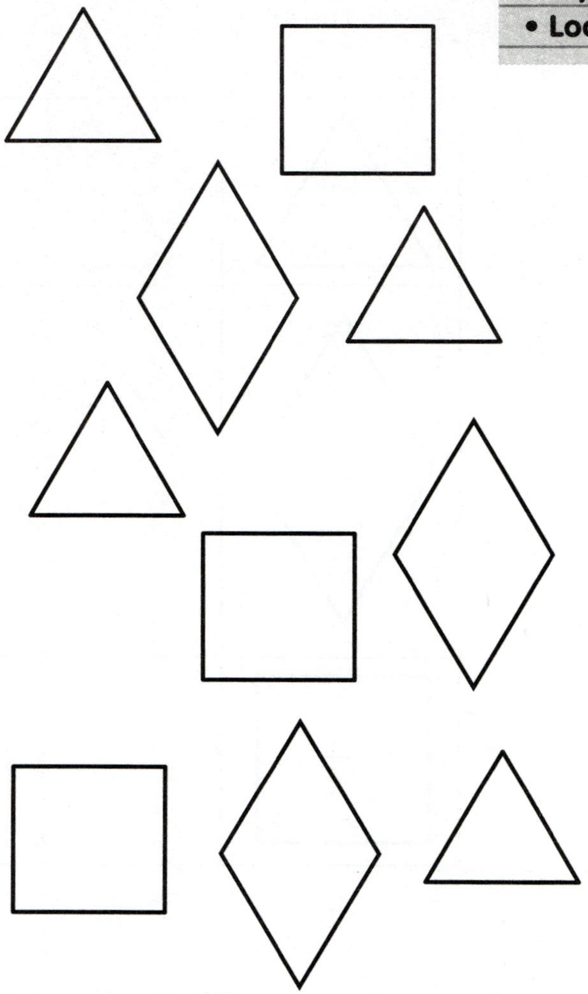

➤ **Understand** Children talk about how they can find out if there is one shape that is pictured the most.

❶

FOLD

Remember!
- Understand
- Plan
- Try it
- Look back

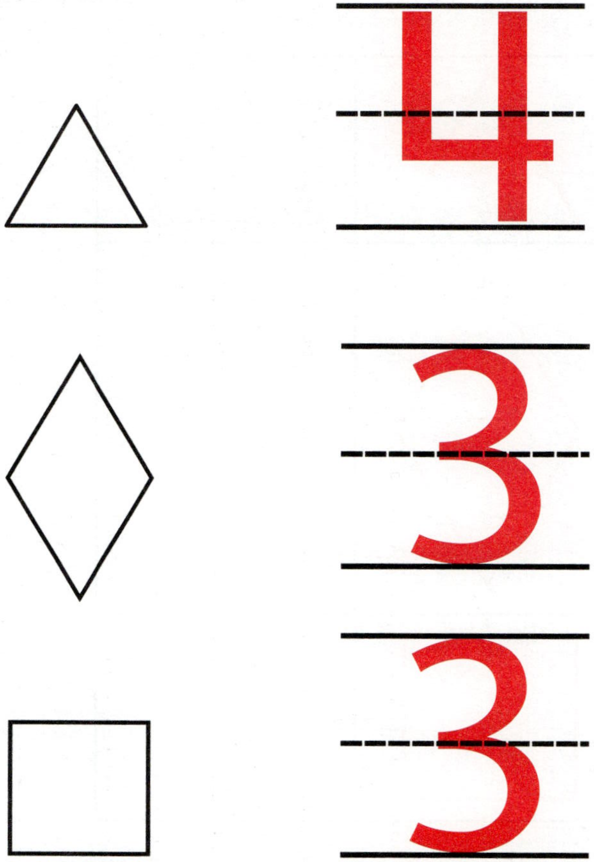

➤ **Look back** Children count how many of each shape there are on the graph and record the number. Ask, "How did your picture help you find these answers?"

Possible answer: I traced the shapes in a row, then counted them. Drawing a picture helped me to find how many, because I can count the shapes.

❹

Remember!
- Understand
- **Plan**
- Try it
- Look back

Remember!
- Understand
- Plan
- **Try it**
- Look back

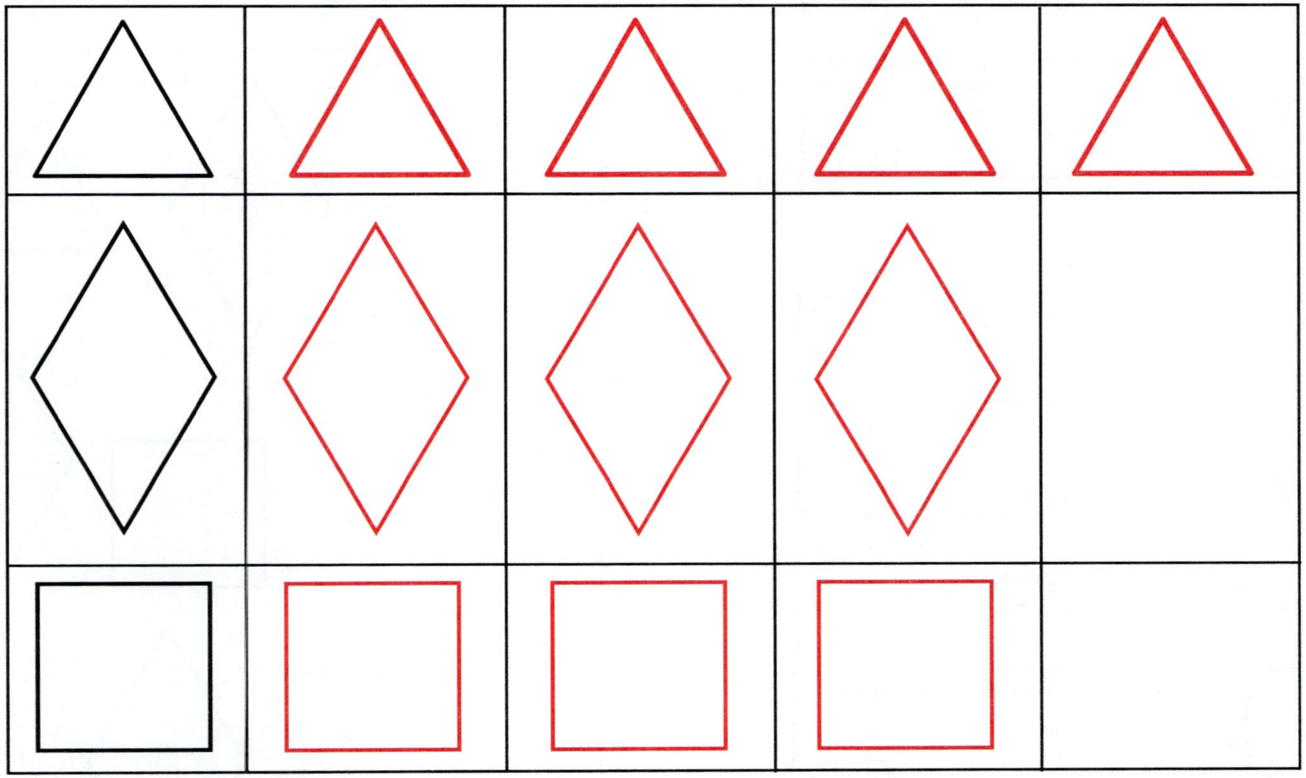

➤ **Plan** Children explain how they can find out how many of each shape there are. I could sort the blocks in rows.

➤ **Try it** Children arrange the blocks in rows on the graph. They trace the blocks.

❷ ❸

Name ____________________

Missing Numbers

Children write the missing numbers.

December: Use when children are familiar with the *Daily Depositor.*

More Time or Less?

Children circle the picture that takes **more** time. Then they explain their reasoning.

Name ___________________________________

When Did it Happen?

Turtle and Frog: Children look at the picture in the box. They circle the picture that shows what happened **before. Fish** and **Bird:** Children look at the picture in the box and put an X on the picture that happened **after.**

December: Use when children are familiar with *Through the Day.*

Match the Shapes

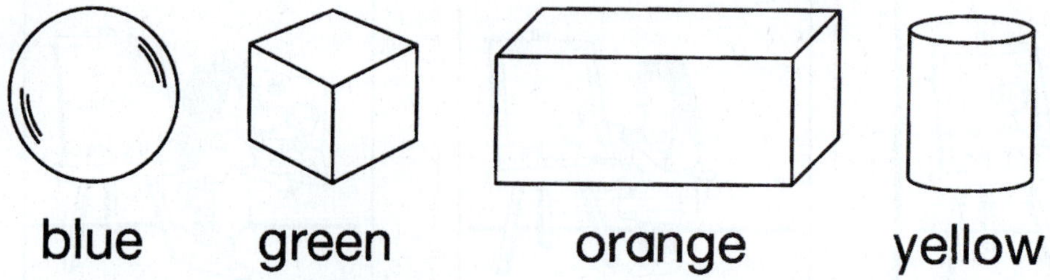

Have children color the key at the top of the page. Then children color the shapes on the picture that match.

Name ______________________________

Length

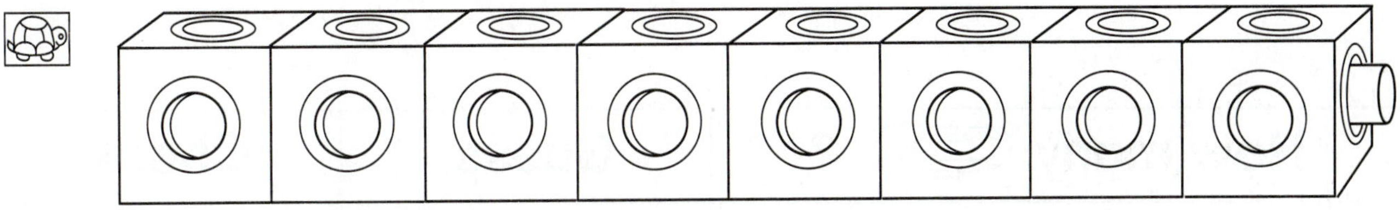

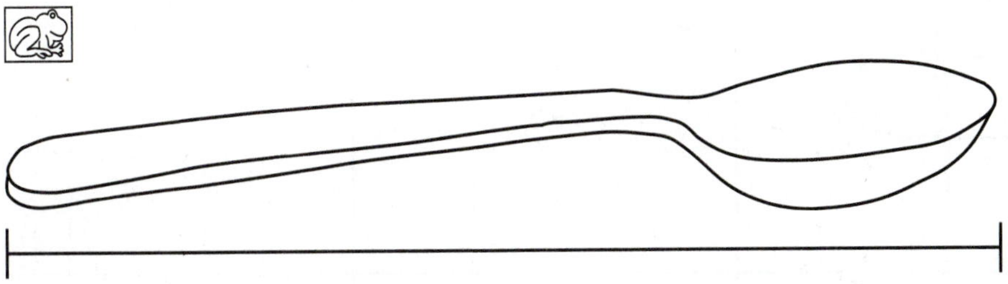

6

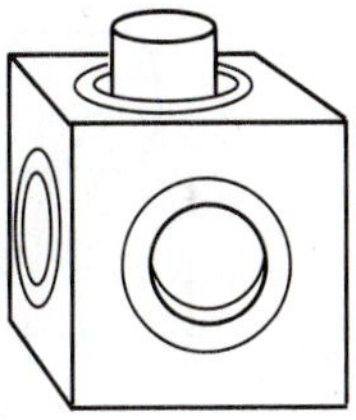

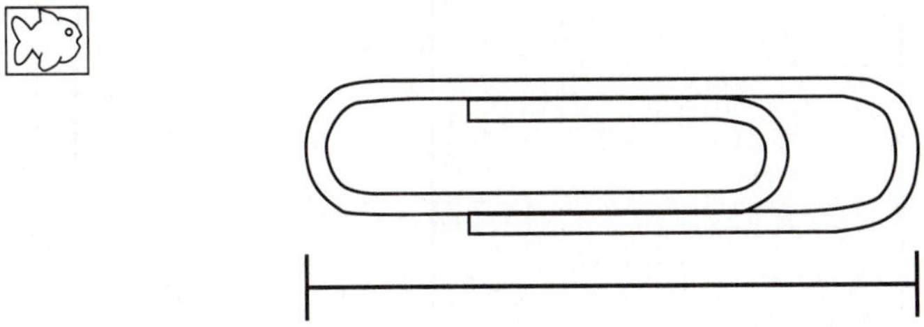

3

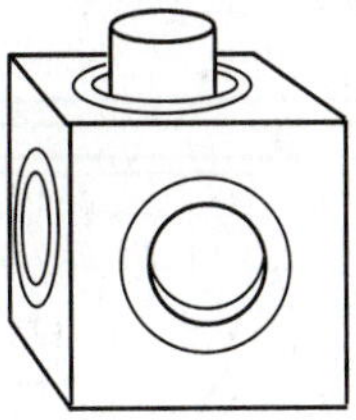

4

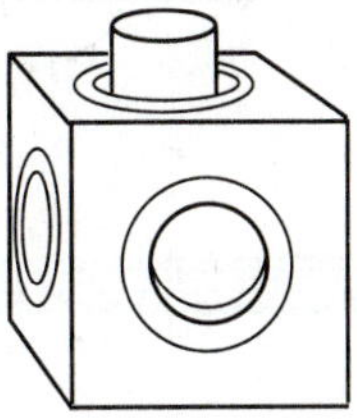

Turtle: Children place connecting cubes on picture to form cube ruler. **Frog, Fish, and Bird:** Children measure object and write the number of cubes. **Squirrel:** Children draw an X on the ribbon they think measures 2 cubes.

December: Use when children are familiar with *Estimate the Length.*

Guess and Check

Answers will vary, depending on size of paper clips.

How many 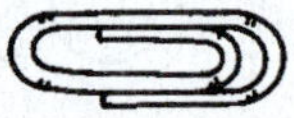 ?	Guess	Check
 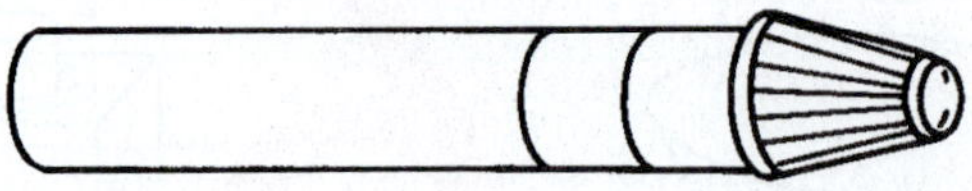		

 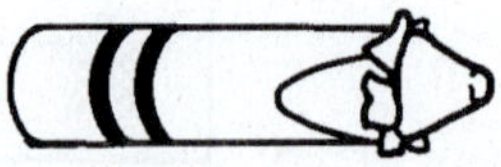		

Children guess how many paper clips each object measures. They record their guesses. Then they use paper clips to check each measurement, and they record the measurement.

Name ______________________________

Creating Patterns

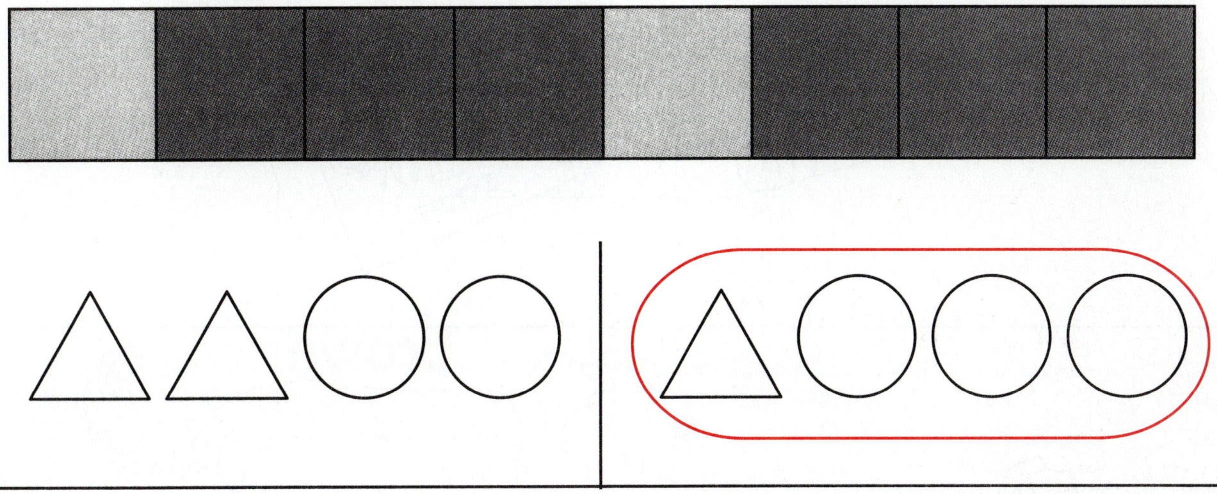

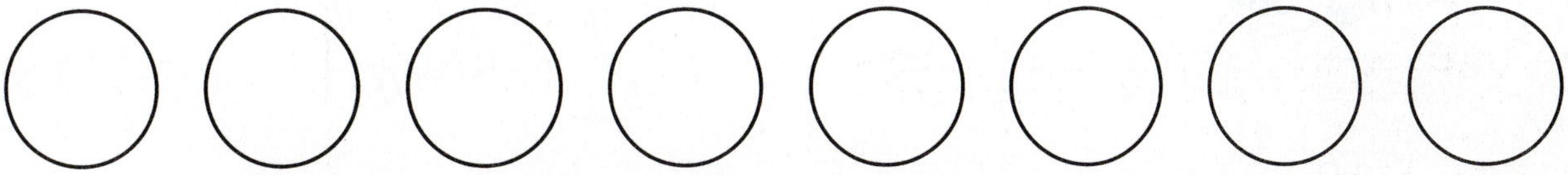

Pattern created in the frog row should be repeated in the fish and bird rows.

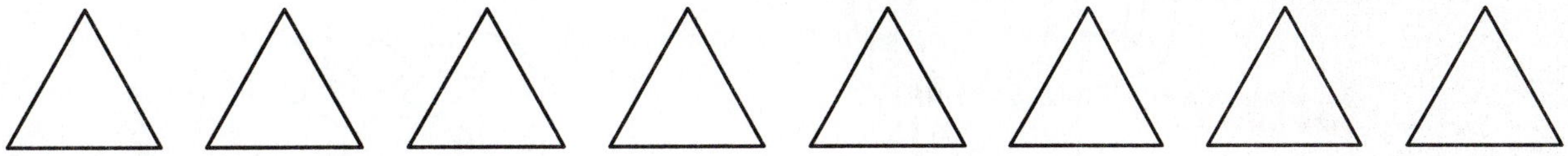

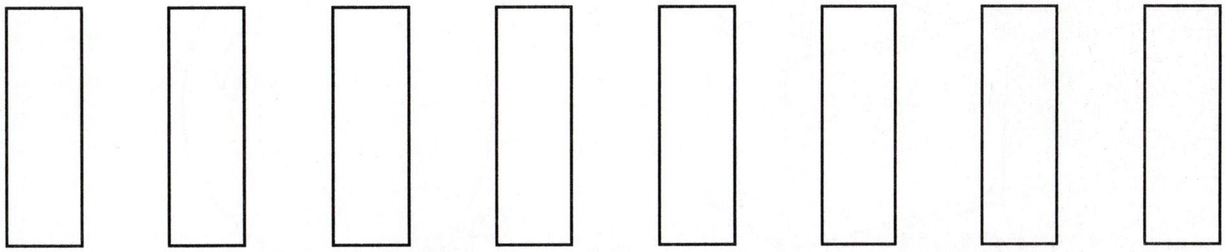

Turtle: Children can use counters or other objects to create patterns before they circle or color. Then children circle the group that shows the same pattern as the shaded-square pattern above. **Frog:** Children color circles to create a pattern. **Fish** and **Bird:** Children repeat the pattern they created.

December: Use when children are familiar with *Make Your Own Patterns.*

Heavier, Lighter

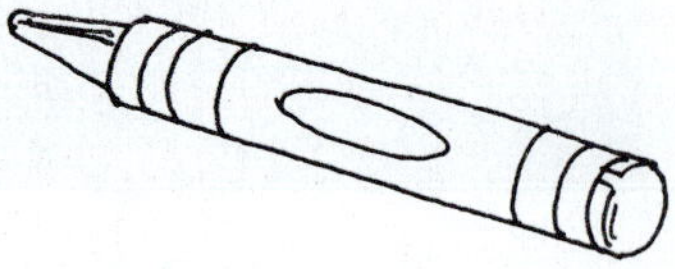

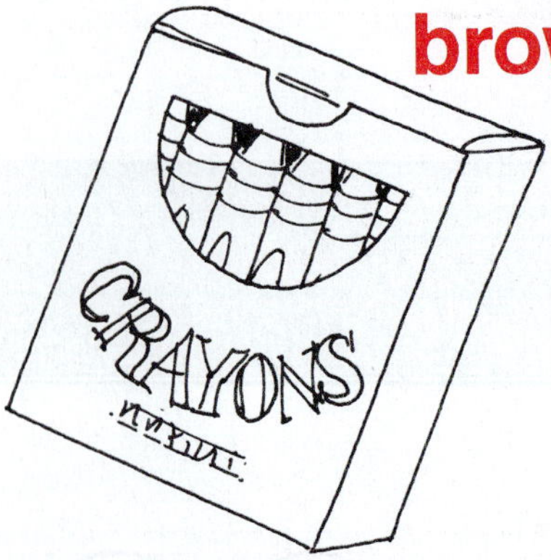

brown

brown

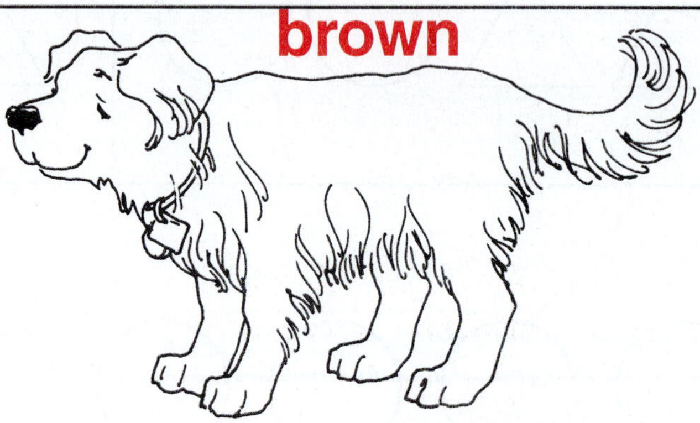

brown

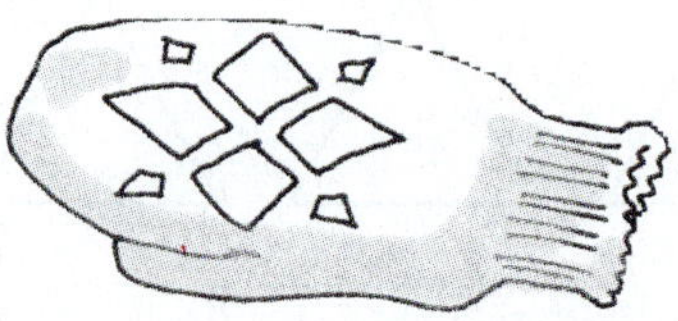

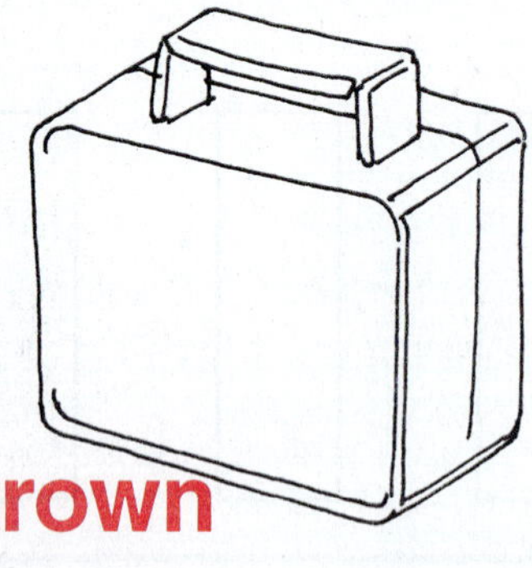

brown

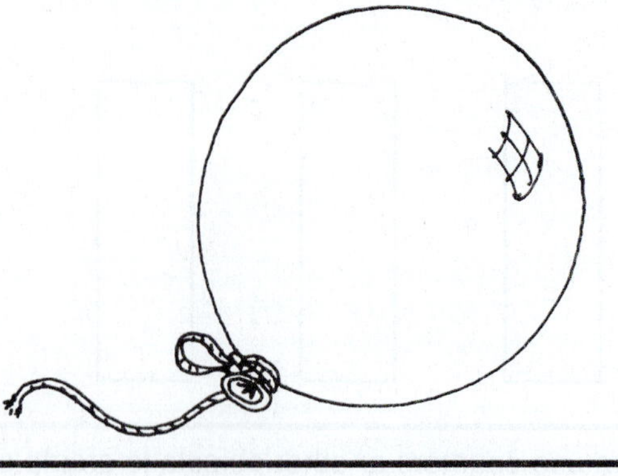

In each row, children color the **heavier** object brown. They can also compare two classroom objects to determine which is heavier.

Name ____________________

Lightest to Heaviest

mouse  **elephant**

hummingbird  **ostrich**

goldfish  **whale**

Children cut out the pictures of the light and heavy animals and paste them in the rows above so that each row shows similar kinds of animals from **lightest** to **heaviest.**

December: Use when children are familiar with *Which Is Heavier?*

Name ____________________________

Numbers to 20

1	2	3	4	5
6	7	8	9	10
11	12	13	14	15
16	17	18	19	20

This is a class activity. Roll a number cube. Children place the corresponding number of counters on the chart, counting numbers as they cover them. Continue until the number 20 is covered.

December: Use when children are familiar with *Collect 20.*

Numbers in Order

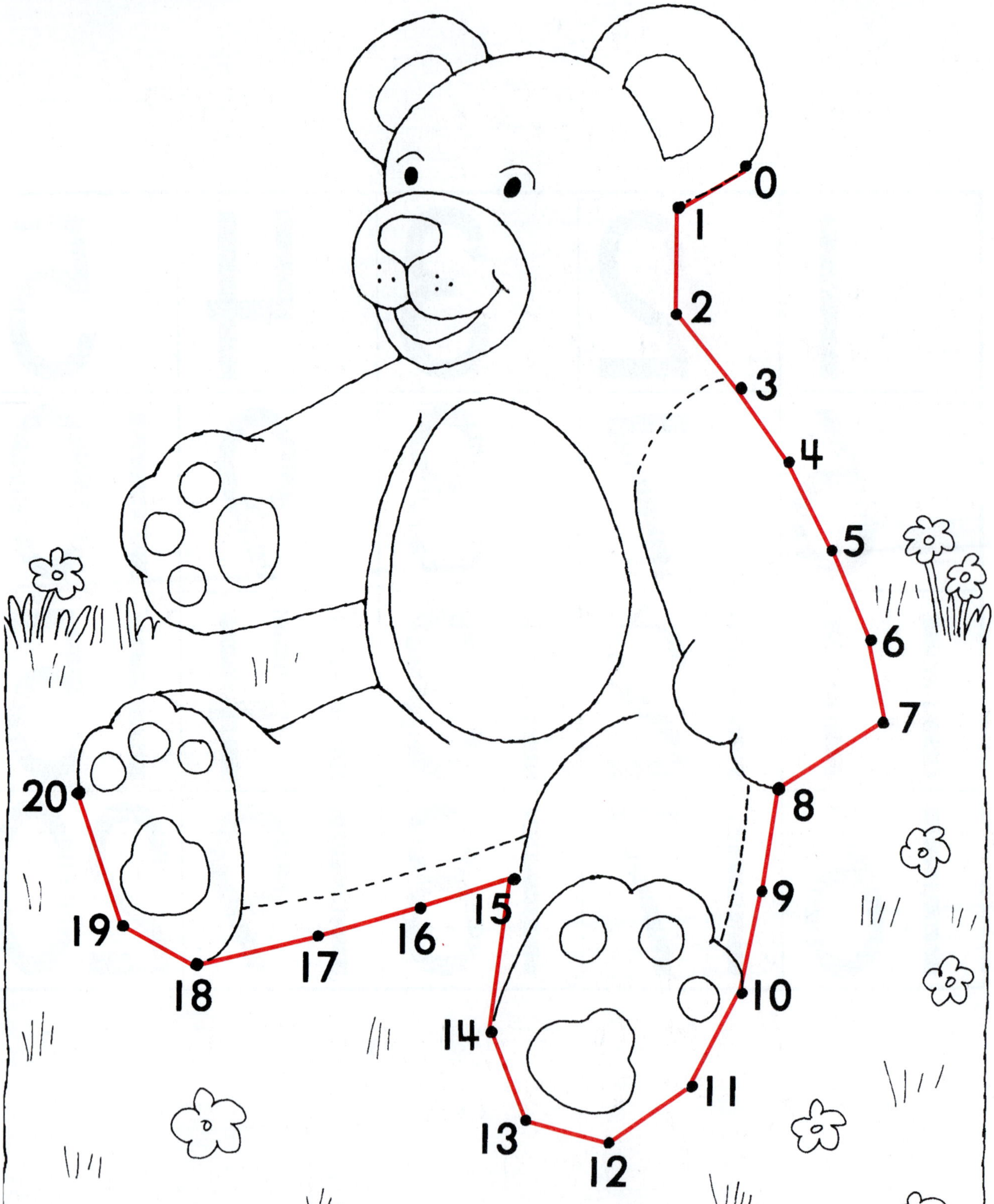

Children follow the numbers to connect the dots in order.

Name ______________________________

Reading a Graph

Favorite Drink

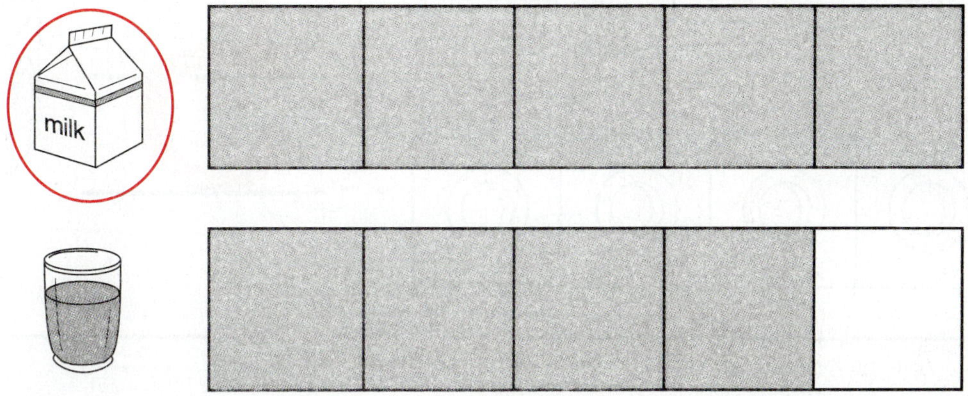

Favorite Activity

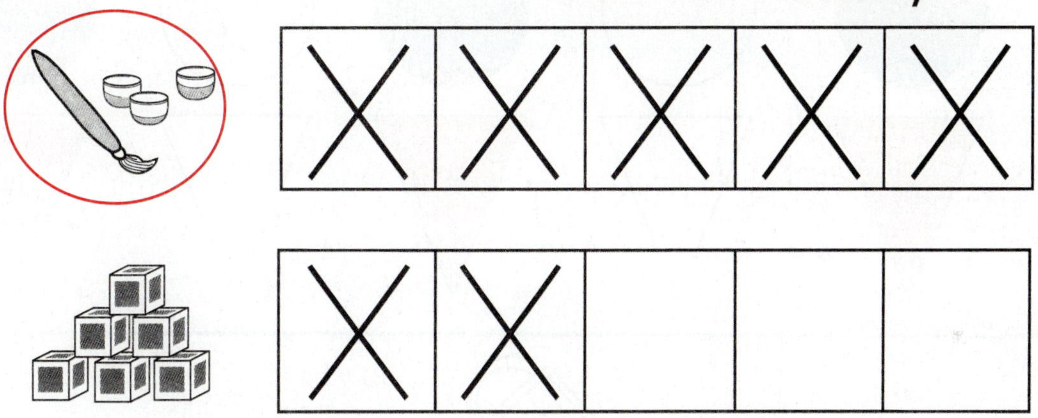

Our Pets

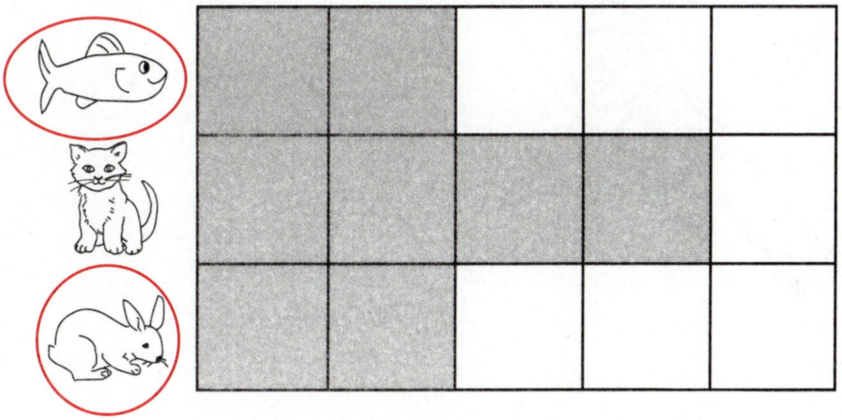

Children circle the item to indicate what the graph shows. **Turtle:** Do more children like milk or juice? **Frog:** Do more children like to paint or play with blocks? **Fish:** Which two pets do the same number of children have? Children can explain their reasoning.

December: Use when children are familiar with the *Classroom Project.*

Review/Test

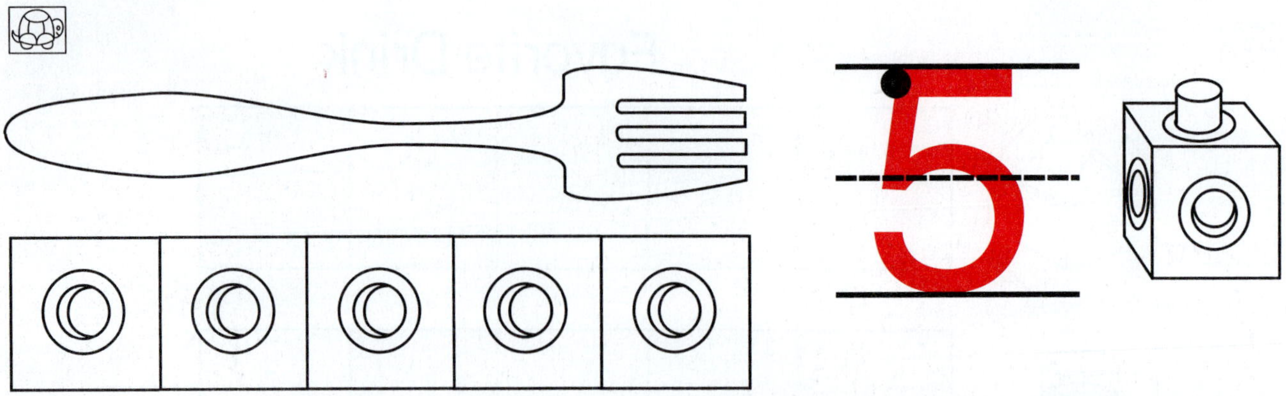

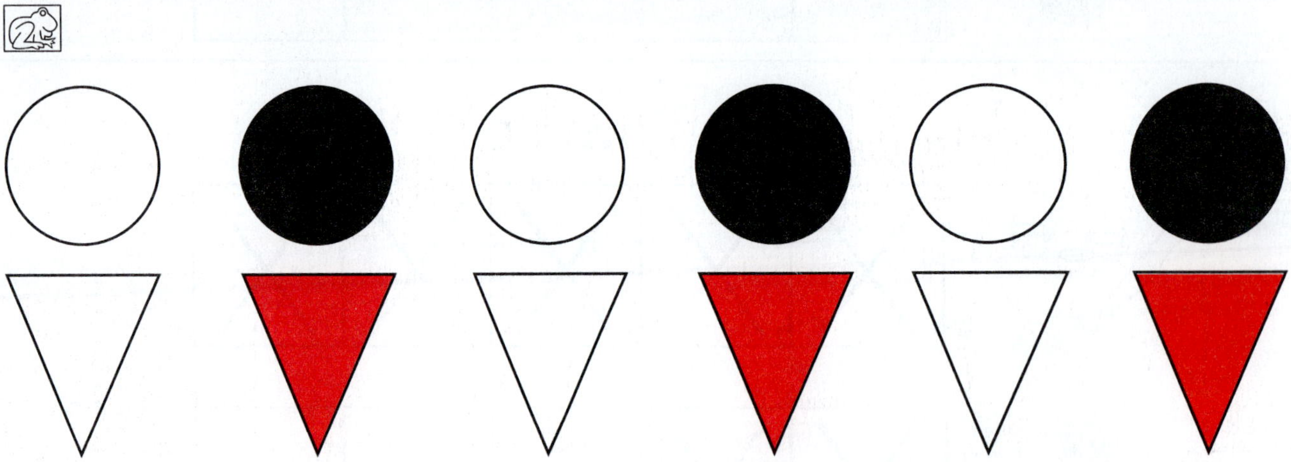

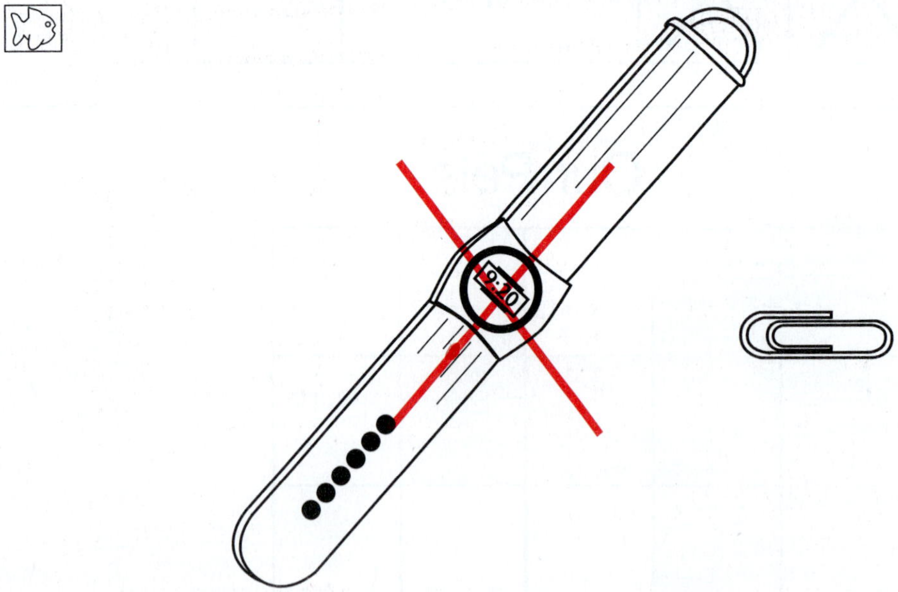

Turtle: Children measure the fork using the cube ruler shown and write the measure. **Frog:** Children color the triangles to match the AB pattern shown by the circles. **Fish:** Children draw an X on the heavier object.

Name ______________________________

Reading a Calendar

January

Sunday	Monday	Tuesday	Wednesday	Thursday	Friday	Saturday
red	orange 1	green 2	blue 3	black 4	yellow 5	purple 6
7	8	9	10	11	12	13
14	15	16	17	18	19	20
21	22	23	24	25	26	27
28	29	30	31			

Children fill in the missing numbers on the calendar. Children draw vertical lines through the days of the week using the following colors: Sundays–red, Mondays–orange, Tuesdays–green, Wednesdays–blue, Thursdays–black, Fridays–yellow, Saturdays–purple. Children draw an X on Tuesday of the second week, a circle on Saturday of the fourth week, and a square on Thursday of the third week.

Adding Objects

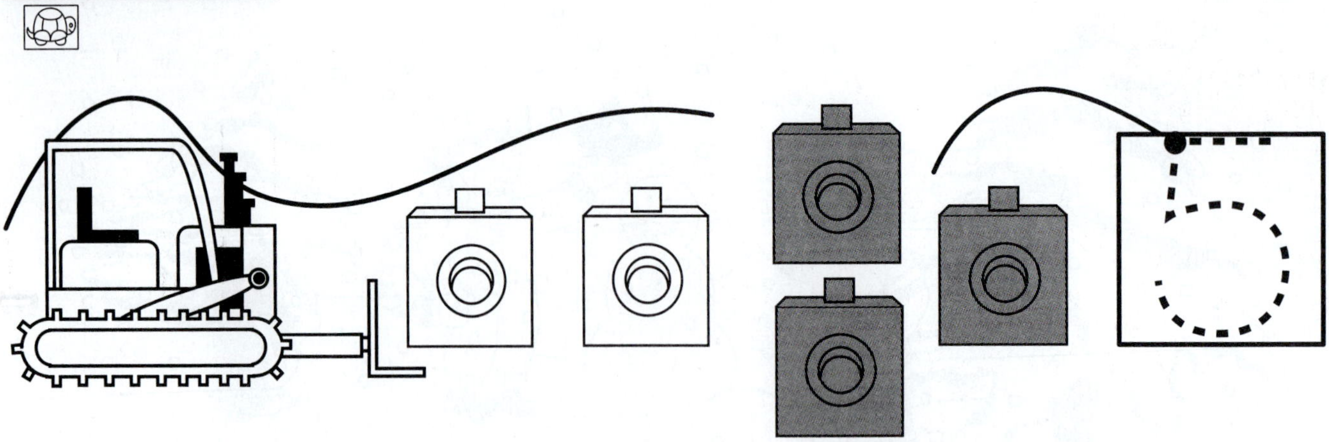

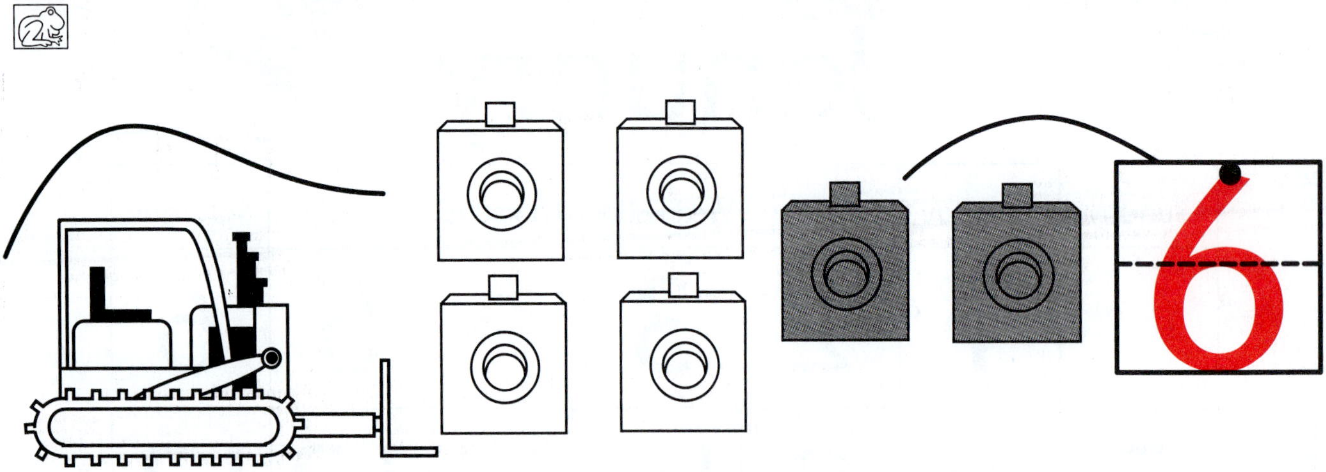

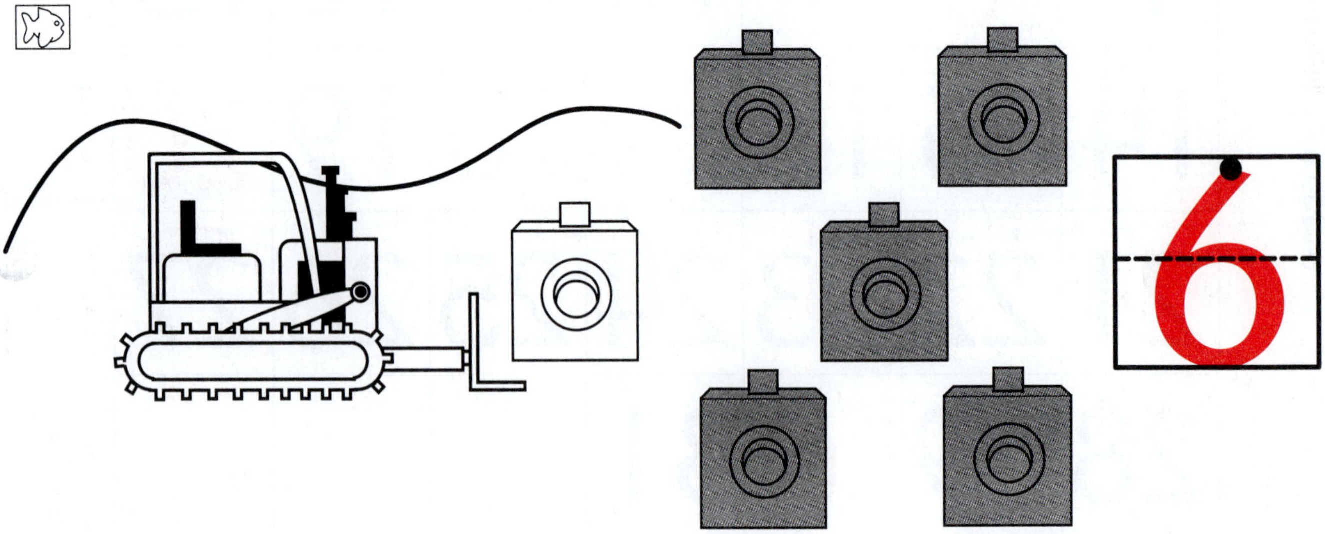

Children place two colors of connecting cubes on the cubes. They count each group and record the total. Children explain what they did.

Remember!
- Understand
- Plan
- Try it
- **Look back**

Answers will vary.

➤ **Look back** Ask, "Did you make a close guess? Was your guess too high? Was it too low?" Children circle the appropriate face.

4

FOLD

Name ______________________

My Problem Solving Book

Strategy: Guess and Check

Remember!
- **Understand**
- Plan
- Try it
- Look back

➤ **Understand** Children talk about how they could determine how many scoops it will take to fill the box.

1

Remember!
- Understand
- **Plan**
- Try it
- Look back

Remember!
- Understand
- Plan
- **Try it**
- Look back

Answers will vary.

about ________ scoops

➤ **Plan** Children talk about the number of scoops they think it will take to fill the box. Then they write their guess. Ask, "What will you do next?" I could count the number of scoops it takes to fill the box to check my guess.

❷

Answers will vary.

________ scoops

➤ **Try it** Children fill the scoop with rice and pour it into the box. Then they record their answers.

❸

Name ______________________________

Top, Middle, and Bottom

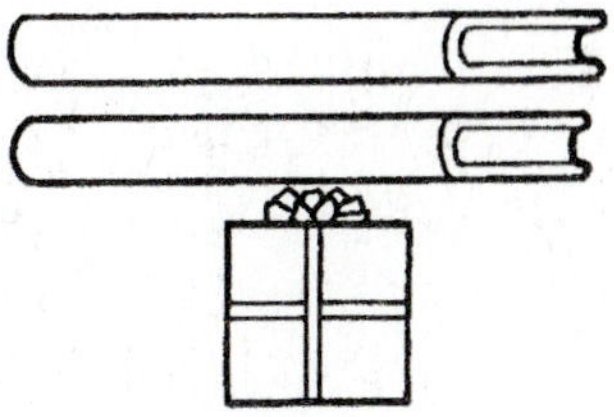

column 2 column 1 column 1 column 3 column 2 column 3

Children cut out the groups of pictures at the bottom of the page. Then they paste each group in the correct column to show if the gift box in each group is on **top,** in the **middle,** or on the **bottom.**

January: Use when children are familiar with *Building Blocks of Geometry.*

Name ____________________

Sides and Corners

O 4

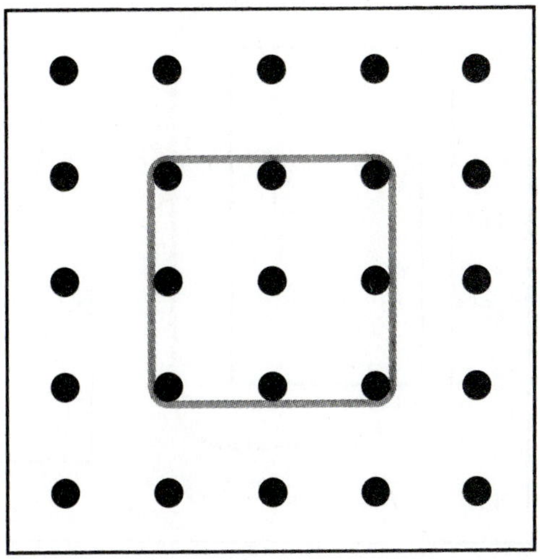

X 4

O 3

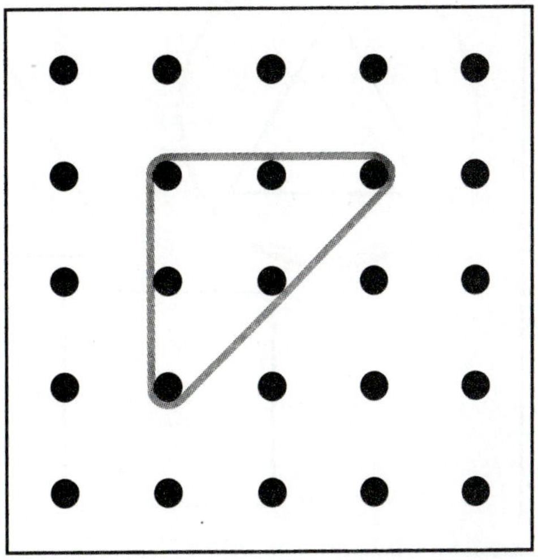

X 3

O 4

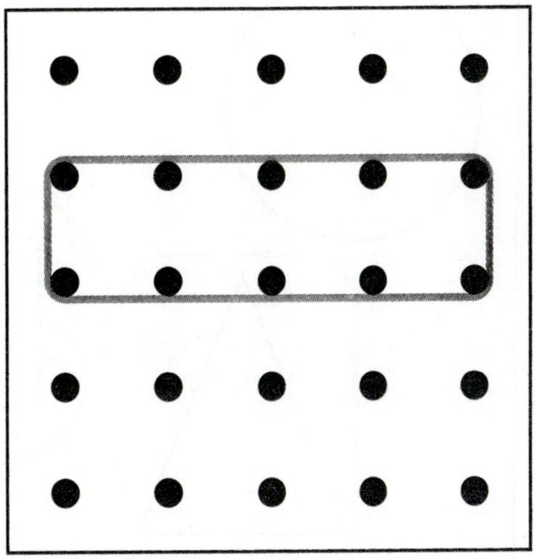

X 4

In each row, children count the number of **sides** and write the numeral in the space under the O. Then they count the **corners** and write the numeral in the space under the X.

January: Use when children are familiar with *Make Your Own Creations.*

Make a Design

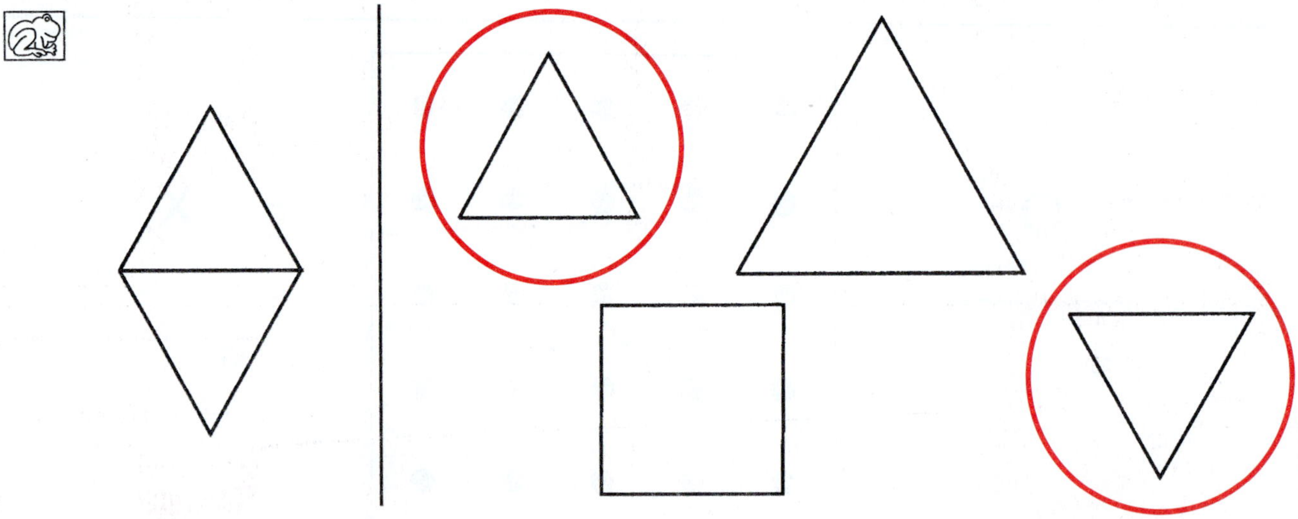

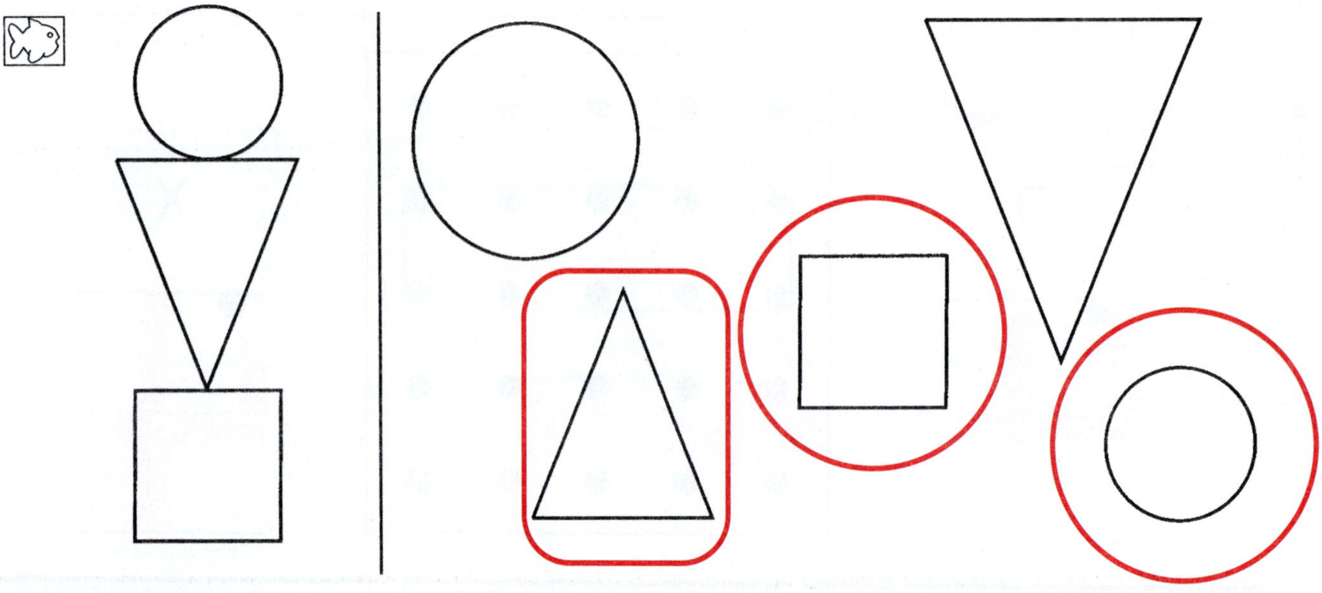

Children circle the shapes they need to make the design at the left in each row.

Name ____________________

How Many in All?

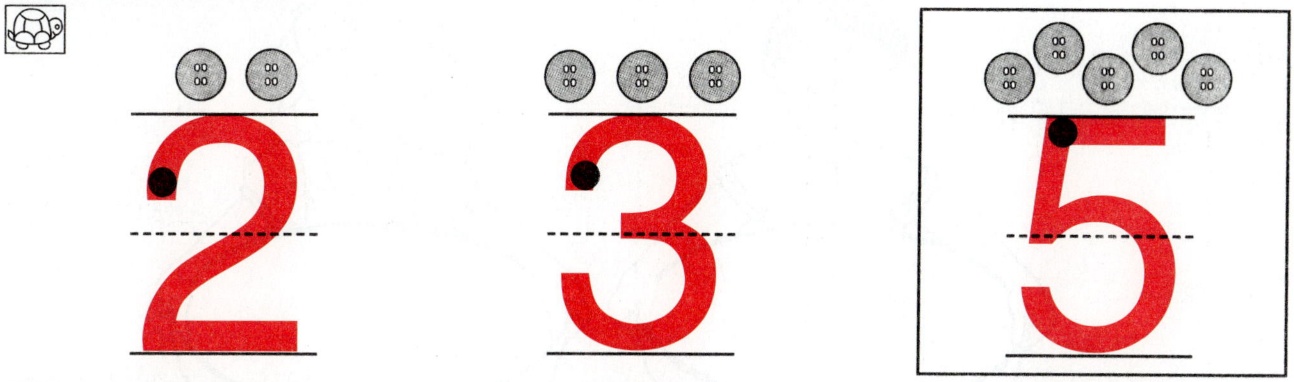

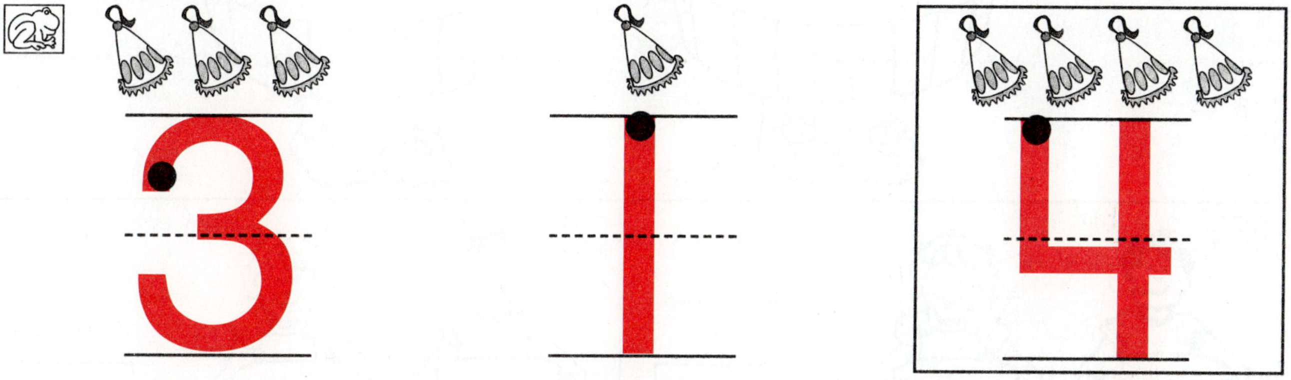

In each row, children count the number of objects in each of the first two groups, tell the number story, and write the corresponding numerals. Then they count and write the numeral showing how many in all. Children may model the situations, using counters or other objects, if needed.

January: Use when children are familiar with *Apple Basket.*

Act Out Sums

$2 + 1 = 3$

$2 + 3 = 5$

$1 + 4 = 5$

$4 + 2 = 6$

Children cut out the pumpkins. They use the cutouts to tell and act out each number story. Then children write how many in all.

Name ______________________________

What Should We Wear?

In each row, children look at the picture and circle the clothing most appropriate to the season.

January: Use when children are familiar with *Weather Pictures*.

Which Holds More?

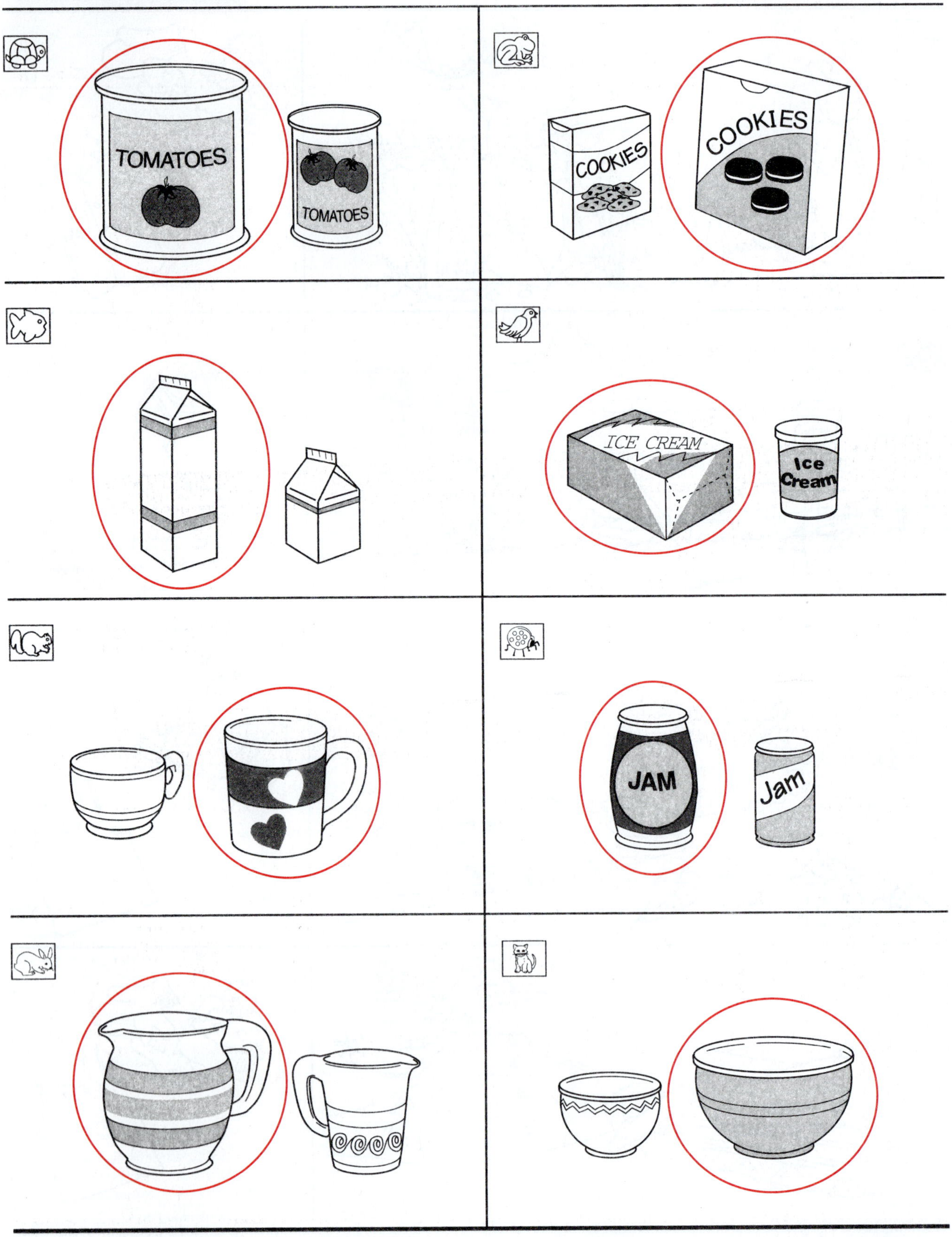

Children compare the size of the containers in each pair. Then they circle the container that can hold more. Using containers in the classroom, children can compare and tell which holds more.

Name ____________________

Greatest to Least

Children cut out each row of containers, one row at a time, order the containers from which holds **most** to which holds **least,** and paste them on paper.

Name

Name ________________________________

Count and Write

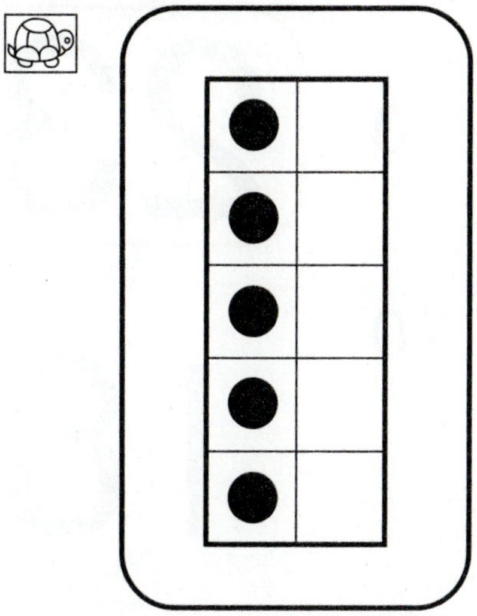

5

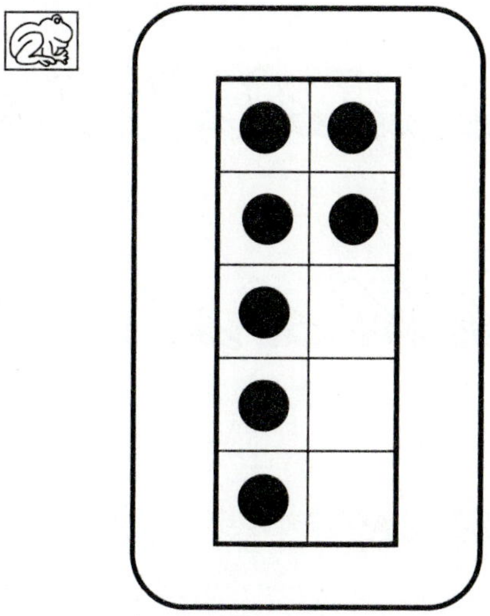

7

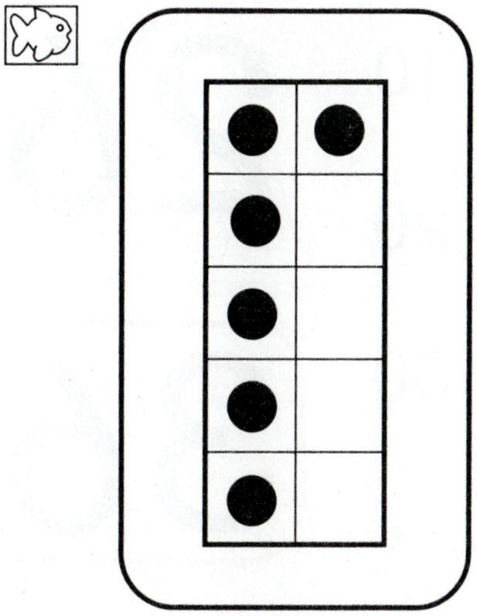

6

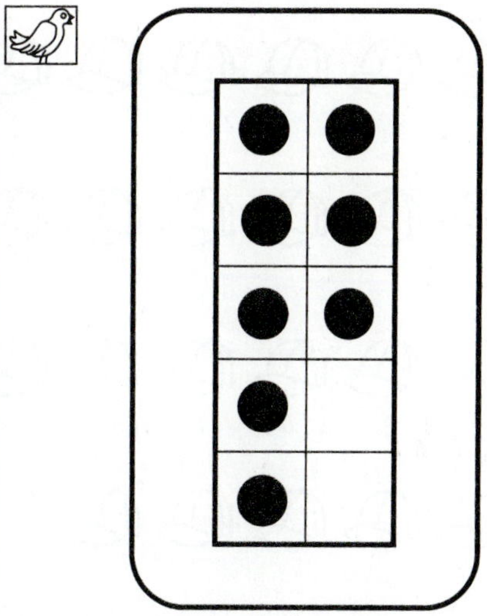

8

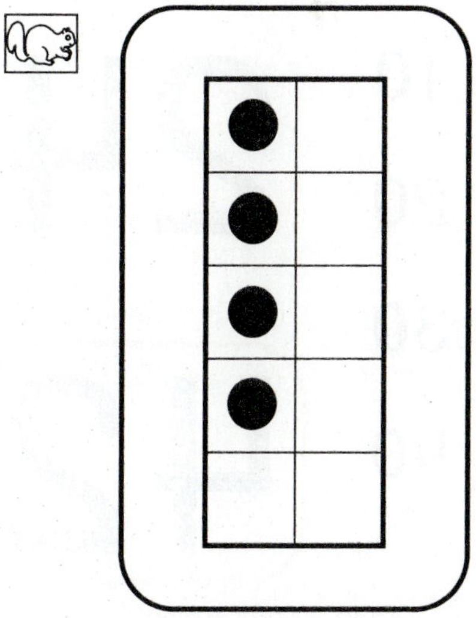

4

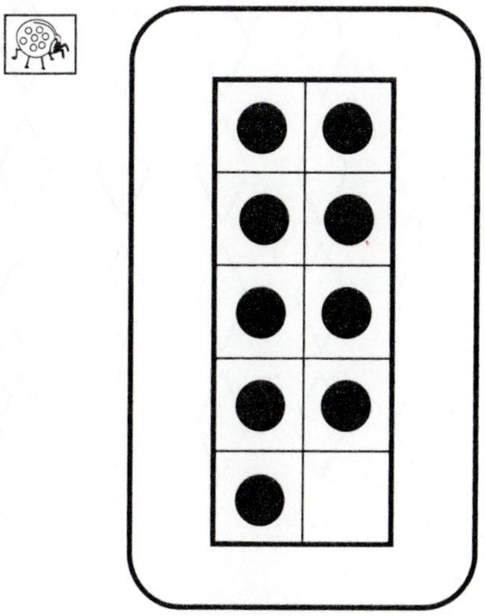

9

In each row, children count the dots on each card and write how many. Some children may need to refer to the counting tape for help writing the numerals.

January: Use when children are familiar with *Ten Grid Number Matchup.*

Tens and More

10

20

23

18

10

20

30

26

36

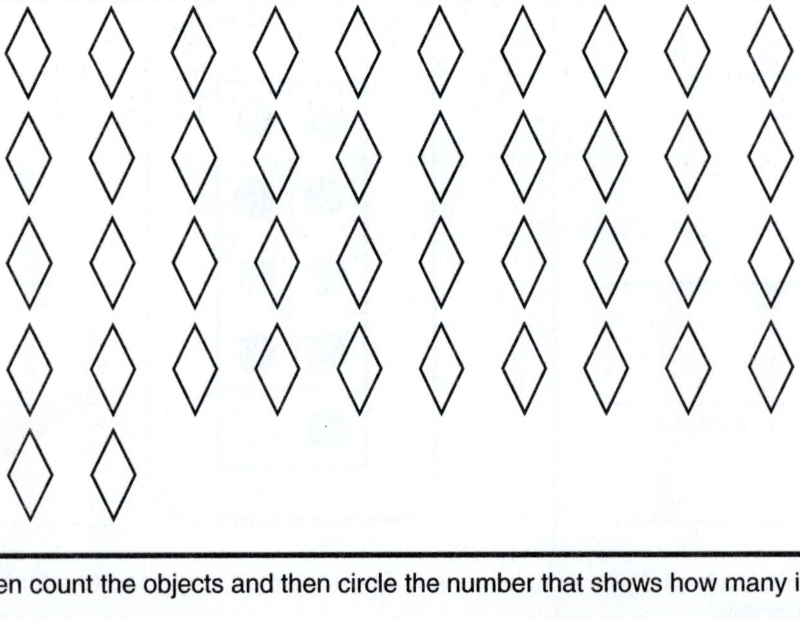

10

20

30

40

24

42

Children count the objects and then circle the number that shows how many in all.

Name ______________________________

Writing Numbers to 30

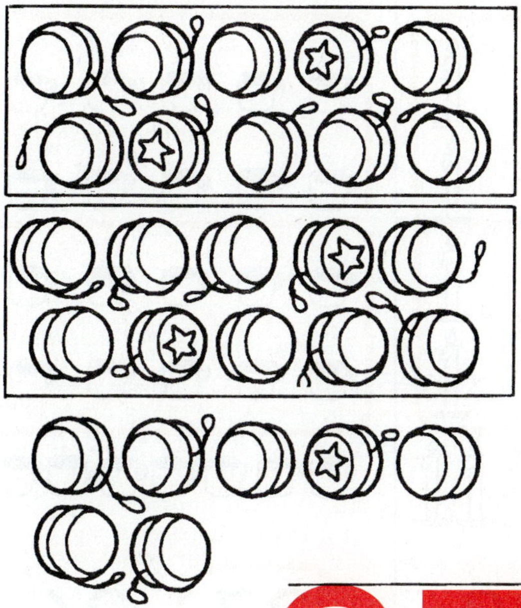

27

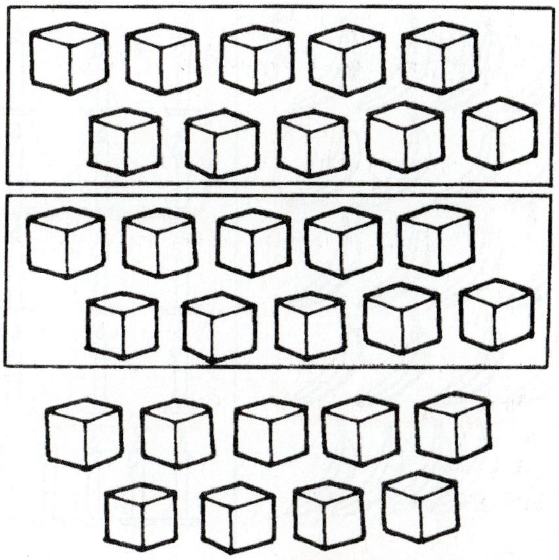

29

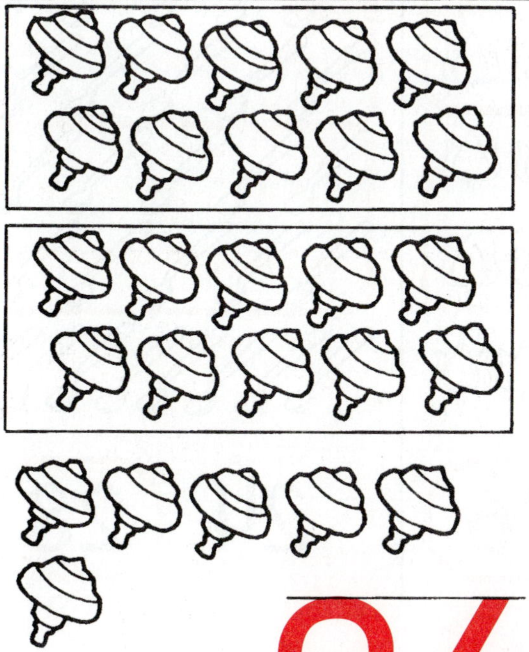

26

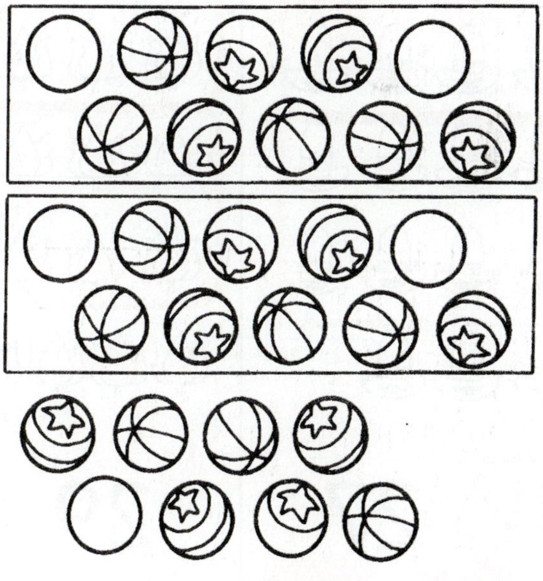

28

Children count the objects and then write the number that shows how many in all.

Numbers to 30

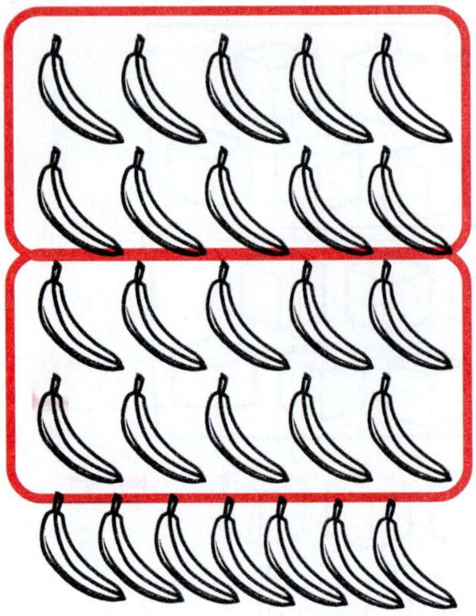

28 27

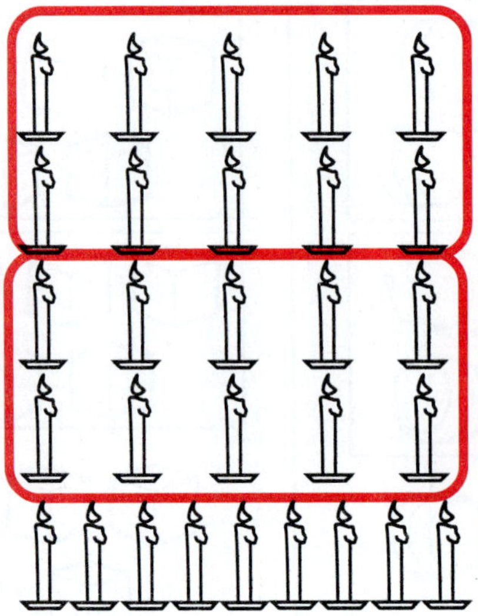

29 28

27 26

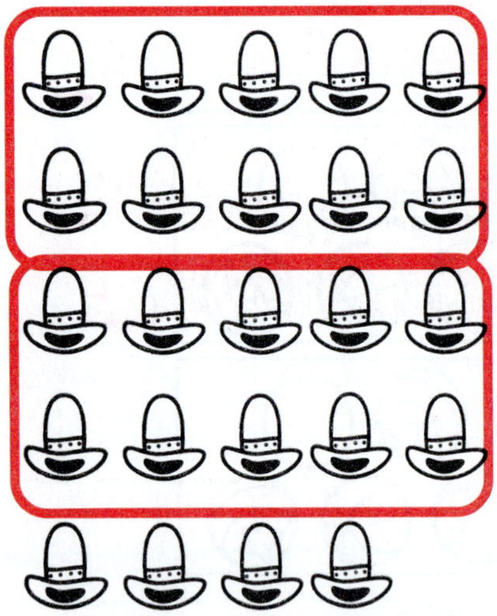

24 27

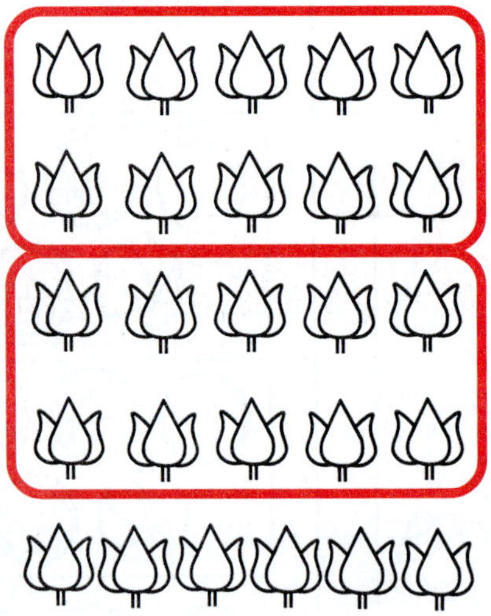

29 26

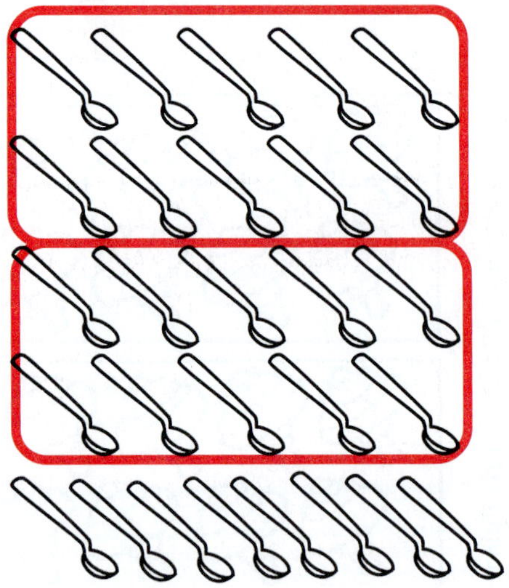

24 28

In each box, children circle groups of 10, count the objects, and circle the number that shows how many in all.

Name ____________________

Color and Write

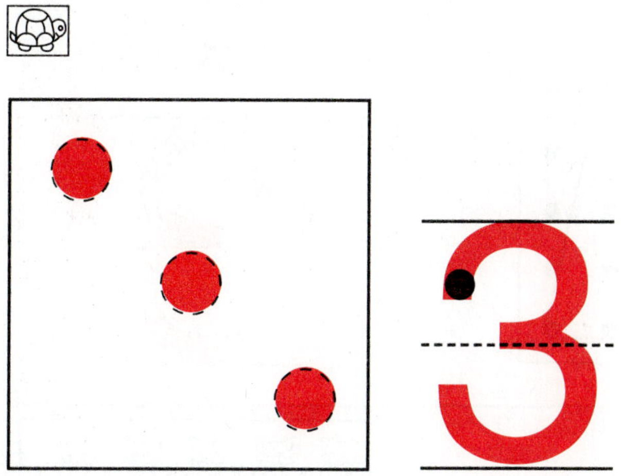

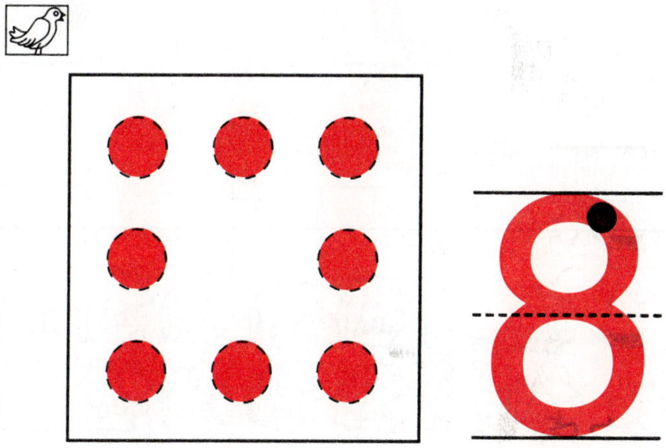

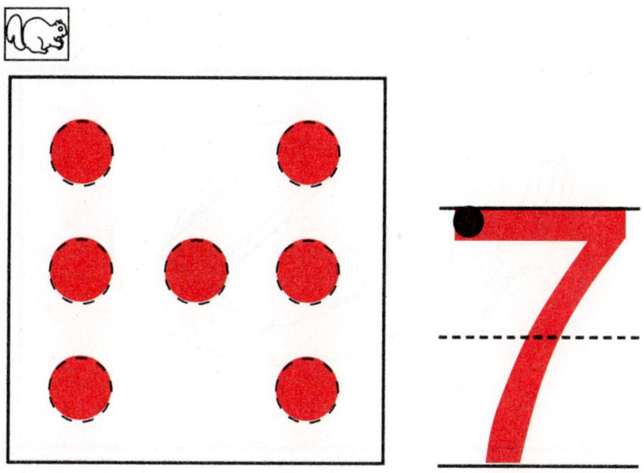

In each row, children color in the dots and then write the numeral.

January: Use when children are familiar with the *Classroom Project.*

Review/Test

O

3

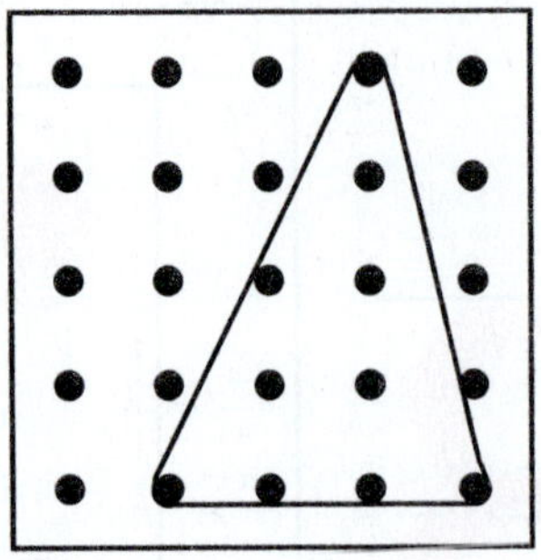

X

3

3

2

5

10

20

25

52

Possible answer is circled. Accept the other if children can justify it.

Spot Check

Turtle: Children write the number of **sides** under the O. Then they write the number of **corners** under the X. **Frog:** Children write the number in each of the first two groups and then write how many in all. **Fish:** Children circle the number that shows how many. **Spot Check:** Children circle the activity that takes longer.

Name ______________________

My Problem Solving Book

Strategy: Look for a Pattern

Remember!
- **Understand**
- **Plan**
- **Try it**
- **Look back**

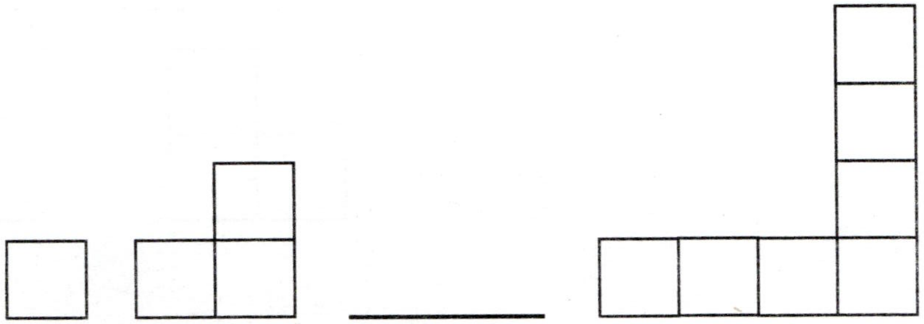

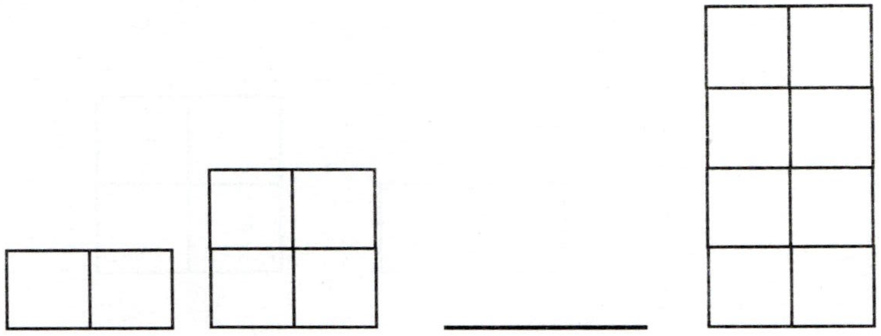

➤ **Understand** Children talk about what they need to find out. Ask, "What is missing?" Accept all reasonable responses, but lead the children that part of the pattern of the blocks are missing.

❶

Remember!
- **Understand**
- **Plan**
- **Try it**
- **Look back**

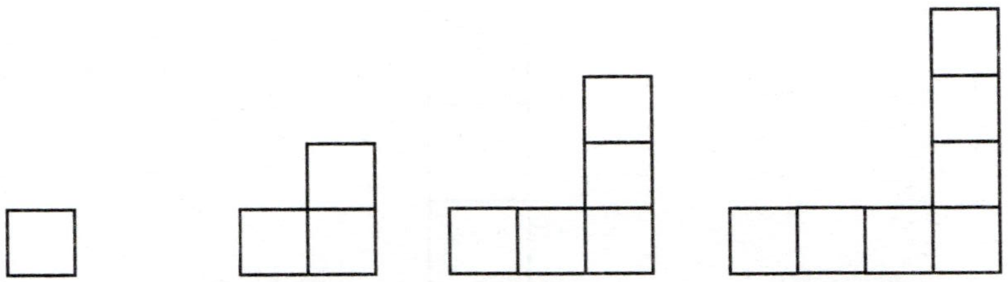

1 3 5 7

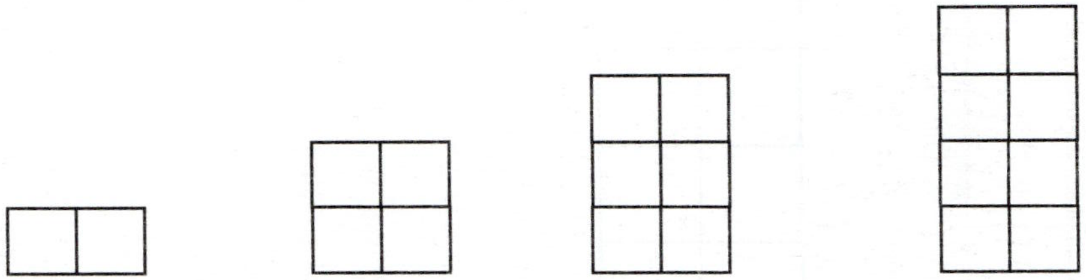

2 4 6 8

➤ **Look back** Children check their drawings and record numbers. Ask, "Do the numbers make sense? Why?" Possible Answer: In the first pattern each shape had two more cubes. In the second pattern each shape showed two more cubes. So, my nubers make sense.

❹

Remember!

- Understand
- **Plan**
- Try it
- Look back

Remember!

- Understand
- Plan
- **Try it**
- Look back

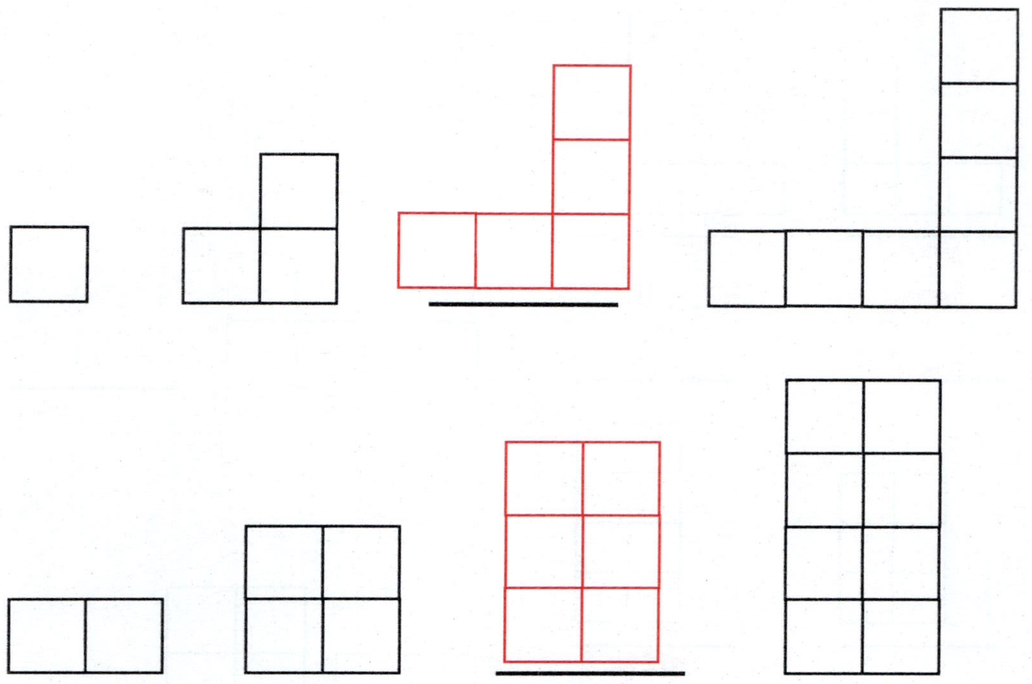

➤ **Plan** Children explain how they can find out what is missing. Possble answer: I can use blocks to make the shapes in the pattern and find the missing shape.

❷

➤ **Try it** Children use connecting cubes to show and complete the pattern. They draw the missing part.

❸

Name ____________________

How Many Are Left?

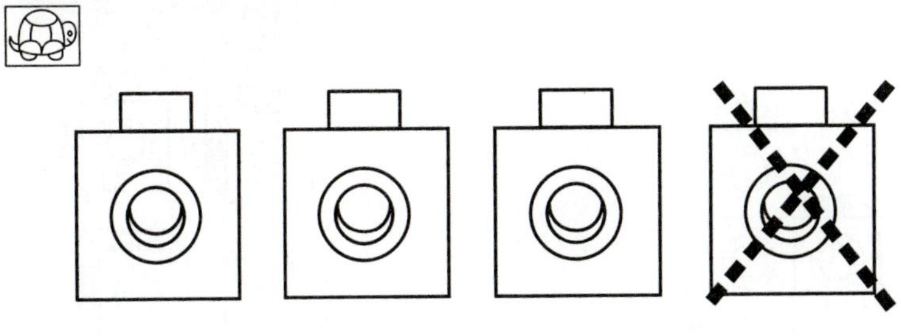

Take away
1

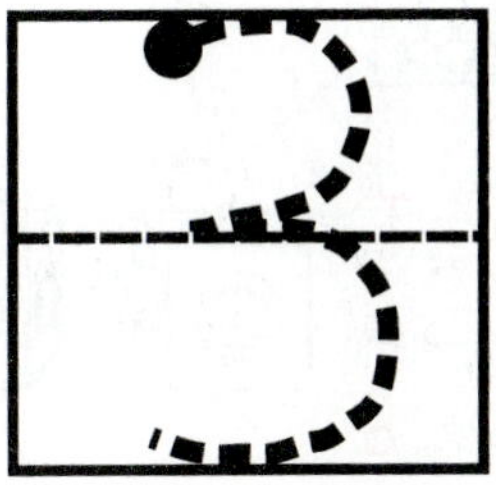

Take away
2

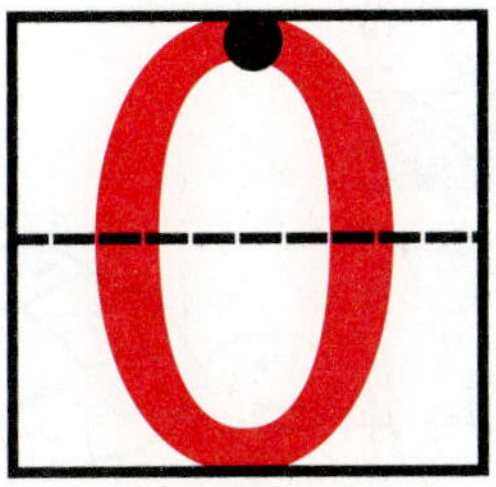

Take away
3

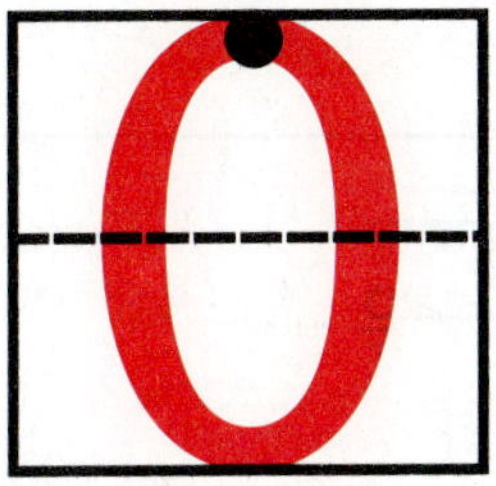

Take away
4

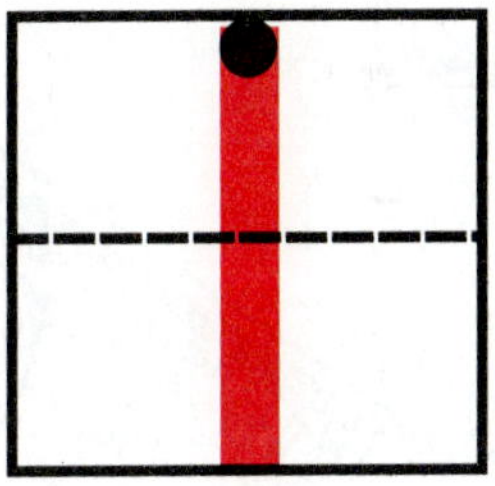

Children place connecting cubes on the picture. They take away cubes according to the numeral given. Children cross out the cubes taken away and write the numeral for how many are left. Children explain what they did.

February: Use when children are familiar with *Add and Take Away.*

Weight

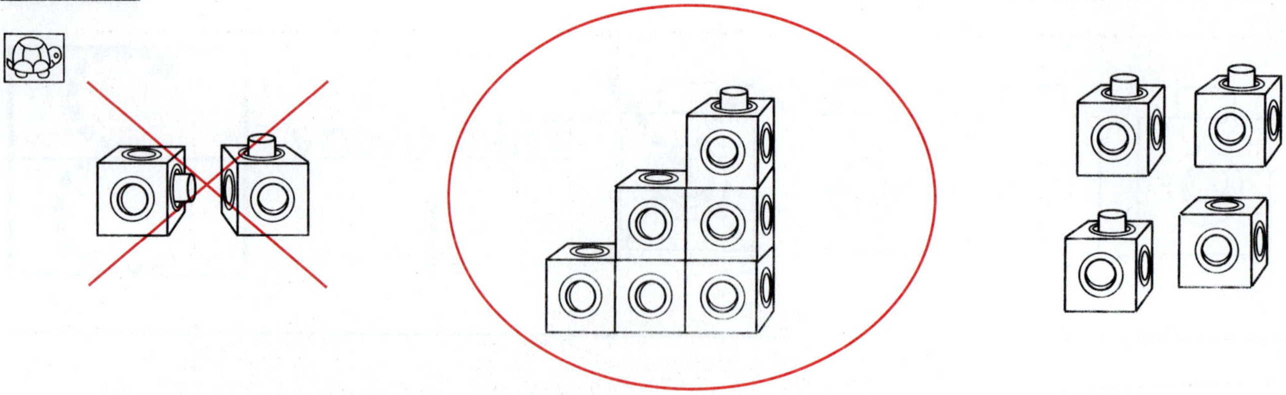

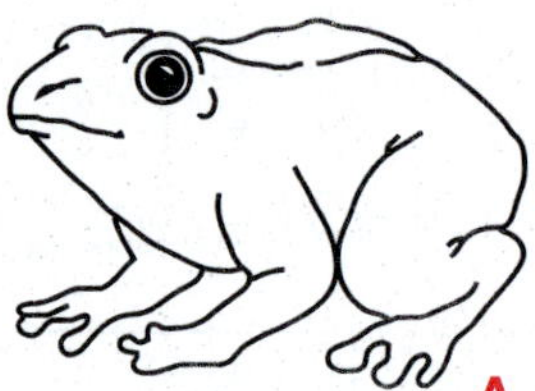

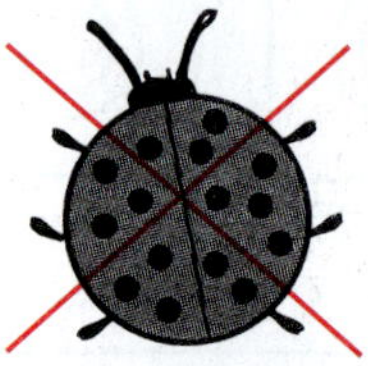

Accept another answer if children can justify it.

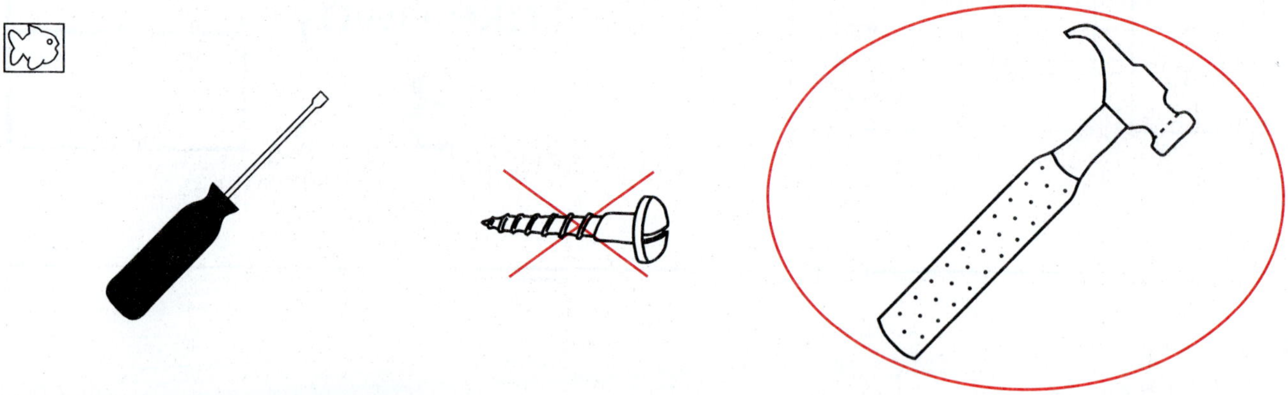

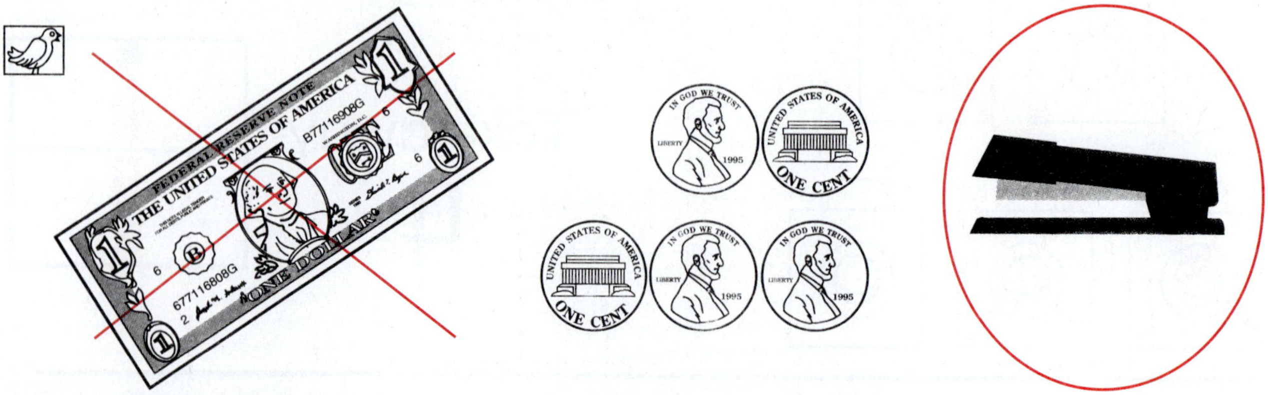

Children circle the **heaviest** object and draw an X on the **lightest** object in each row. Children find and compare classroom objects to see which is heaviest, which is lightest.

Name ______________________________

Make a Pattern

Children cut out the flowers and bees at the bottom and then paste them in the boxes to complete the pattern.

February: Use when children are familiar with *Make a Pattern of Pasta.*

Name

Real Graph

Answers will vary.

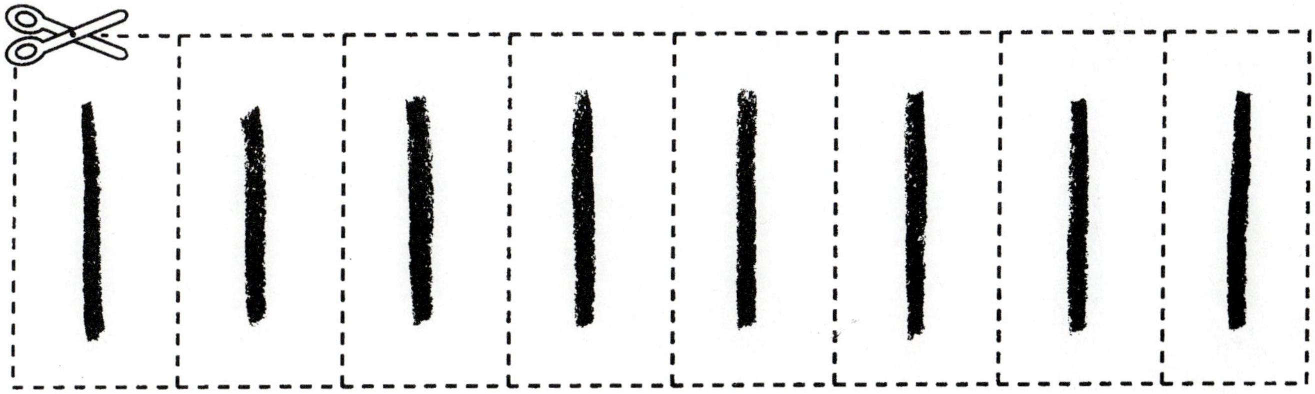

Children toss a real or play penny and record the toss by pasting a cutout tick mark in the column that matches the toss. They continue until all cutout tick marks have been used. When completed, ask children questions about the data.

February: Use when children are familiar with *Guess and Graph.*

Name ______________________________

Cylinders

Circled items should be colored.

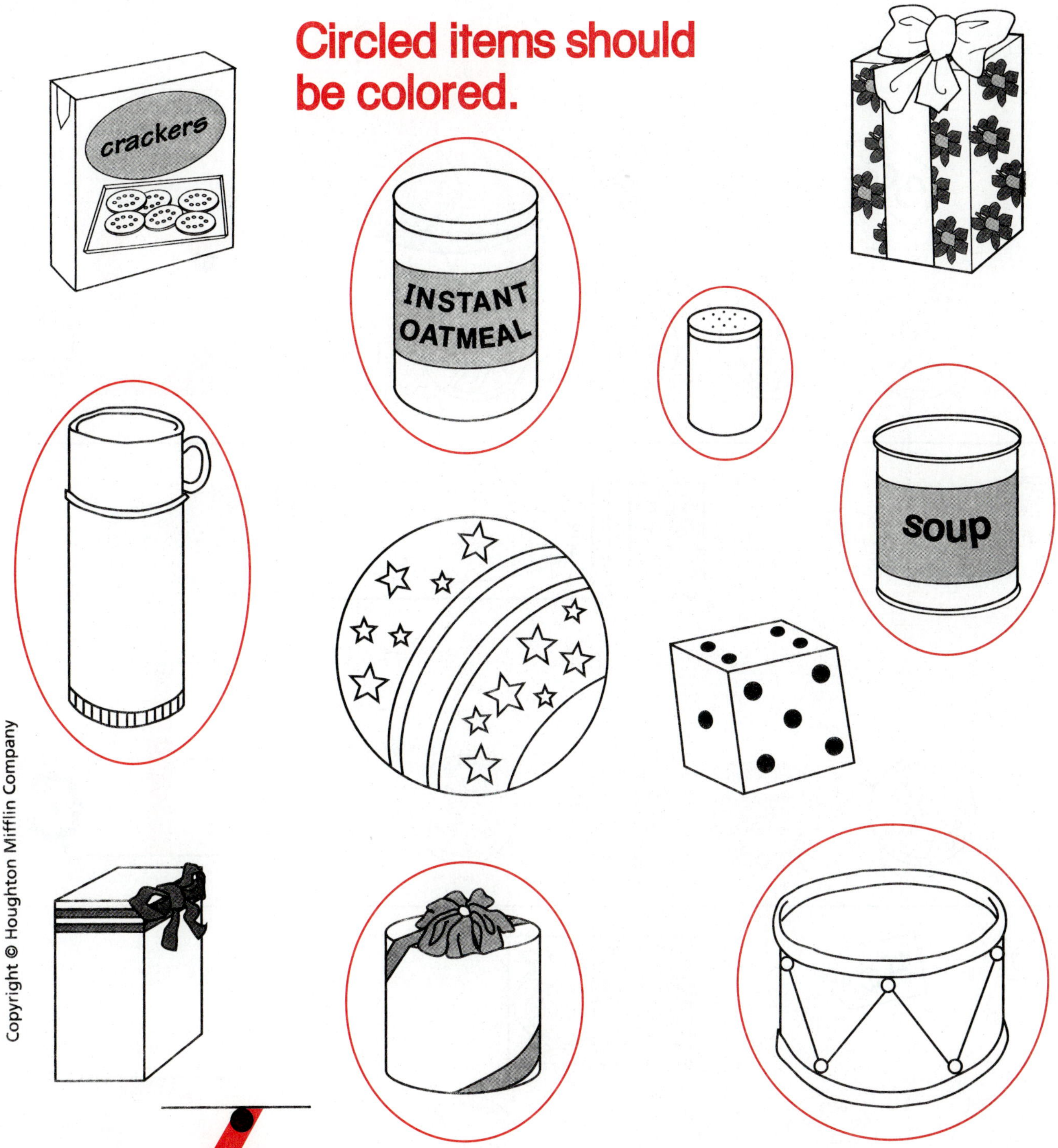

6

Children color the cylinders above the answer space. Then they count the cylinders and write the number.

At the Store

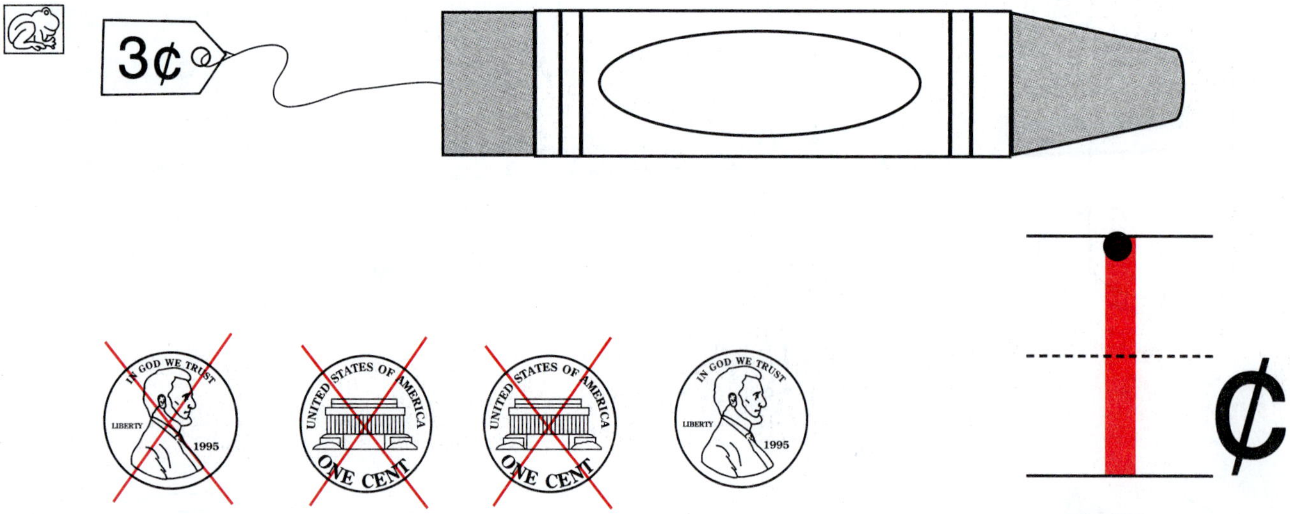

Children count the pennies and cross out the numver equal to the price of the object. Children then count the pennies left and write the amount of money left.

Name ______________________________

How Much Is Left?

Start with	You buy	Money left
		1 ¢
		1 ¢
		4 ¢
	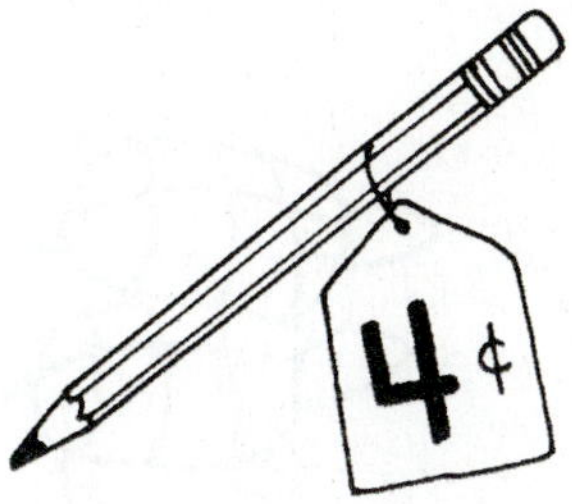	2 ¢

For each row, children use pennies to count out the number of pennies shown. They move away the number of pennies they need to buy the object shown. Then they cross out that same number of pennies and write how much money is left.

February: Use when children are familiar with *Break the Bank.*

Match the Number Sentence

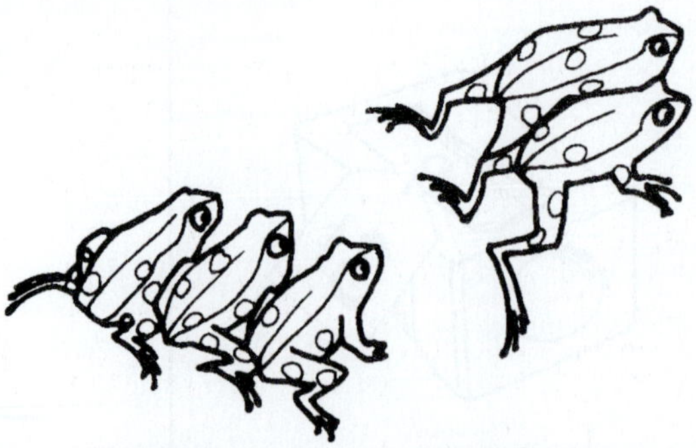

5 - 2

3 - 3

2 + 3

2 + 2

Children look at what is happening in the picture story. If the number sentence matches the story, they circle the number sentence. Children may act out the story, if necessary.

Name ______________________________

Number Path

1 2 3 4 5 6 7 8 9 10 11 12 13 14 15 16 17 18 19 20 21 22 23 24 25 26 27 28 29 30 31

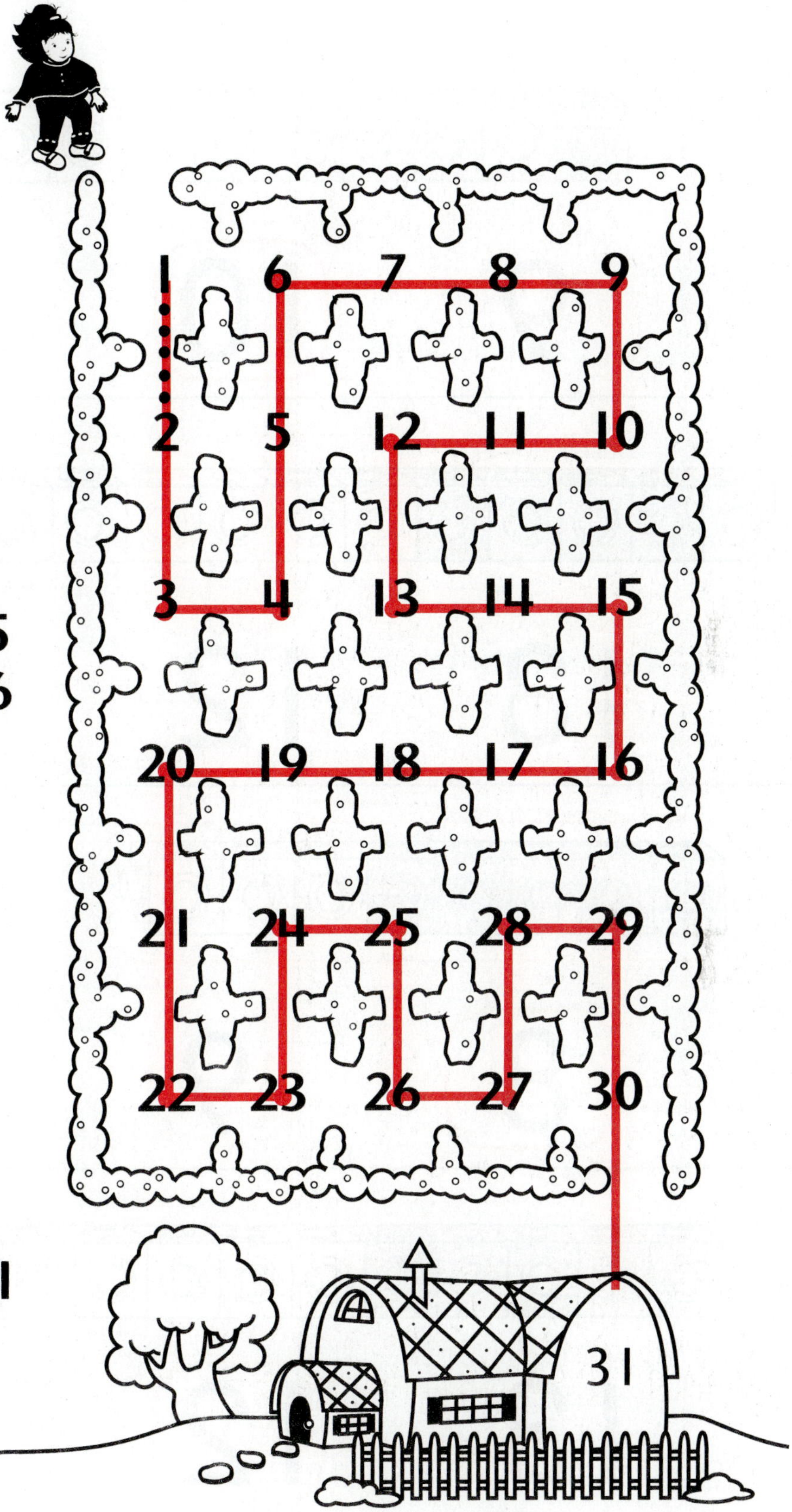

Children connect the numbers in the maze in order to show the path to the house.

February: Use when children are familiar with *Race to 31*.

How Long?

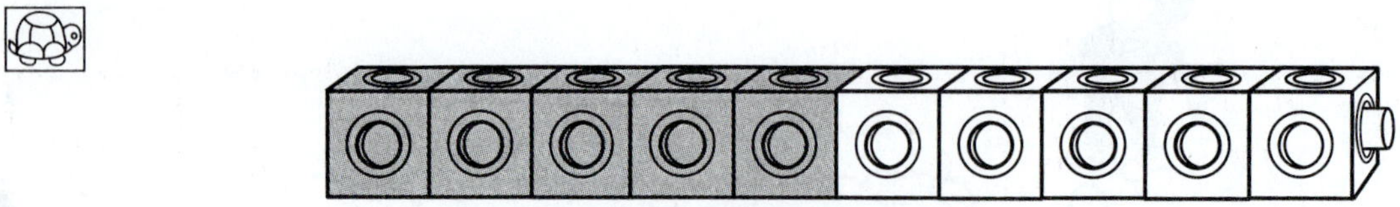

9 10 11

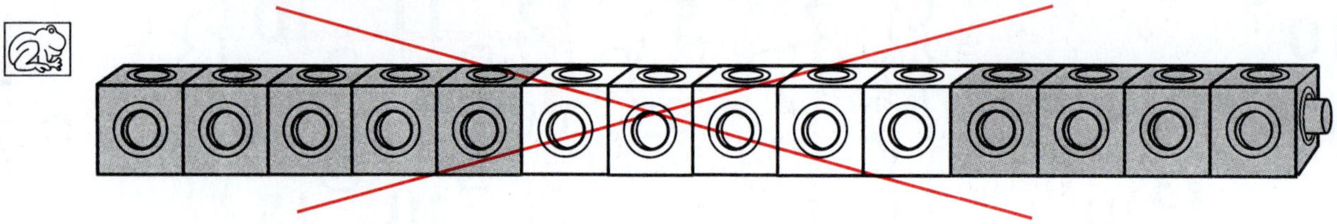

13 12 14

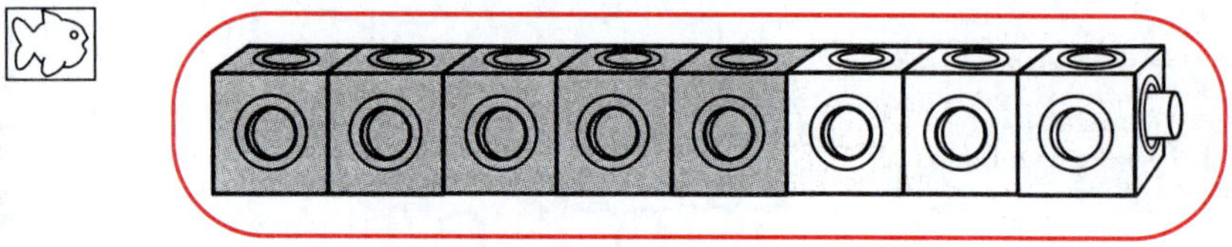

8 9 7

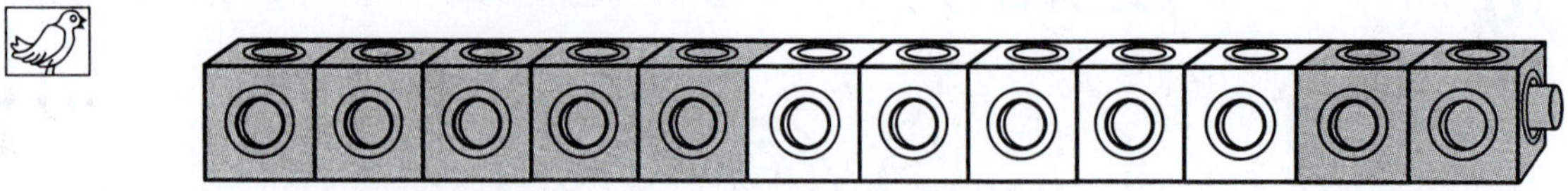

13 12 14

Children count the cubes and then circle the corresponding numeral to show how many. Then they circle the **shortest** cube train and put an X on the **longest** cube train.

Name ______________________________

Numbers to 100

Shaded squares should be colored red.

1	2	3	4	5	6	7	8	9	10
11	12	13	14	15	16	17	18	19	20
21	22	23	24	25	26	27	28	29	30
31	32	33	34	35	36	37	38	39	40
41	42	43	44	45	46	47	48	49	50
51	52	53	54	55	56	57	58	59	60
61	62	63	64	65	66	67	68	69	70
71	72	73	74	75	76	77	78	79	80
81	82	83	84	85	86	87	88	89	90
91	92	93	94	95	96	97	98	99	100

Whole Class: Children count by multiples of 10 to 100, placing a counter on each number. Children then find and color red the squares with the numbers 32, 33, 37, 38, 41, 44, 46, 49, 51, 55, 59, 62, 68, 73, 77, 84, 86, and 95. When children have finished the activity, they can count from 1 to 100 to each other.

Count to One Hundred

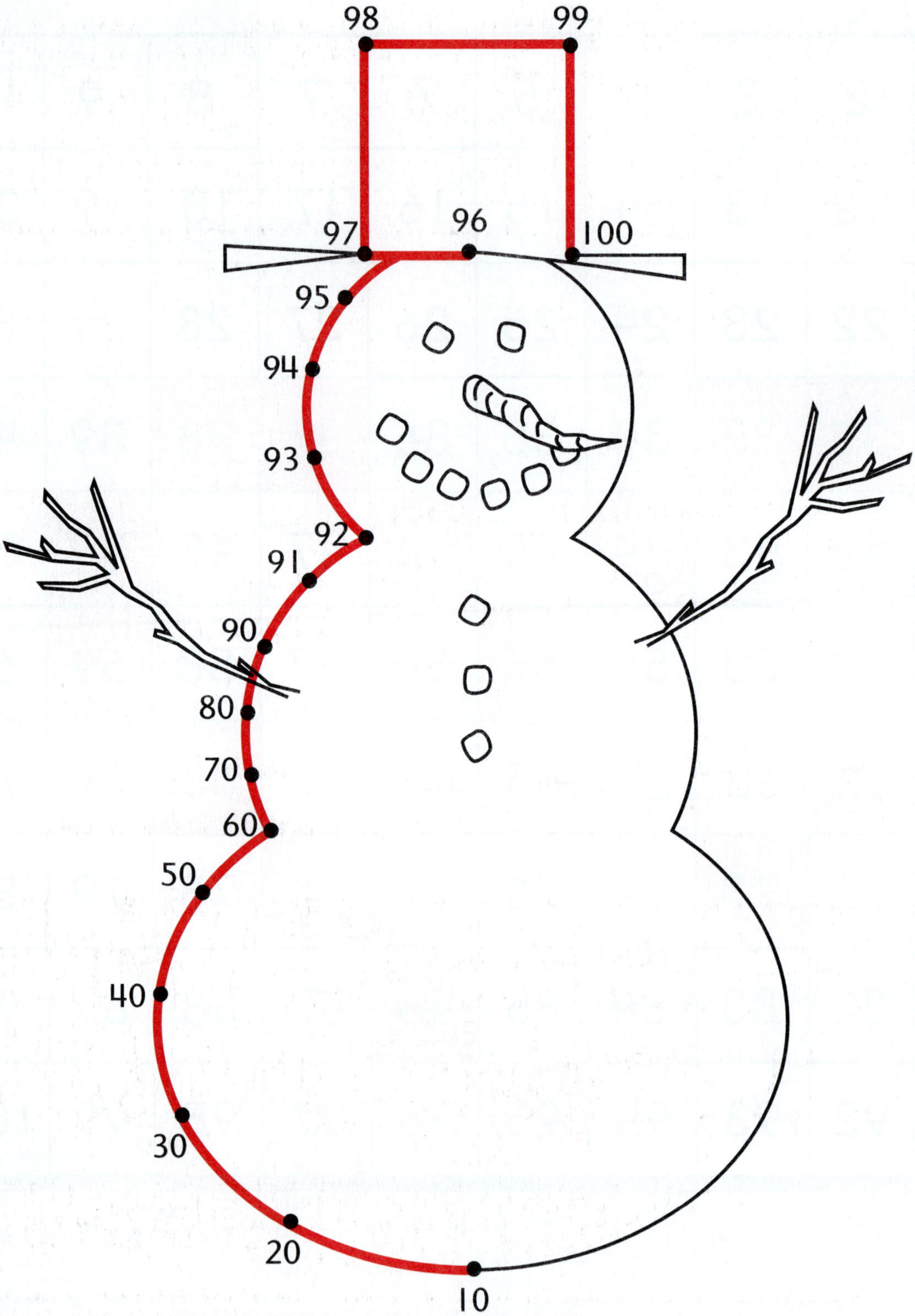

Children connect the dots from 10 to 90 counting by tens. They connect the dots from 90 to 100 counting by ones.

Name ______________________

Count and Write

13

16

19

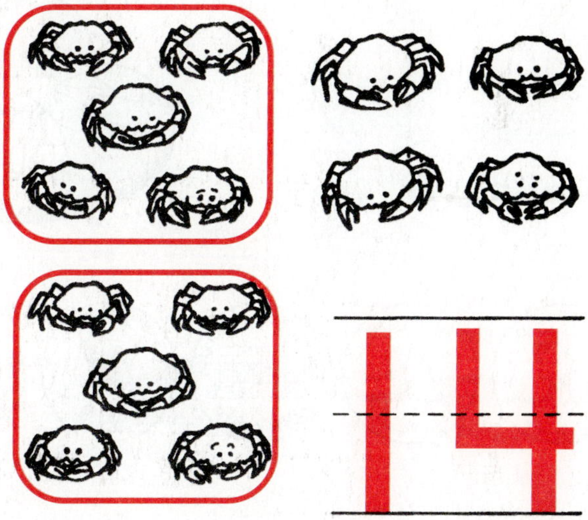

14

15

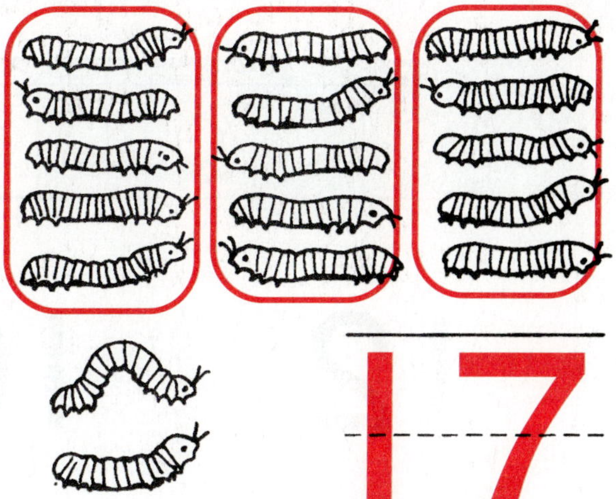

17

In each box, children circle groups of 5. Then they write how many in all.

Review/Test

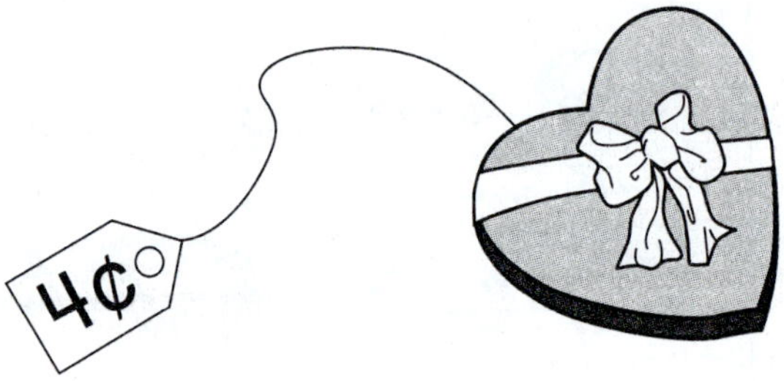

2¢

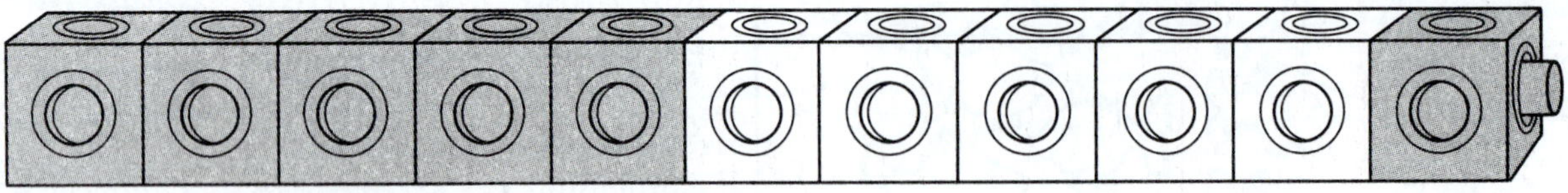

12 10 11

Turtle: Children circle the cylinder. **Frog:** Children cross out the number of pennies representing the price and then write the amount left. **Fish:** Children count the cubes and circle the corresponding numeral.

Remember!
- Understand
- Plan
- Try it
- **Look back**

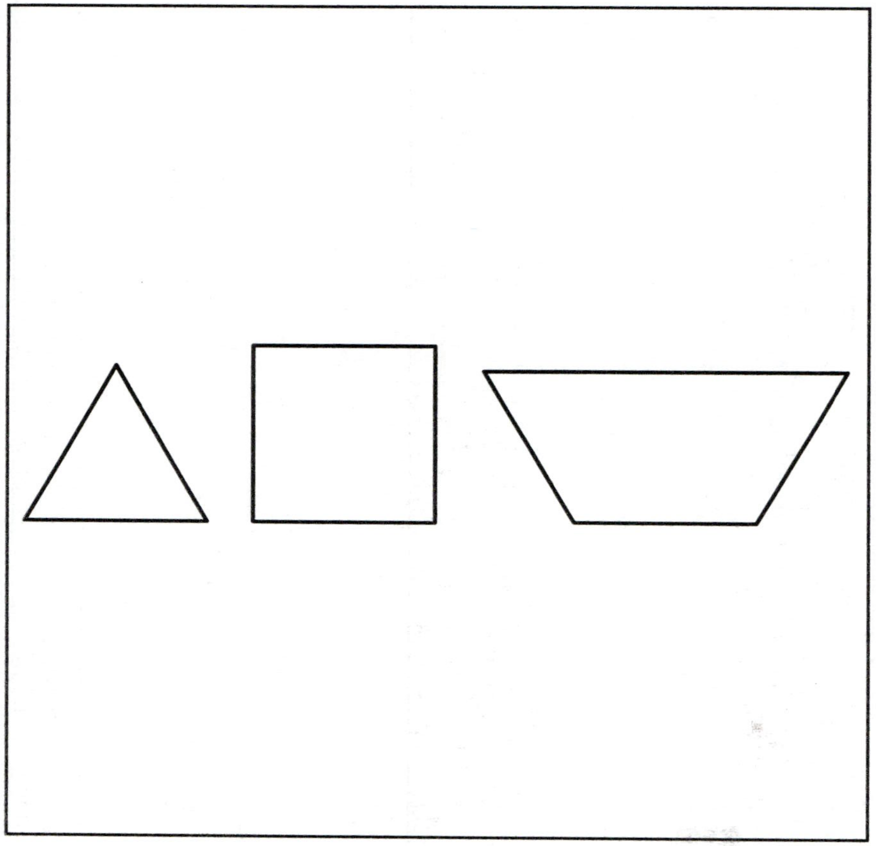

➤ **Look back** Children compare the drawing to their work.

FOLD

Name ______________________________

Remember!
- **Understand**
- Plan
- Try it
- Look back

My Problem Solving Book

Strategy: Draw a Picture

I need to find out where the triangle is.

➤ **Understand** Read this problem aloud to children: There are 3 blocks in a row. The square is in the middle. The trapezoid is last. Where is the triangle? Children tell what they need to find out.

Remember!

- Understand
- **Plan**
- Try it
- Look back

I'll listen to the directions and arrange all the blocks.

➤ **Plan** Children explain how they will find out where the triangle is in the row.

❷

Remember!

- Understand
- Plan
- **Try it**
- Look back

➤ **Try it** Read the problem again. Children arrange the blocks in the correct order and trace them to make a picture.

❸

Name ______________________________

Counting On

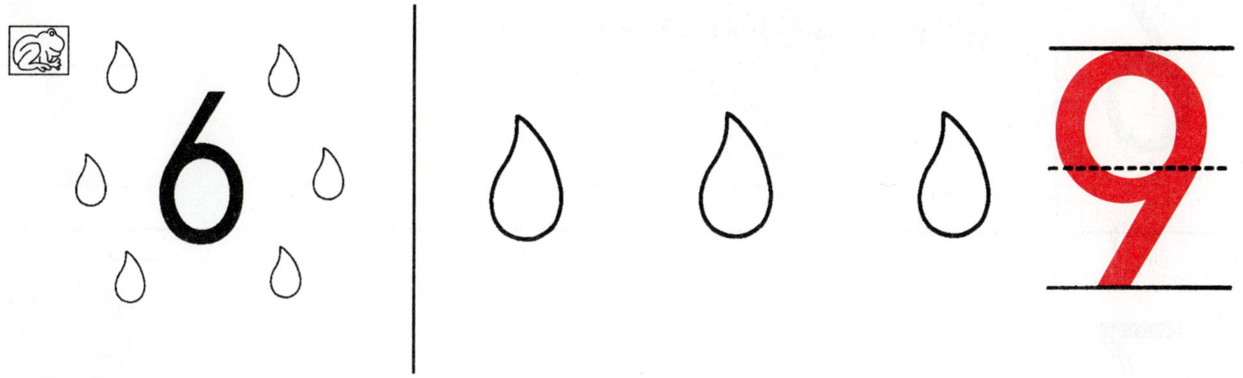

Children count on from the number in the first box to find how many objects are in each row. Then they write the number to show how many objects there are in all. Children may model the situations using counters or other objects.

March: Use when children are familiar with the *Daily Domino.*

One More

5 six raindrops 6

6 seven raindrops 7

7 eight raindrops 8

8 nine raindrops 9

9 ten raindrops 10

In each row, children draw one more raindrop than the number shows. Then they write the number that shows one more.

Name ______________________________

Pennies

= 5¢

4¢

3¢

2¢

4¢

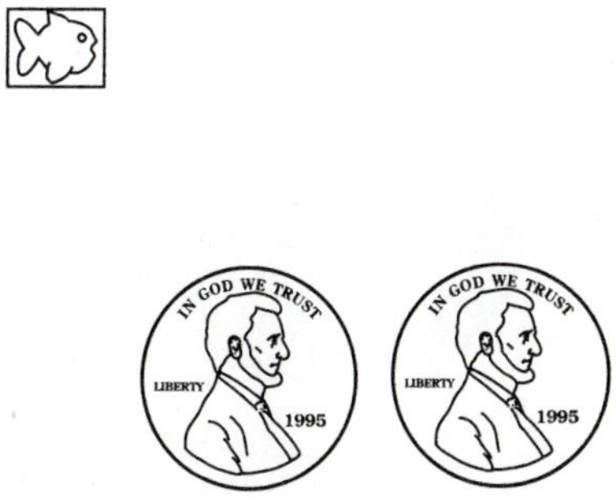

2¢

3¢

2¢

1¢

In each row children write the numbers to show the amounts. Then they circle the greater amount in each row. Children model the situations using real or play pennies.

March: Use when children are familiar with the *Graph.*

Box It!

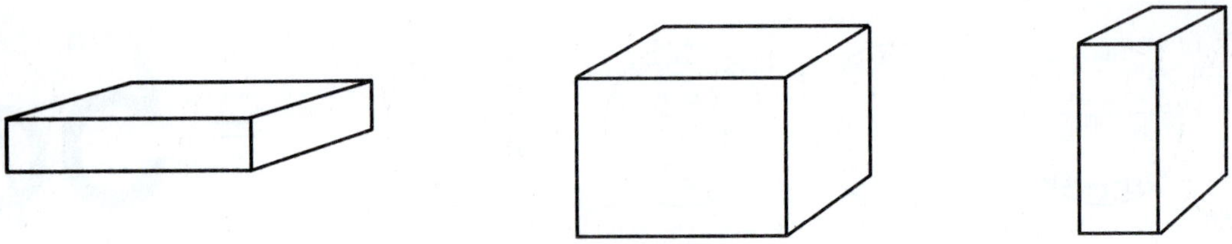

7

Answer may be 4 or 7, depending on whether or not children count examples.

Children circle each object that is a rectangular solid, using the examples at the top of the page for reference. Then they count and write the total number of rectangular solids.

Name ______________________________

Counter Toss

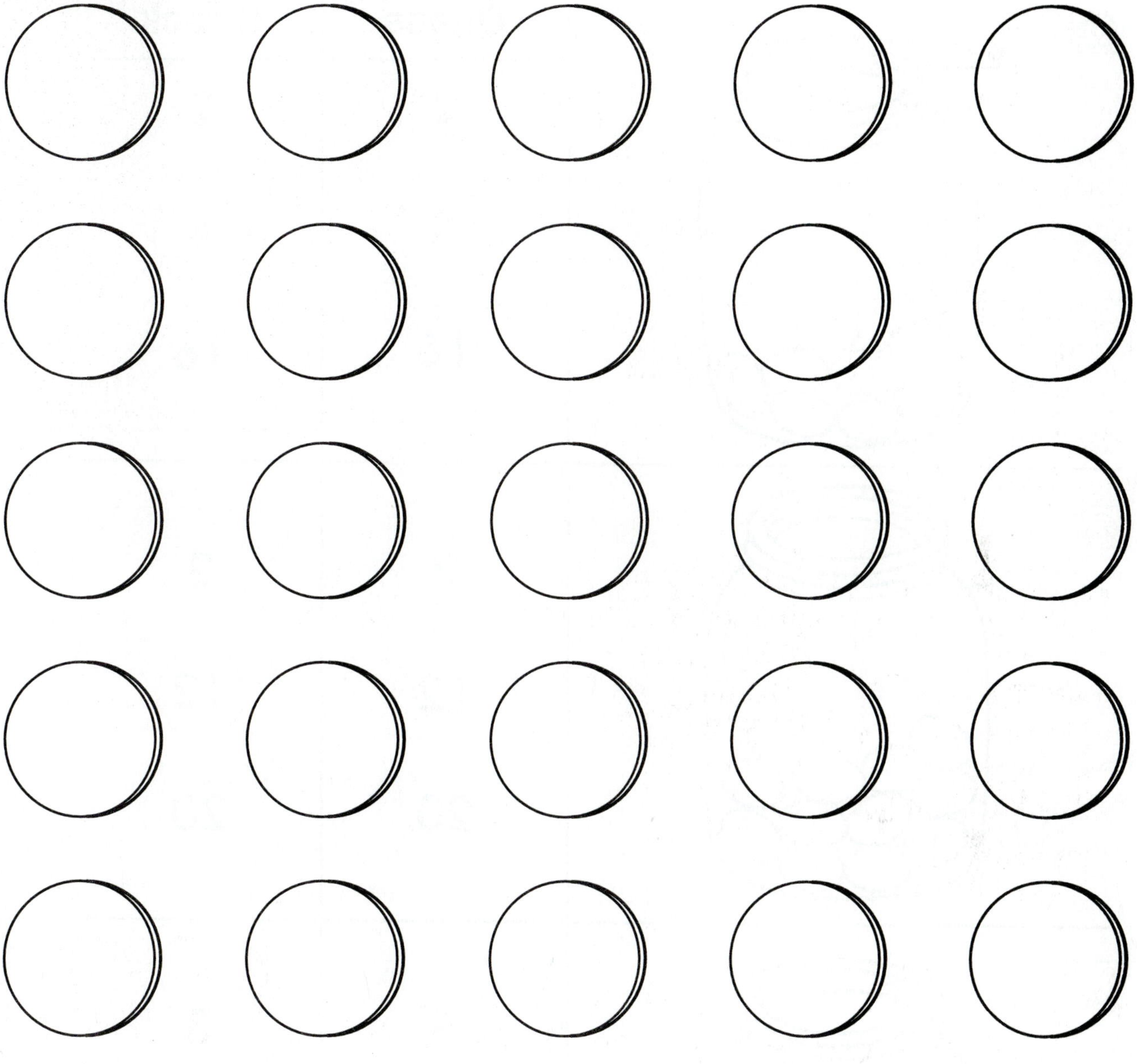

______

______ red ○

______

______ white ○

Answers will vary.

Place 25 counters in a container. Children shake and carefully spill the counters. Each child records the spill by coloring the number of red and putting an X on the numbers of white counters. Then children write the results. Have children share their results.

March: Use when children are familiar with *Grab a Handful!*

Guess How Many

Guesses will vary.

	Guess	Check
 	2 8 16	2 8 16
 	2 12 20	2 12 20
 	3 13 18	3 13 18

Children look quickly at the jar in each row. They guess how many objects are in the jar, circle their guess, and then count and color the objects. Then they circle the actual number in the Check column.

Name ______________________________

Groups of 10

Circles will vary, but should always enclose 10 objects.

18 19 20

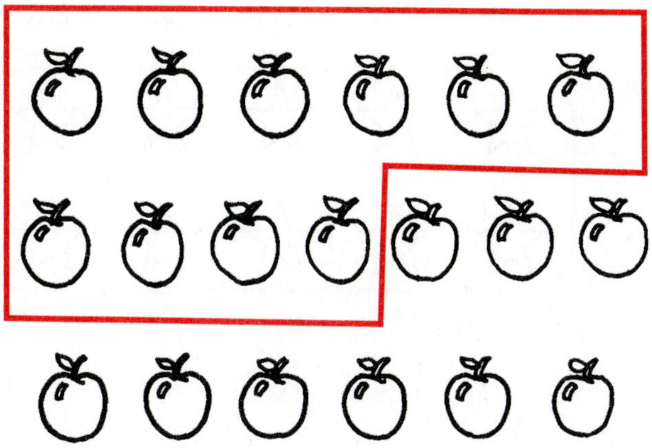

18 19 20

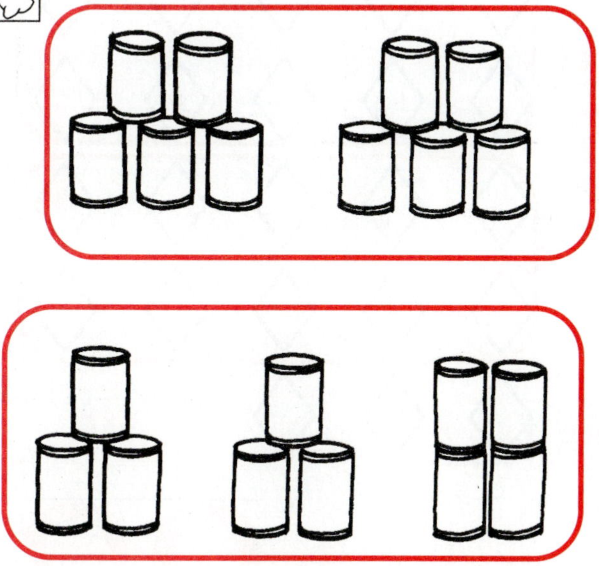

19 20 21

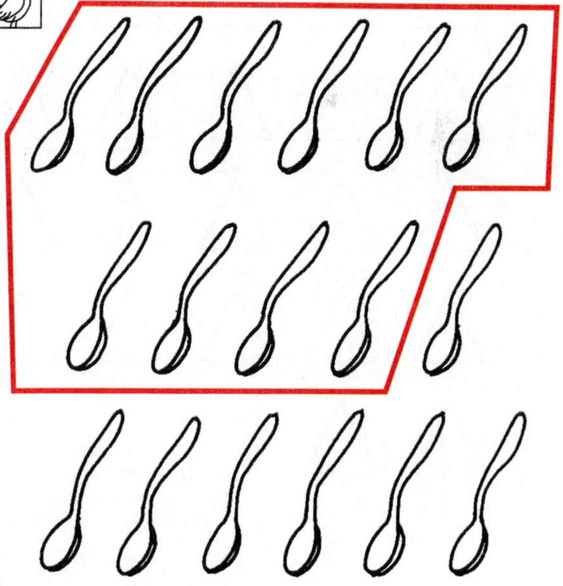

17 18 19

Children circle groups of 10 for each picture. Then they circle the number that shows how many objects are in that group.

March: Use when children are familiar with *Counting Tens and Ones.*

Circle Tens

20

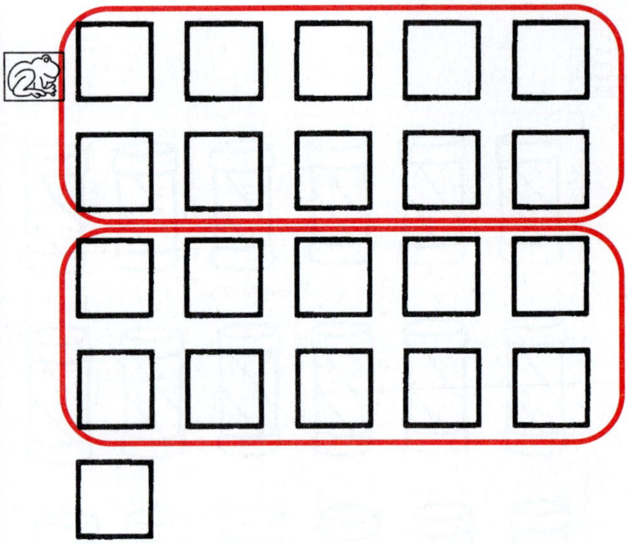

21

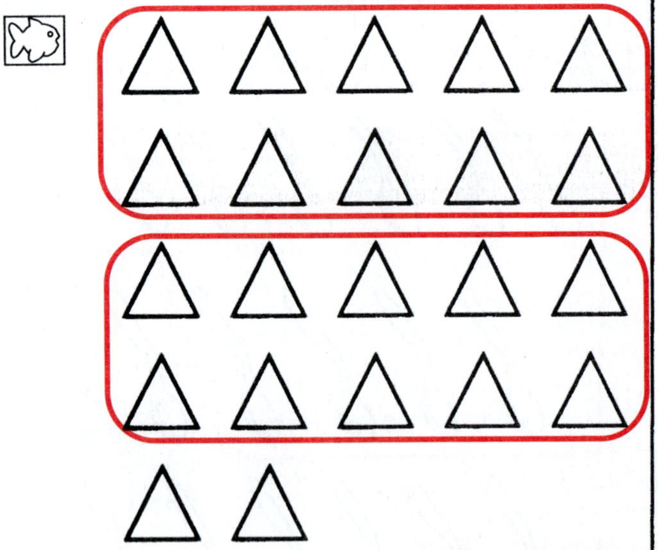

22

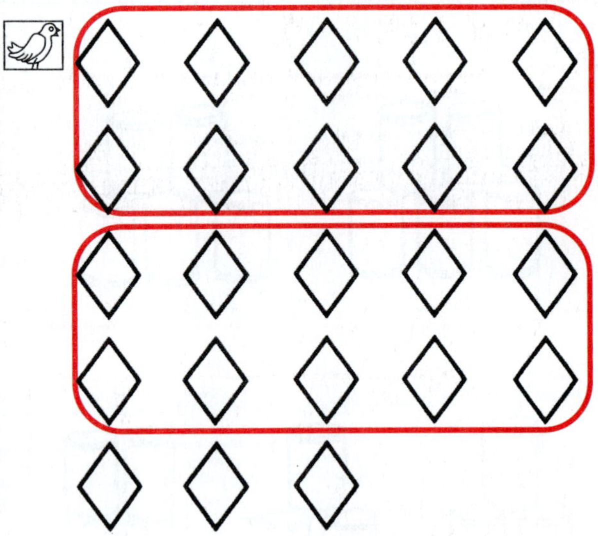

23

Children circle groups of 10 for each picture. Then they write the number that shows how many objects are in that group.

Name ____________________

Fill It Up Faster, Slower

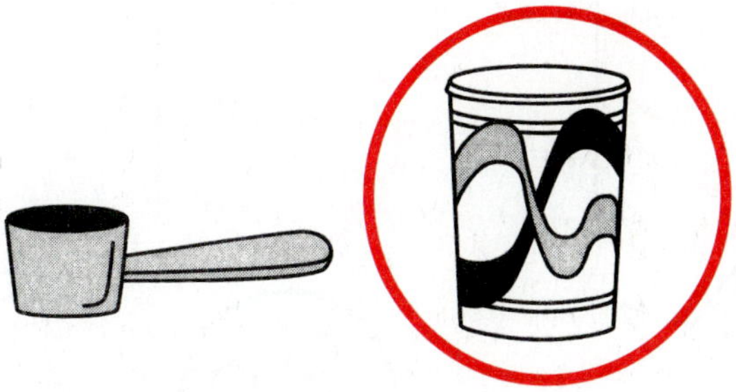

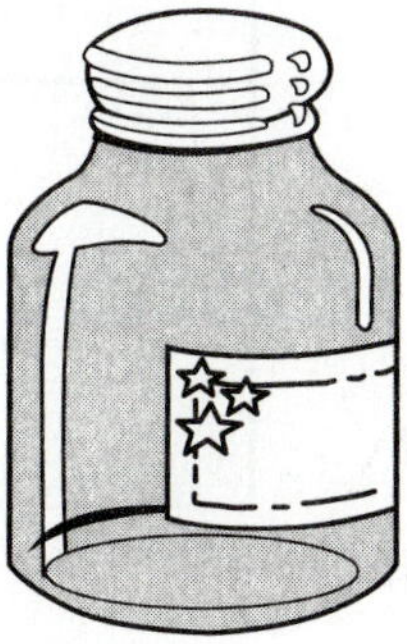

Turtle and **Frog:** Children circle the object they would use to fill the container at left if they wanted to fill it more quickly. **Fish:** Children circle the object they would use to fill the container more slowly. Children can experiment by filling containers with rice or sand in the classroom.

March: Use when children are familiar with *How Much Does It Hold?*

ABC Patterns

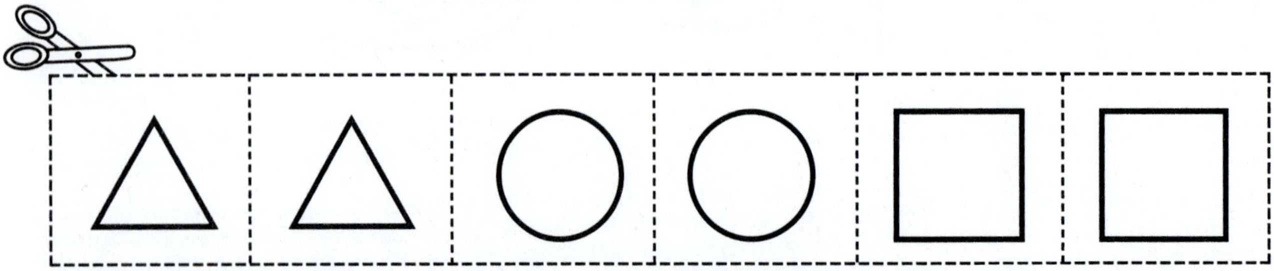

Have children turn the page so the turtle row is on top. **Turtle and Frog:** Children draw the next picture to complete the pattern. **Fish:** Children use three colors of crayons to create an ABC pattern. **Bird:** Children cut and paste the shapes to make an ABC pattern.

Name ____________________

Count and Compare

4 more

2 more

3 more

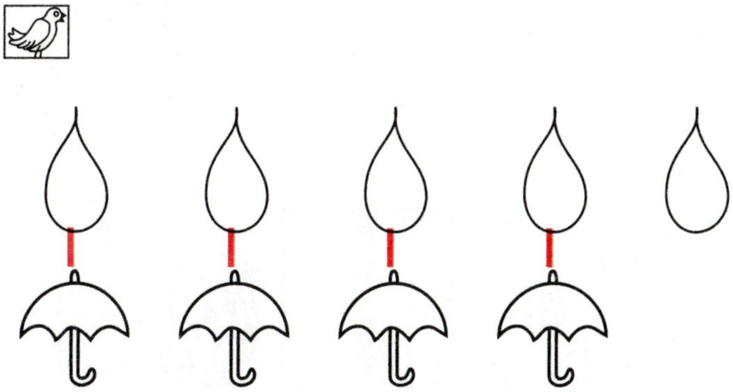

1 more

In each row, children determine which has more by drawing lines to show one-to-one correspondence. Children write the numeral showing how many more and draw a picture showing the correct object.

March: Use when children are familiar with *The Penny Tosser.*

Whole to Parts

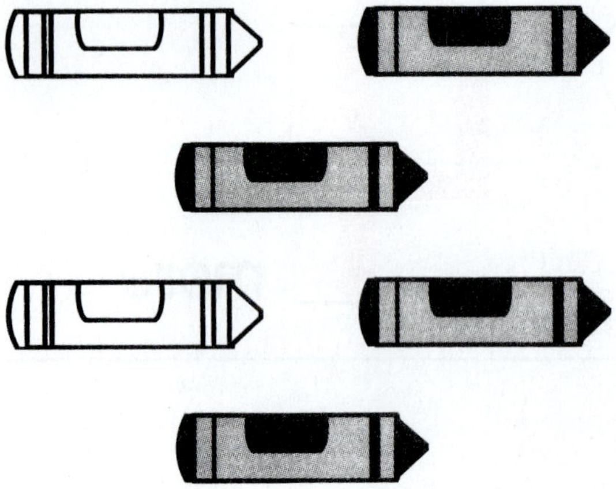

6

4  and 2 

5

4  and 1 

For each group, children write how many are in the whole set. Then they write how many are in each part. Children can use two colors of counters to model these situations.

Name ______________________________

Shape Sort

Children cut out the pictures of the bowls and paste them on shelves next to bowls with the same shape and size. Children explain their placement of the objects.

March: Use when children are familiar with the *Classroom Project.*

Children look at the different kinds of balls and then color a box in the graph to represent each ball. Children may cross out each item as they record it in the graph.

Name ______________________________

Sort the Tools

	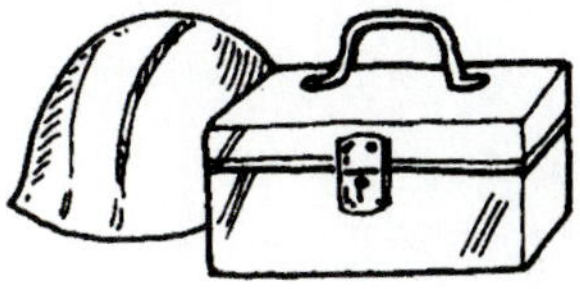

doctor

carpenter

carpenter

doctor

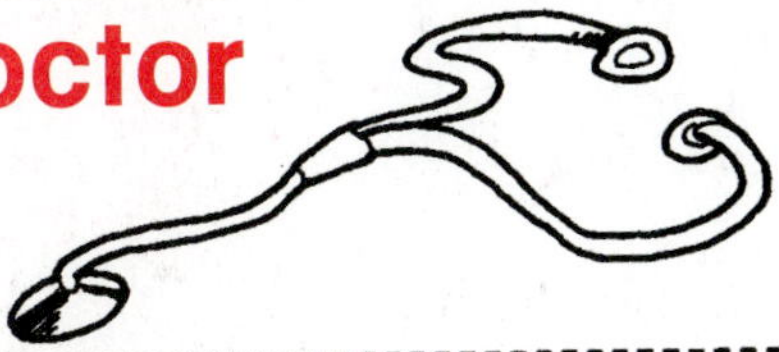

carpenter

doctor

Children cut and paste the tools used by a doctor below the bag and the tools used by a carpenter below the toolbox. Have children explain their reasoning.

March: Use when children are familiar with the *Classroom Project*.

Name ______________________________

Add the Counters

Counters circled may vary.

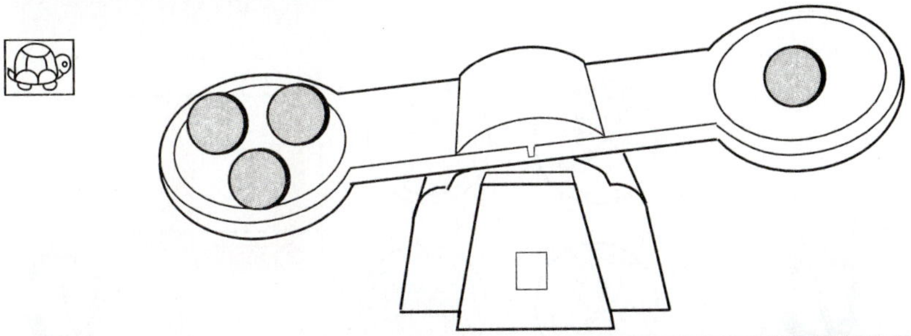

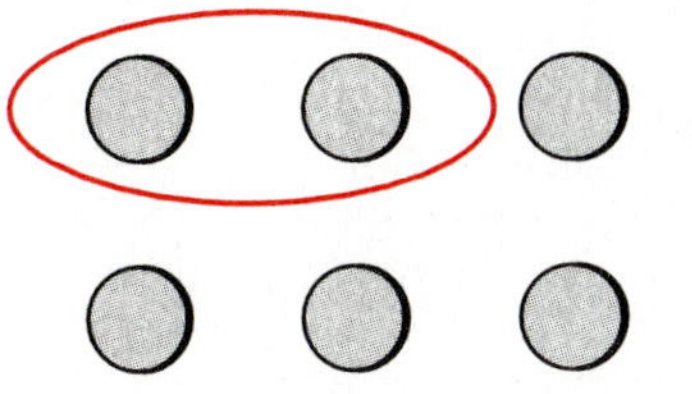

Circle any 2.

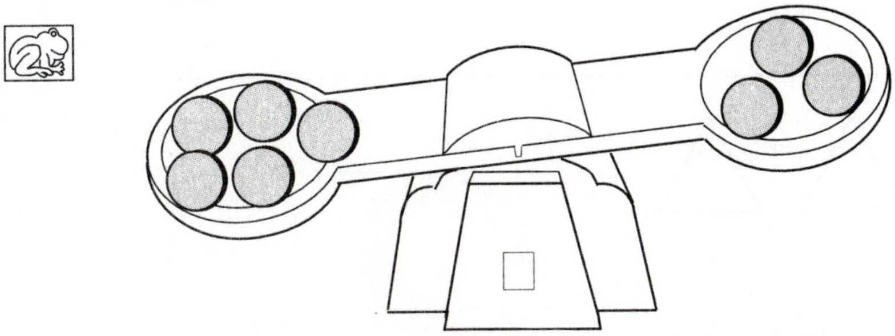

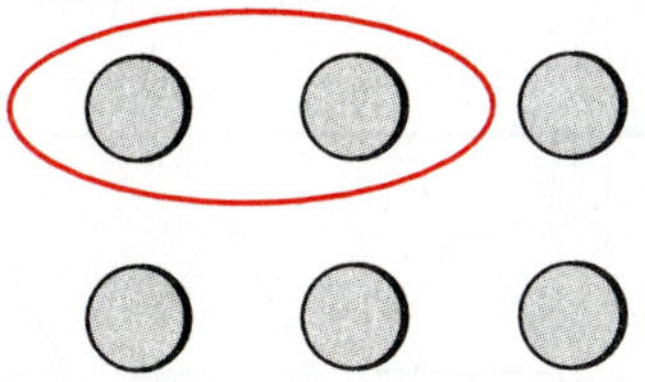

Circle any 2.

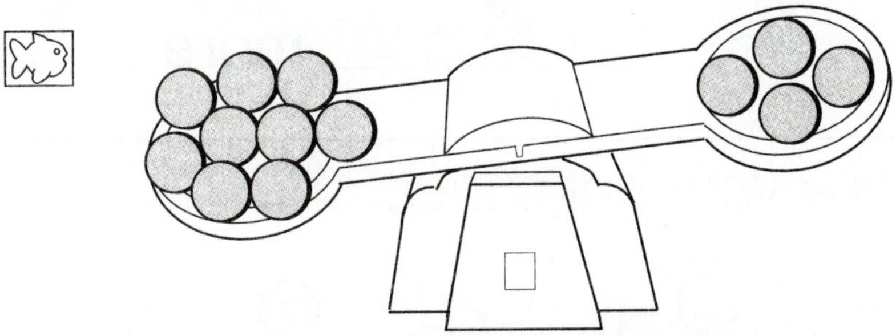

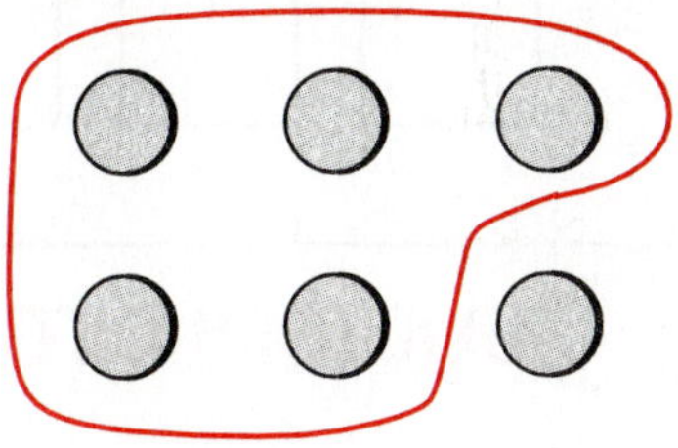

Circle any 5.

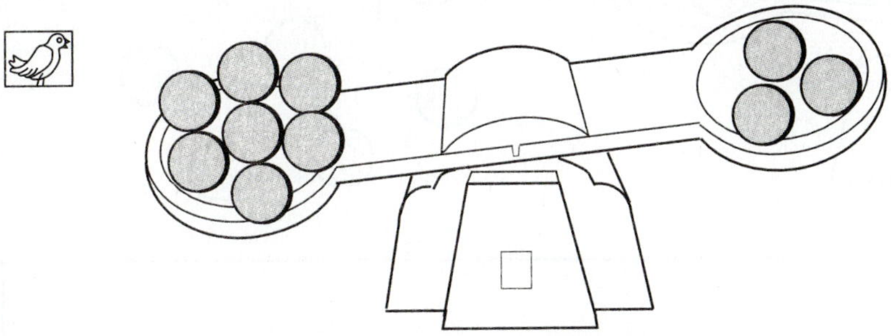

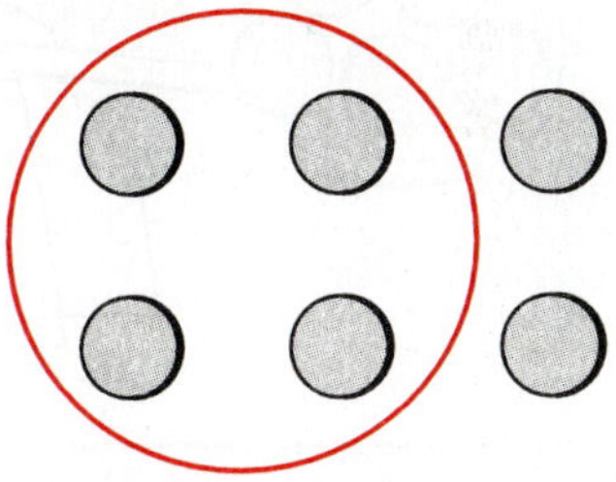

Circle any 4.

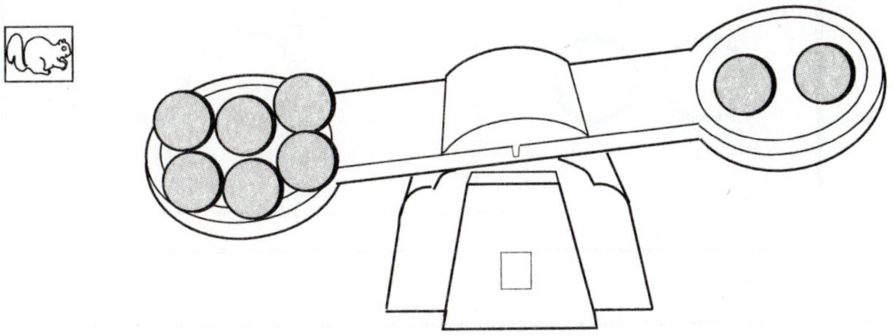

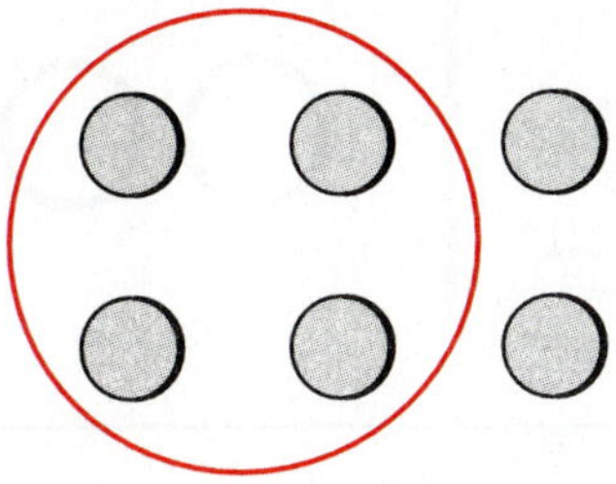

Circle any 4.

In each row, children circle the number of counters it will take to balance the scale.

March: Use when children are familiar with *Domino Fill Up.*

Review/Test

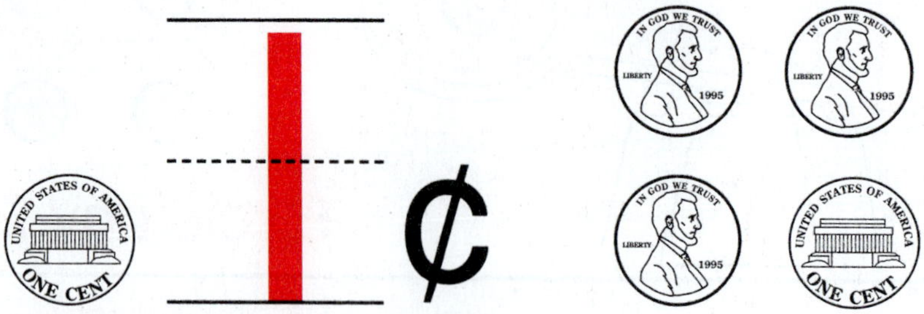

1 ¢

4 ¢

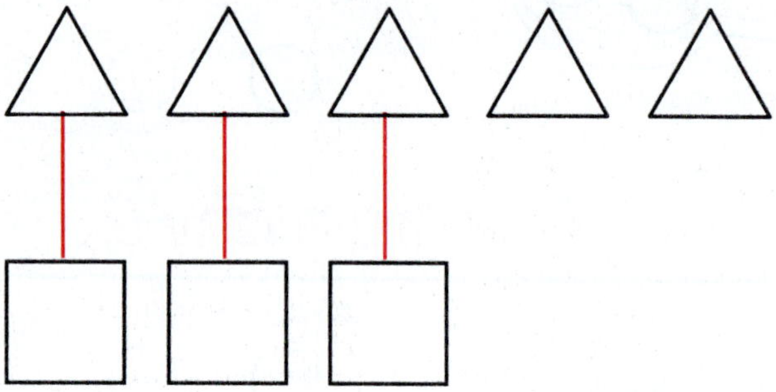

2 more

Counters circled may vary but should show 2.

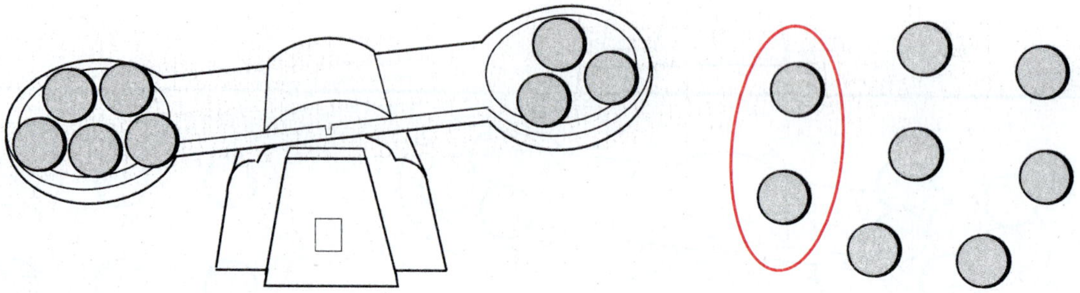

Spot Check

Turtle: Children write the amounts and then circle the greater amount. **Frog:** Children draw lines to show one-to-one correspondence. Then they write the numeral showing how many more and draw the correct shape. **Fish:** Children circle the number of counters it will take to balance the scale. **Spot Check:** Children repeat the AABB pattern.

Remember!
- Understand
- Plan
- Try it
- **[Look back]**

Number sentences will vary.

_____ ☐ _____ = _____

➤ **Look back** Children write the number sentence for their story. Ask, "Does your story fit your numbers? How do you know that your answer make sense?"

❹

FOLD

Name ____________________

My Problem Solving Book

Strategy: Act It Out

Remember!
- **[Understand]**
- Plan
- Try it
- Look back

➤ **Understand** Children choose two number cards. They talk about how they can use the number cards to tell a story and act it out.

❶

Remember!
- Understand
- **Plan**
- Try it
- Look back

Remember!
- Understand
- Plan
- **Try it**
- Look back

Answers will vary.

➤ **Plan** Children explain what their stories might be about.

❷

➤ **Try it** Children use people counters to act out their stories. Then they draw their stories.

❸

Name ______________________________

Money in the Bank

Children count the coins and then circle the piggy bank that shows that amount.

April: Use when children are familiar with the *Daily Depositor.*

Equal Parts

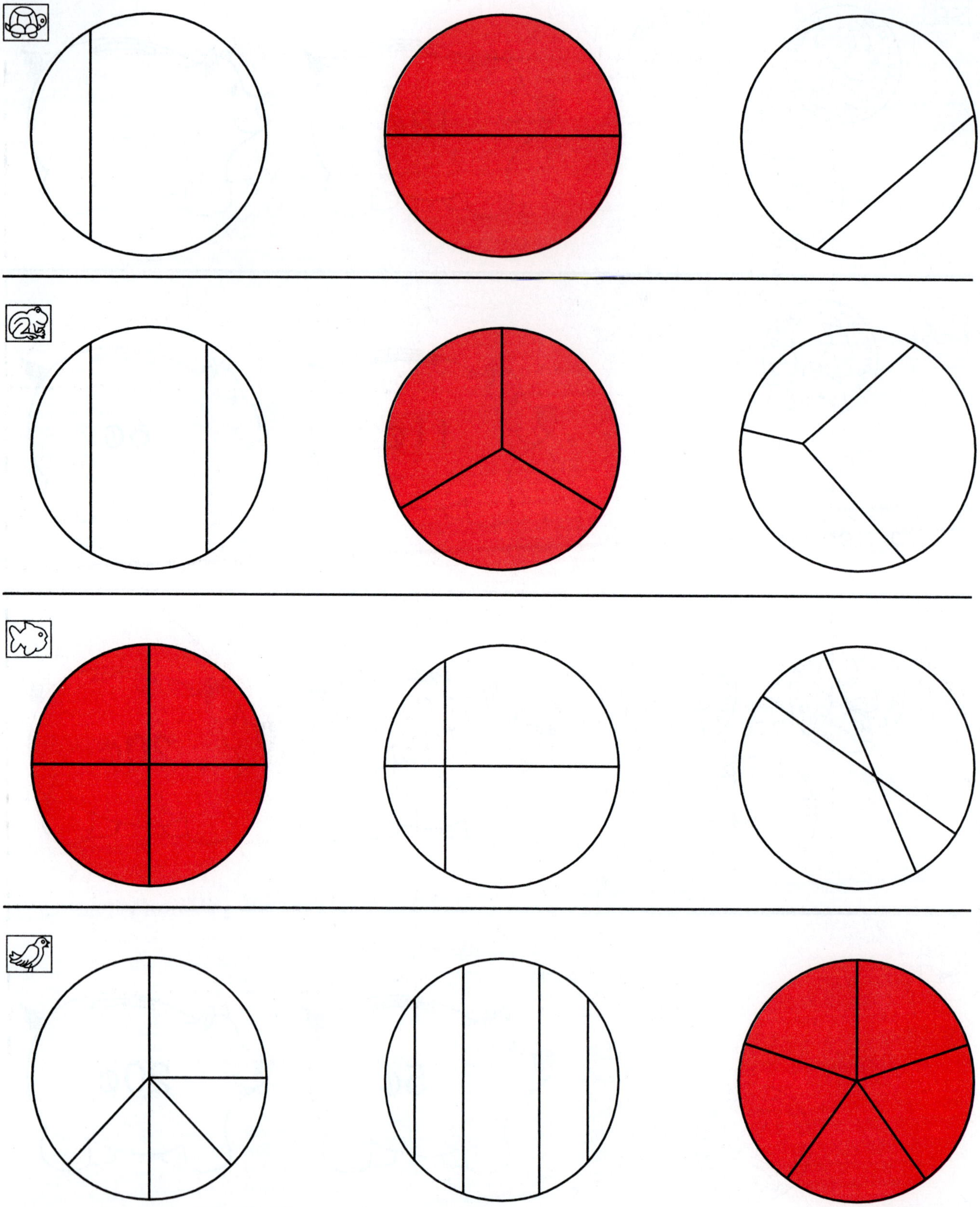

In each row, children color the circle that shows equal parts.

Name ____________________

Shapes in Half

Answers will vary.

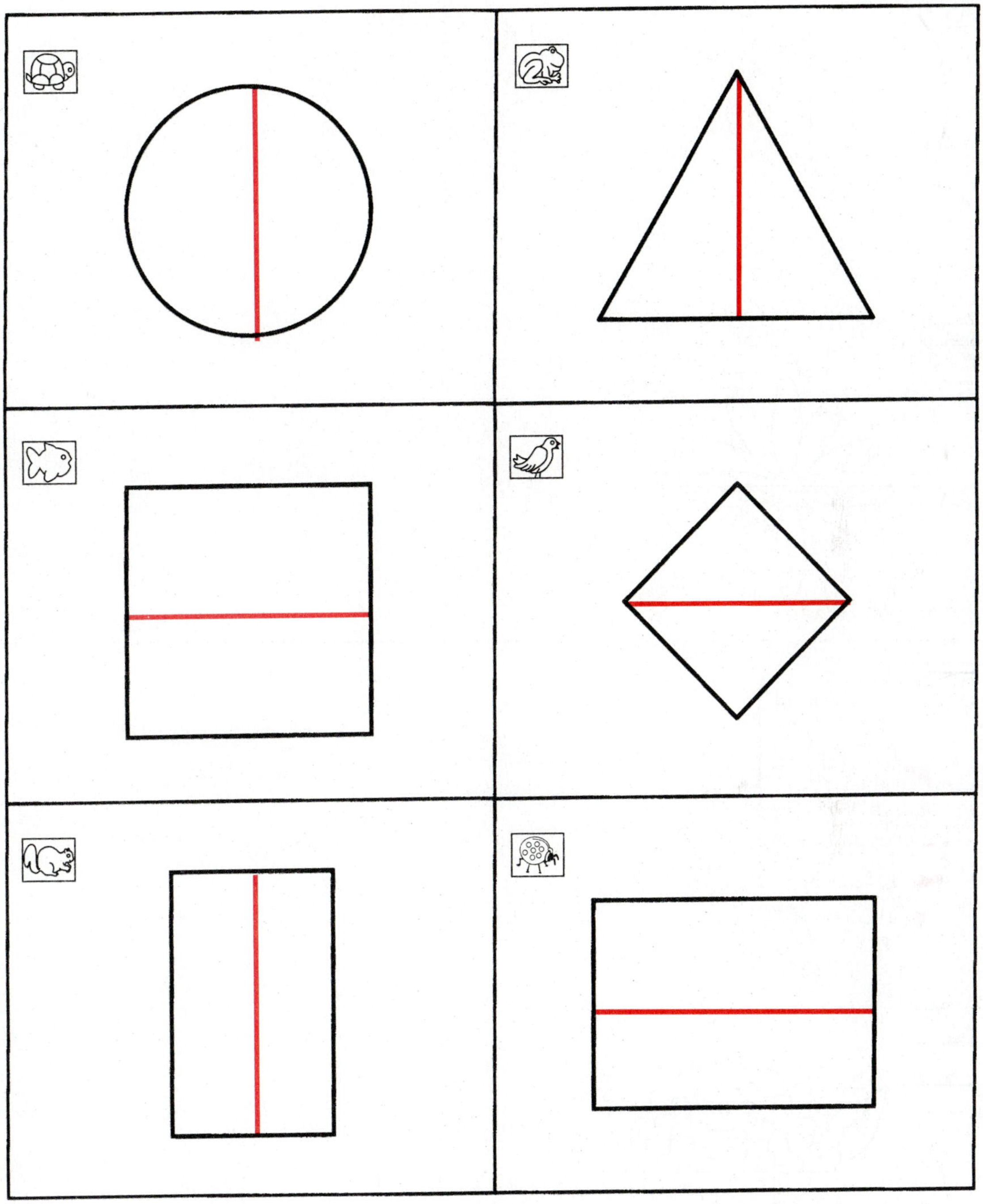

Children draw a line to divide each shape in half. Have children explain how they divided each shape.

April: Use when children are familiar with *Fractional Play.*

Make It Whole

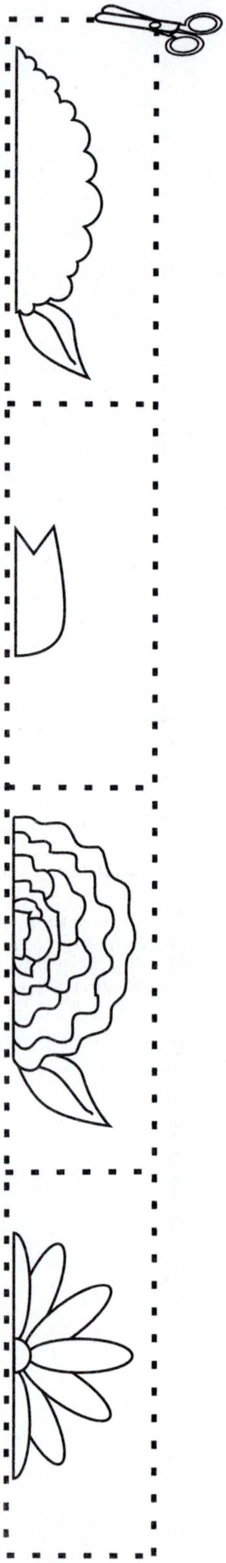

Children cut out the flower halves, match, and paste them to make a whole flower. Then they explain their choices.

Name ______________________________

Choose a Cube

How Many Cubes?

 red						
 blue		Graphs will vary.				
 green						

______________  red ______________

______________ 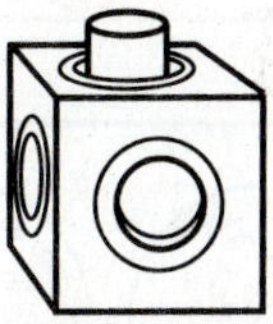 blue ______________

______________  green ______________

Answers will vary.

Working in pairs or small groups, children color cubes on the page according to the labels. They place a red cube, a blue cube, and a green cube in a paper bag. Without looking, one child pulls out a cube. Each child records the color of the cube on his or her graph. The cube is replaced, and the steps are repeated until one row in the graph is filled. Then children record how many cubes of each color were picked.

April: Use when children are familiar with *Penny Probability.*

2¢ + 2¢ = 4¢

3¢ + 4¢ = 7¢

4¢ + 4¢ = 8¢

Children place pennies where they are shown in each row. They count the pennies in each group and write each amount. Then they combine the two groups of pennies, count, and write the total amount.

Name ____________________

Subtract Money

3¢ – 1¢ 2¢

7¢ – 1¢ 6¢

6¢ – 1¢ 5¢

In each row, children use pennies and nickels to show how much money they start with. They move coins to show how much they spend. Then they cross out the same coins and write how much money is left.

Before and After

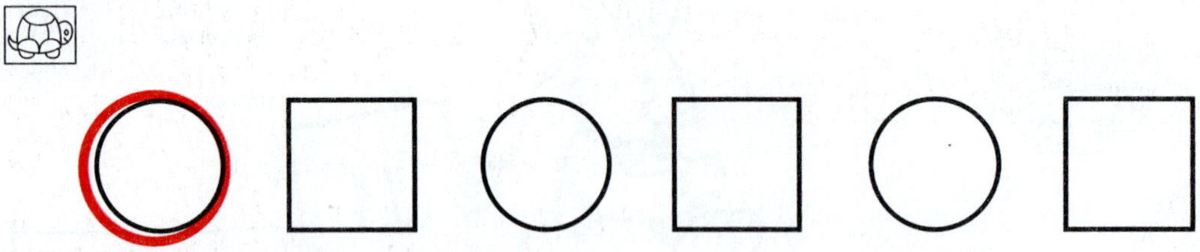

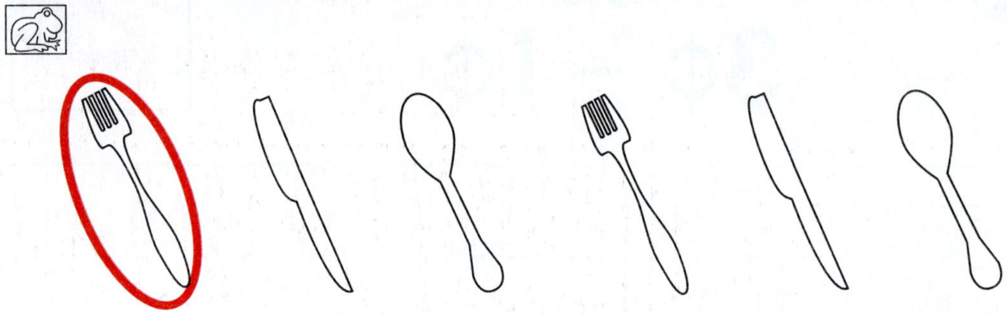

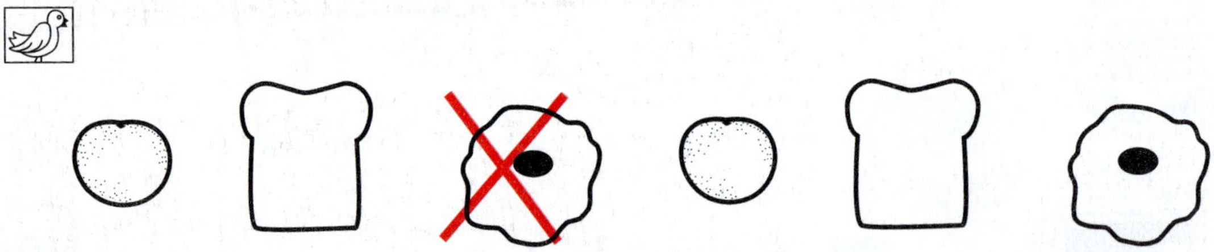

Turtle: Children circle the shape that comes **before** the square. **Frog:** Children circle the implement that comes **before** the knife. **Bird:** Children put an X on the food that comes **after** the bread. **Fish:** Children put an X on the animal that comes **after** the frog.

 April: Use when children are familiar with *Make New Patterns.*

Name ______________________________

Group and Add

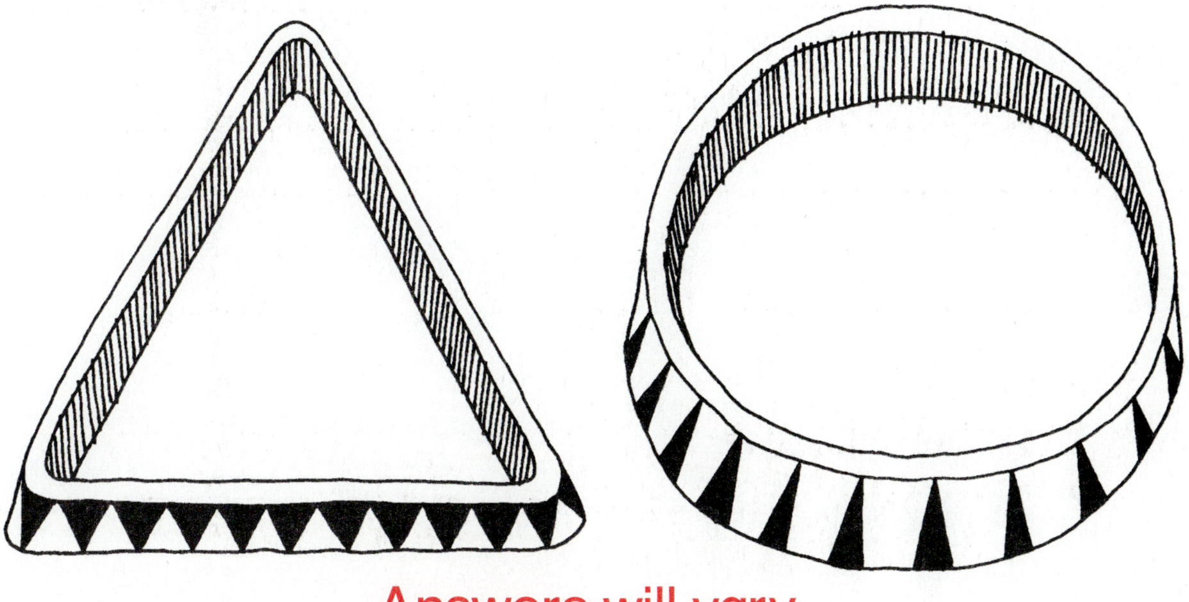

Answers will vary.

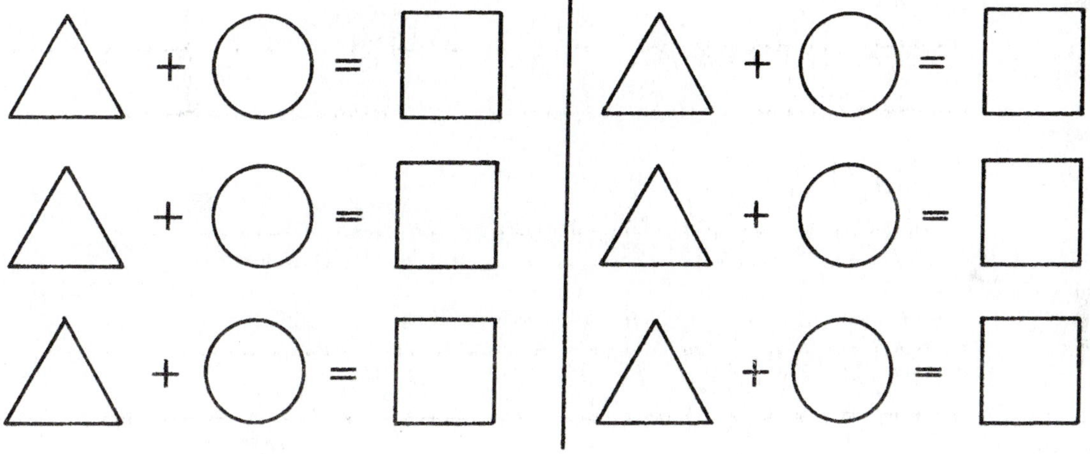

Children cut out the elephants. They put some in the triangle and some in the circle and tell a story. Then they record the numbers in a triangle and a circle below and write the sum in the box. They continue until all the boxes are filled.

April: Use when children are familiar with *Addition and Subtraction Stories.*

Name ______________________________

Open and Closed Shapes

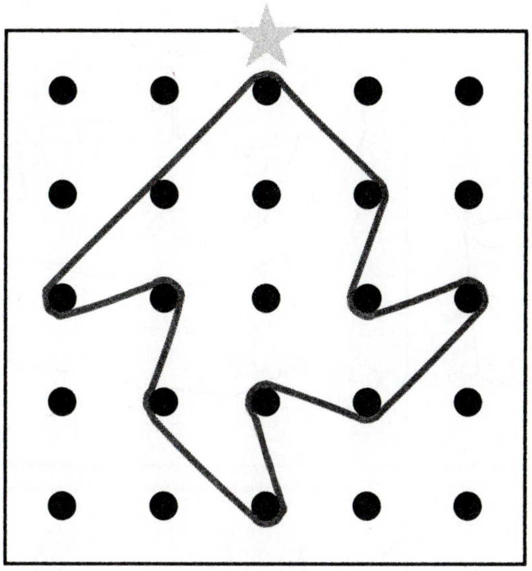

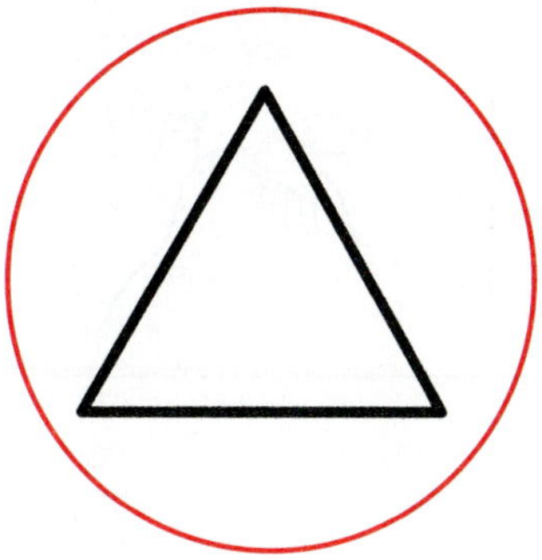

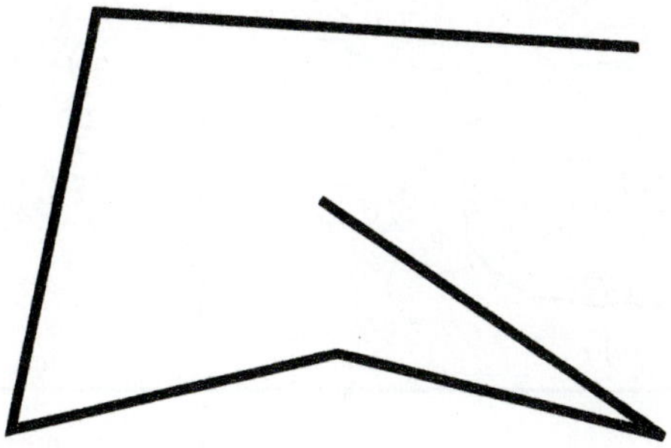

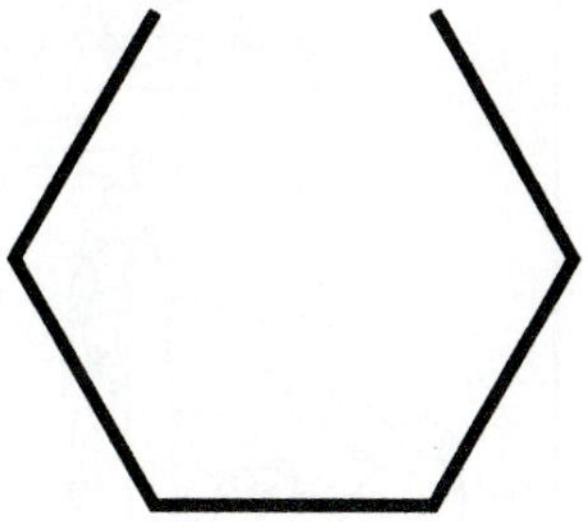

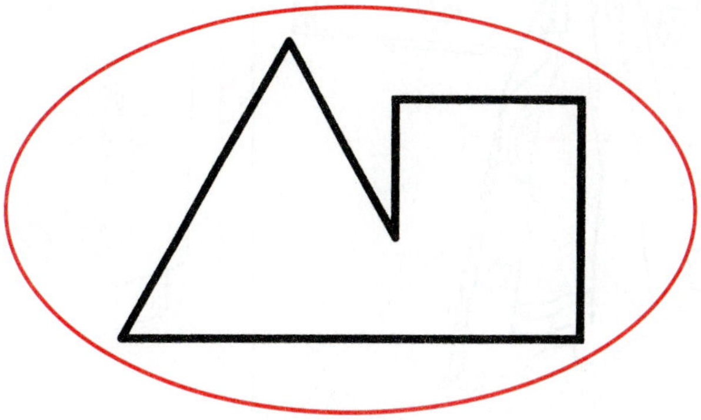

Turtle: Children circle the geoboard that shows a shape made with the geoband touching 12 pegs. Children may want to use the star as a guide to start and stop counting. **Frog:** Children circle each closed shape.

April: Use when children are familiar with *Geoboard Follow the Leader.*

How Long?

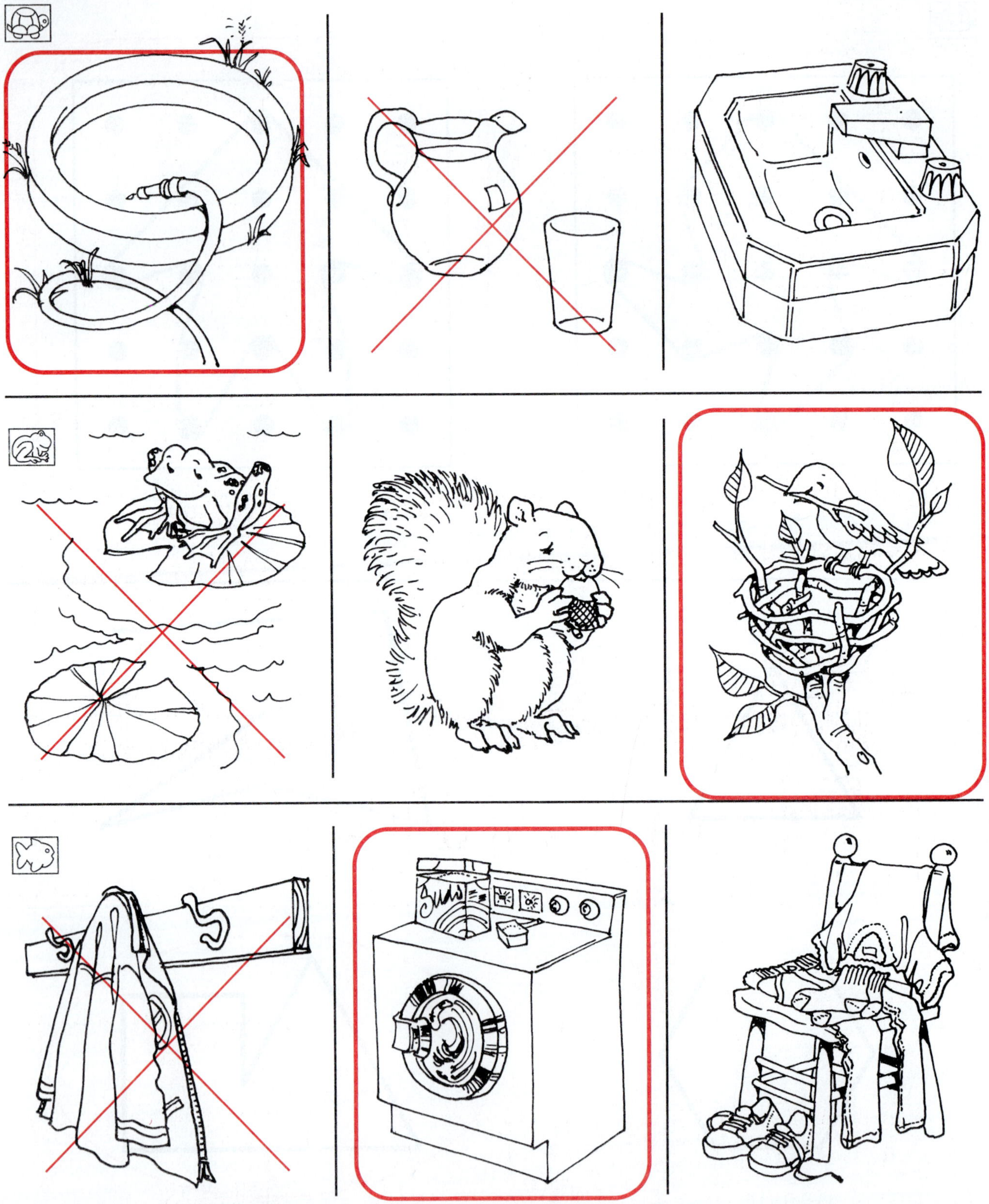

In each row, children circle the activity that takes the most time and draw an X on the activity that takes the least time. **Turtle:** filling a pool, a glass, or a sink; **Frog:** frog jumping from one lily pad to the next, squirrel eating acorn, or bird building nest; **Fish:** hanging up jacket, washing clothes, or laying out clothes.

Name ____________________

Calculator Counting

19 [+] [1] [=] 20

21 [+] [1] [=] 22

4 [+] [1] [0] [=] 14

14 [+] [1] [0] [=] 24

Children use calculators to display the number shown in the box and then input the key sequence depicted. Then they write the answer.

April: Use when children are familiar with *Counting with a Calculator.*

How Many More?

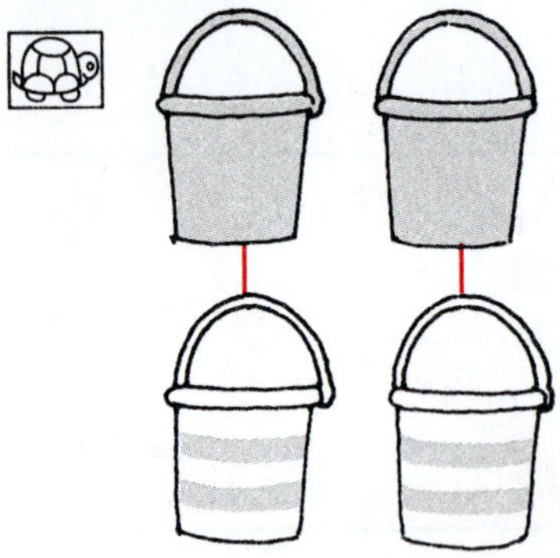

2 more

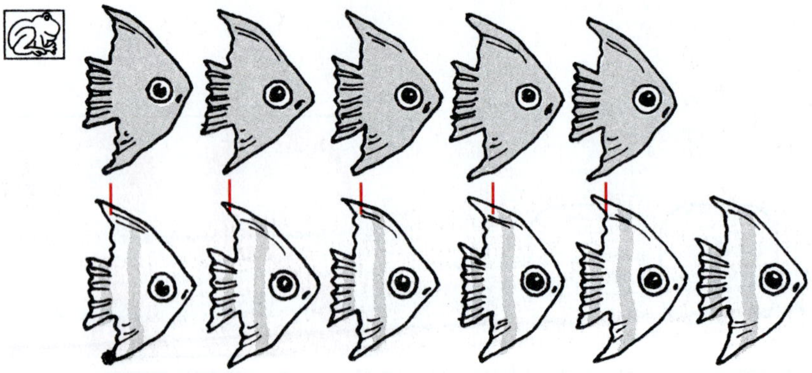

1 more

4 more

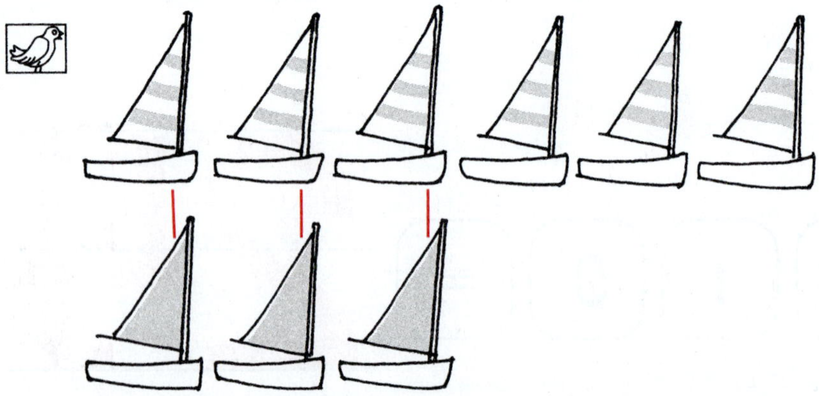

3 more

In each row, children draw lines between rows of objects to show one-to-one correspondence. Then they write the numeral to show how many more and color or draw stripes on the rebus to show which kind has more.

Name ____________________

Trading Pennies

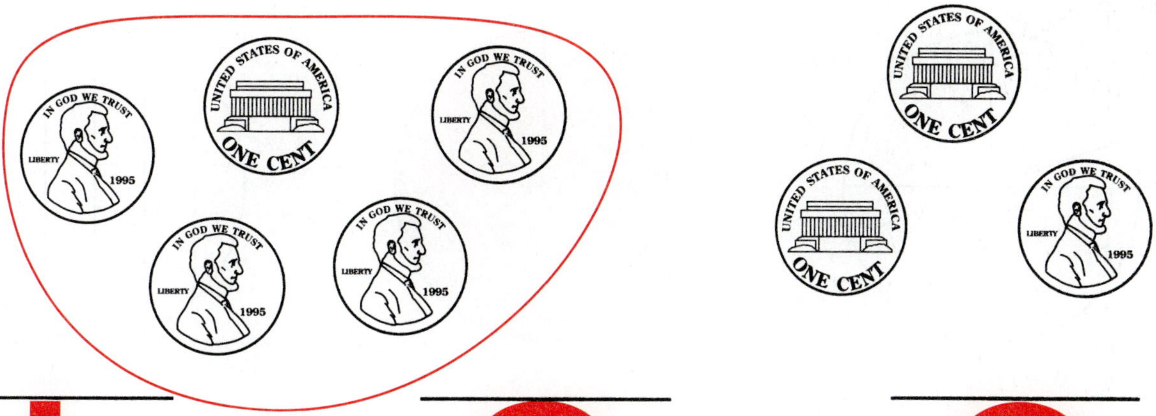

1  3  8¢

2  2  12¢

In each row, children circle groups of 5 pennies. They write the number of nickels they could trade for and the number of pennies left over. Then they write how much in all.

April: Use when children are familiar with *5! 10! 15! 20!*

Review/Test

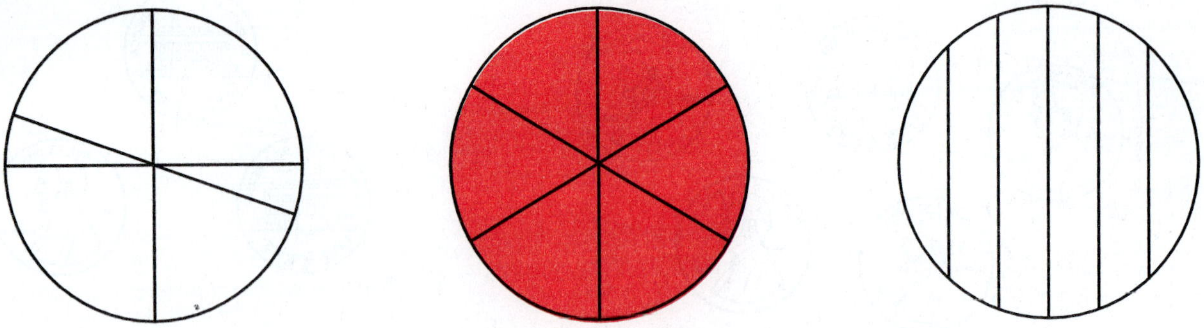

2¢ + 4¢ = 6¢

1 more 

Turtle: Children color the circle that is divided into 6 equal parts. **Frog:** Children count the pennies and then write each amount and the total. **Fish:** Children draw lines to show one-to-one correspondence, write how many more, and then show which kind has more.

Name ______________________________

Reading Months, Weeks, Days

MAY

Sunday	Monday	Tuesday	Wednesday	Thursday	Friday	Saturday
						1
2	3	4	5	6	7	8
9	10	11	12	13	14	15
16	17	18	19	20	21	22
23	24	25	26	27	28	29
30	31					

JUNE

Sunday	Monday	Tuesday	Wednesday	Thursday	Friday	Saturday
		1	2	3	4	5
6	7	8	9	10	11	12
13	14	15	16	17	18	19
20	21	22	23	24	25	26
27	28	29	30			

Children answer these questions: What month is shown on the first calendar? What day of the week is June 11? What day is the last day of June? What is Thursday's date in the third week of May? What are the dates of each Saturday in May? **May; Friday; Wednesday; May 20; May 1, 8, 15, 22, 29**

May/June: Use when children are familiar with the *Calendar.*

Money Sums

2¢ + 1¢ = 3¢

5¢ + 1¢ = 6¢

3¢ + 1¢ = 4¢

Children write the sum of the money in the bag and the money being added. Children can use real pennies to model these facts.

 May/June: Use when children are familiar with *Acting Out Number Stories.*

Remember!
- Understand
- Plan
- Try it
- Look back

Money Spent

Answers will vary depending on toy chosen.

__________ ¢

Money Left

__________ ¢

➤ **Look back** Children draw coins and write the amount to show the amount of money they spent. Then they draw and write the money they have left. Ask, "Did you have enough money? Did you make a good guess?"

4

FOLD

Name ____________________

Remember!
- Understand
- Plan
- Try it
- Look back

My Problem Solving Book

Strategy: Guess and Check

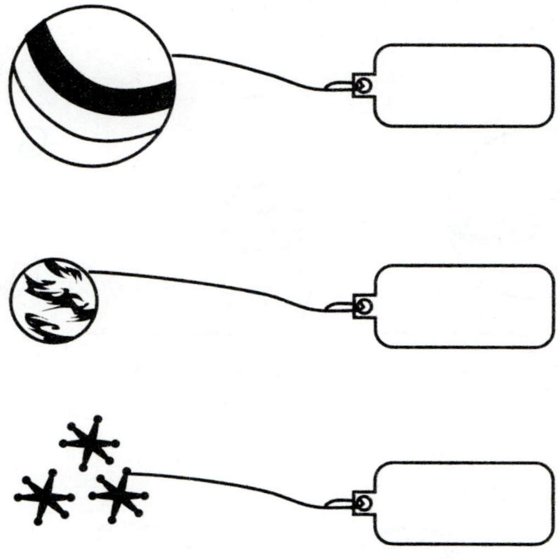

➤ **Understand** Children choose a toy they might like to buy. They guess whether or not they have enough money.

1

Remember!
- Understand
- **Plan**
- Try it
- Look back

Remember!
- Understand
- Plan
- **Try it**
- Look back

Children have enough money to buy the ball, the marbles, the ring, and the jump rope.

➤ **Plan** Children explain how they will decide if they have enough money.

❷

➤ **Try it** Children count out real coins near the toy they chose. They decide if they have enough money to buy the toy.

❸

Name ______________________________

+ or –

2 [+] 1

7 [–] 2

6 [–] 2

middle

top

bottom

Children cut out the pictures and paste them where they belong. Then they write + or – in the box.

May/June: Use when children are familiar with *Acting Out Number Stories.*

Name ______________________________

Counting Back

4 − 1 = 3

3 − 1 = 2

5 − 1 = 4

Children tell a number story about each picture. Then they count back 1 and write the difference. When they do the Turtle and Frog rows, children can use the people counters to model the situations.

May/June: Use when children are familiar with *Acting Out Number Stories.*

The Sum Is Five

Possible combinations are: 5 + 0, 1 + 4, 2 + 3, 3 + 2, 4 + 1, and 0 + 5.

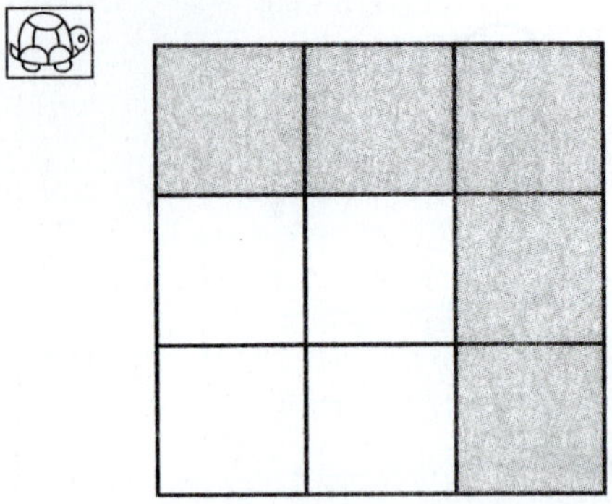

_____ + _____ = 5

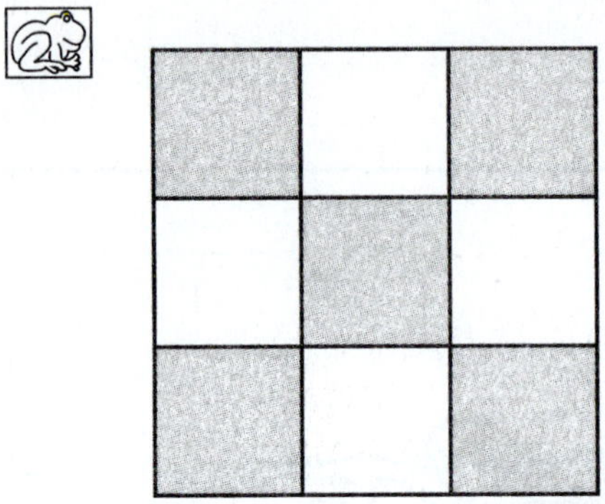

_____ + _____ = 5

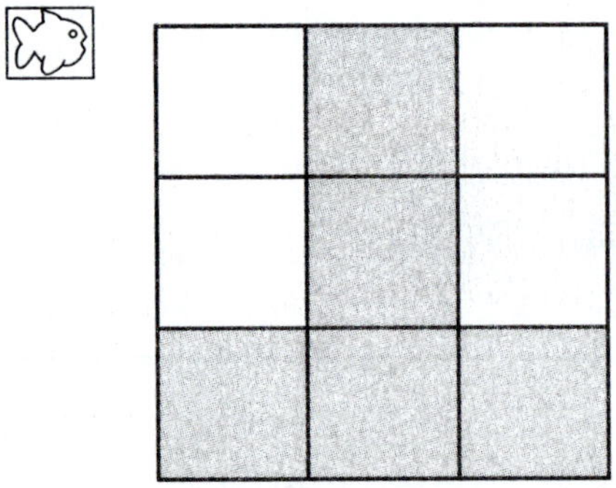

_____ + _____ = 5

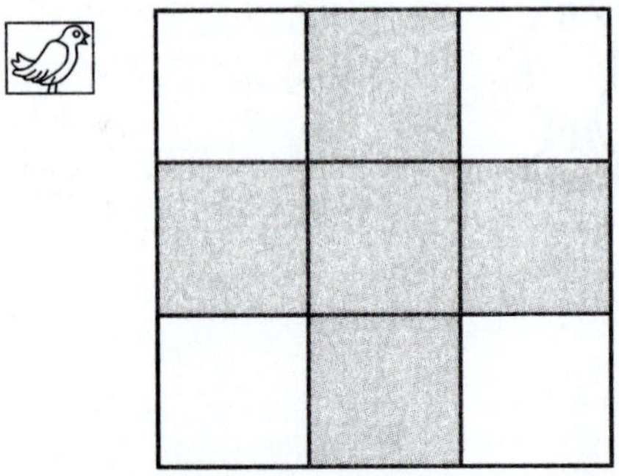

_____ + _____ = 5

In each row, children look at the shading on the 3 x 3 grid. Then they record a different combination to go with each arrangement of 5 shaded squares.

Name ______________________________

Calculate and Color

1	2	3	4	5	6	7	8	9	10 g
11	12	13	14	15	16	17	18	19	20 g
21	22	23	24	25	26	27	28	29	30 g
31	32	33	34	35	36	37	38	39	40 g
41	42	43	44	45	46	47	48	49	50 g
51	52	53	54	55	56	57	58	59	60 g
61	62	63	64	65	66	67	68	69	70 g
71	72	73	74	75	76	77	78	79	80 g
81	82	83	84	85	86	87	88	89	90 g
91 y	92 y	93 y	94 y	95 y	96 y	97 y	98 y	99 y	100 g

Children input [10] on the calculator and color 10 on the chart green. Then they press [+] [10] [=] and color 20 green. Children continue to press [+] [10] [=] and color the answer green each time until they reach 100. Then they press [–] [1] [=] until they reach 91, coloring each answer yellow on the chart.

May/June: Use when children are familiar with *Counting with a Calculator.*

How Many Dots?

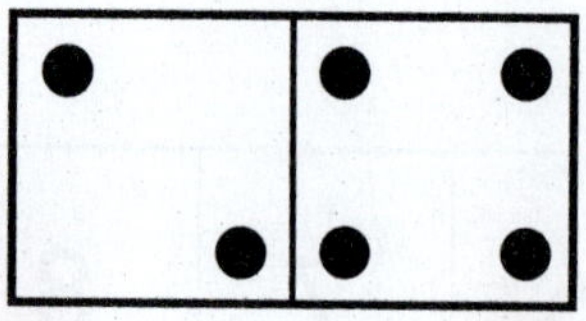

$2 + 4 = 6$

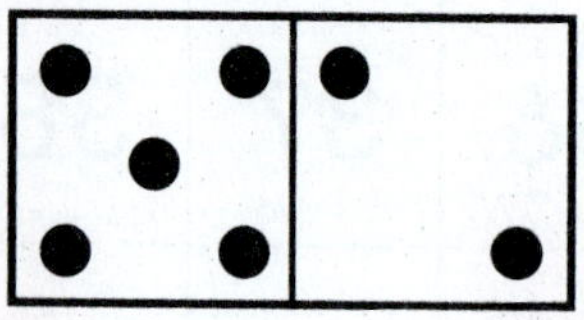

$5 + 2 = 7$

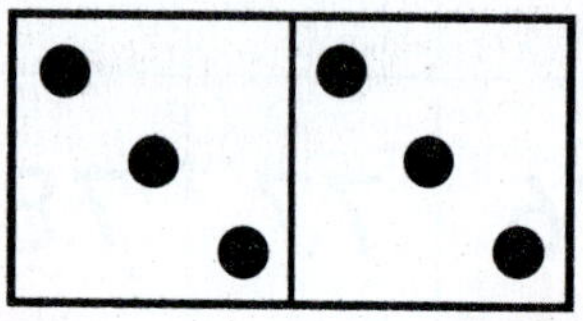

$3 + 3 = 6$

In each row, children count the dots on the left domino half and then write the number. They do the same for the right half. Then they count the total number of dots and write the sum.

Name ______________________________

Trade for Dimes and Nickels

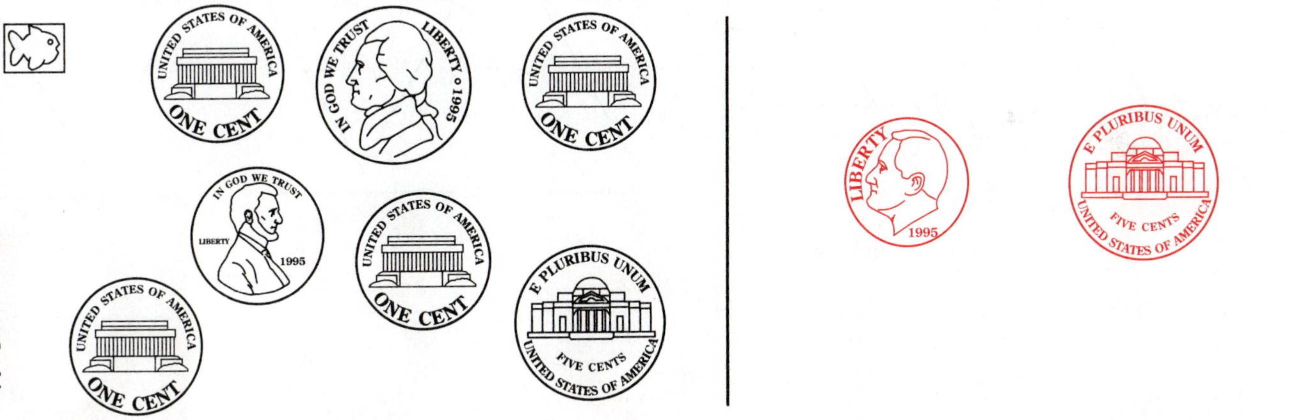

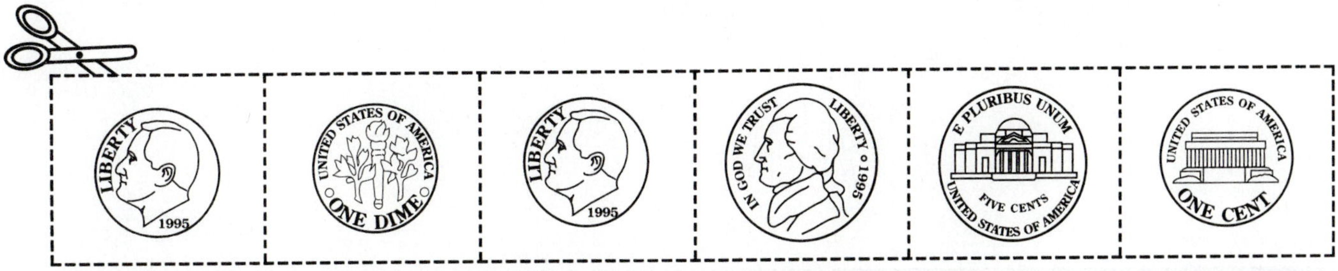

In each row, children trade pennies for nickels and nickels for dimes. They cut and paste to show their trades. Children may use coins to help them.

May/June: Use when children are familiar with *5! 10! 15! 20! with Dimes.*

Count by Twos

2 4 6 8

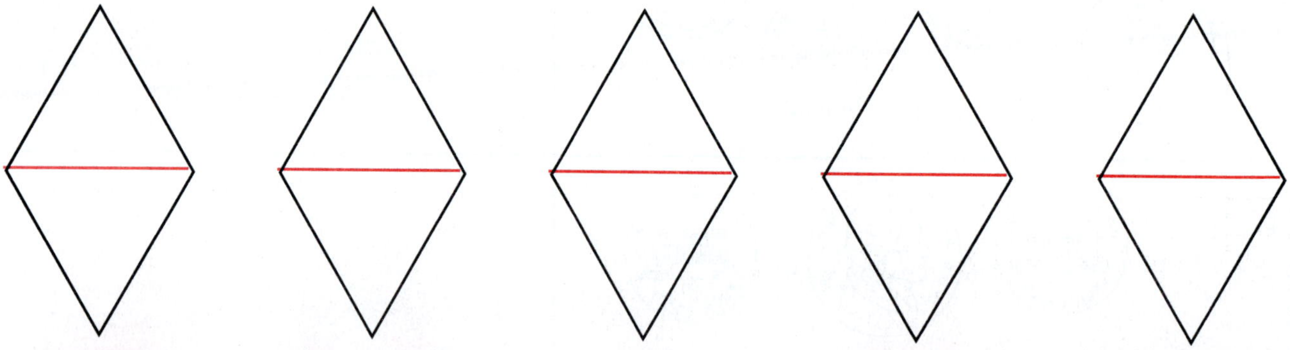

2 4 6 8 10

In each row, children place their triangle pattern blocks on the outlines. Removing one pattern block, they draw a line on each rhombus to show the two triangles that form the rhombus. Then they write the numbers to show counting by 2's.

Name ____________________

Making Change

____

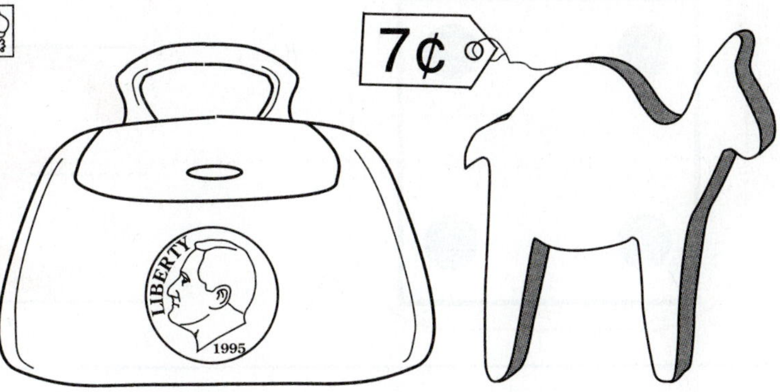

____

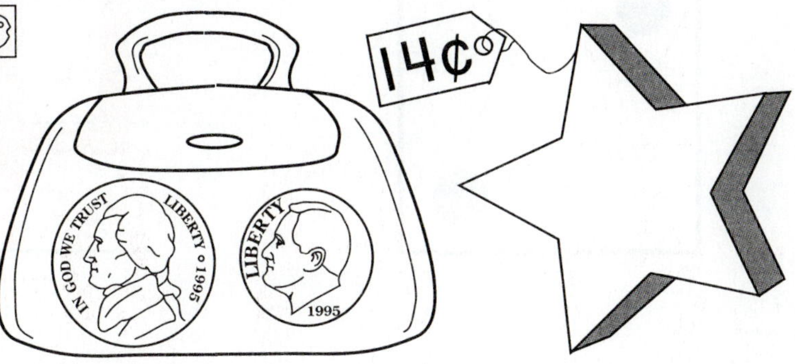

____

All rows: Children determine the change due after they buy each item. Then they cut and paste to show the correct amount of change. Children can use real or play coins to exchange and subtract.

May/June: Use when children are familiar with *Pay Your Partner.*

Comparing Dominos

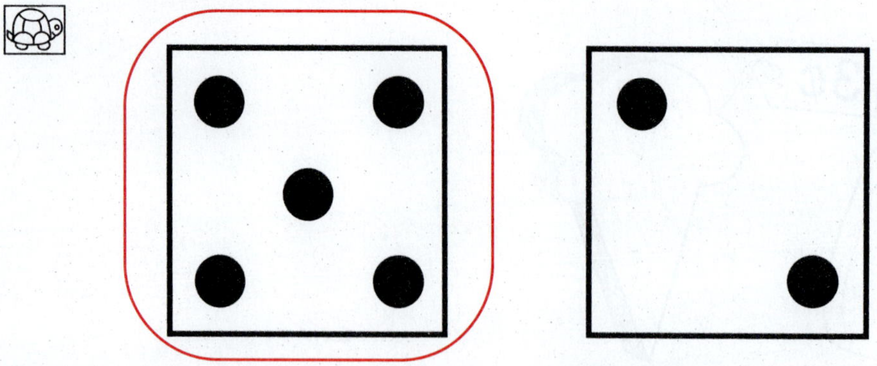

3

3

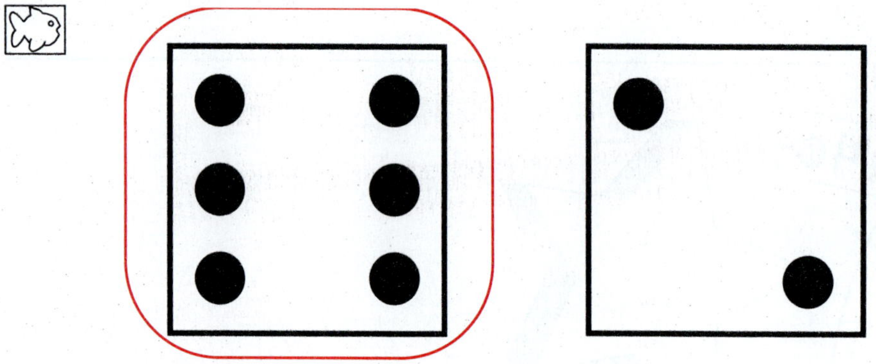

4

In each row, children circle the domino with more dots. Then they write the numeral to show how many more.

Name ________________________________

Shape Up!

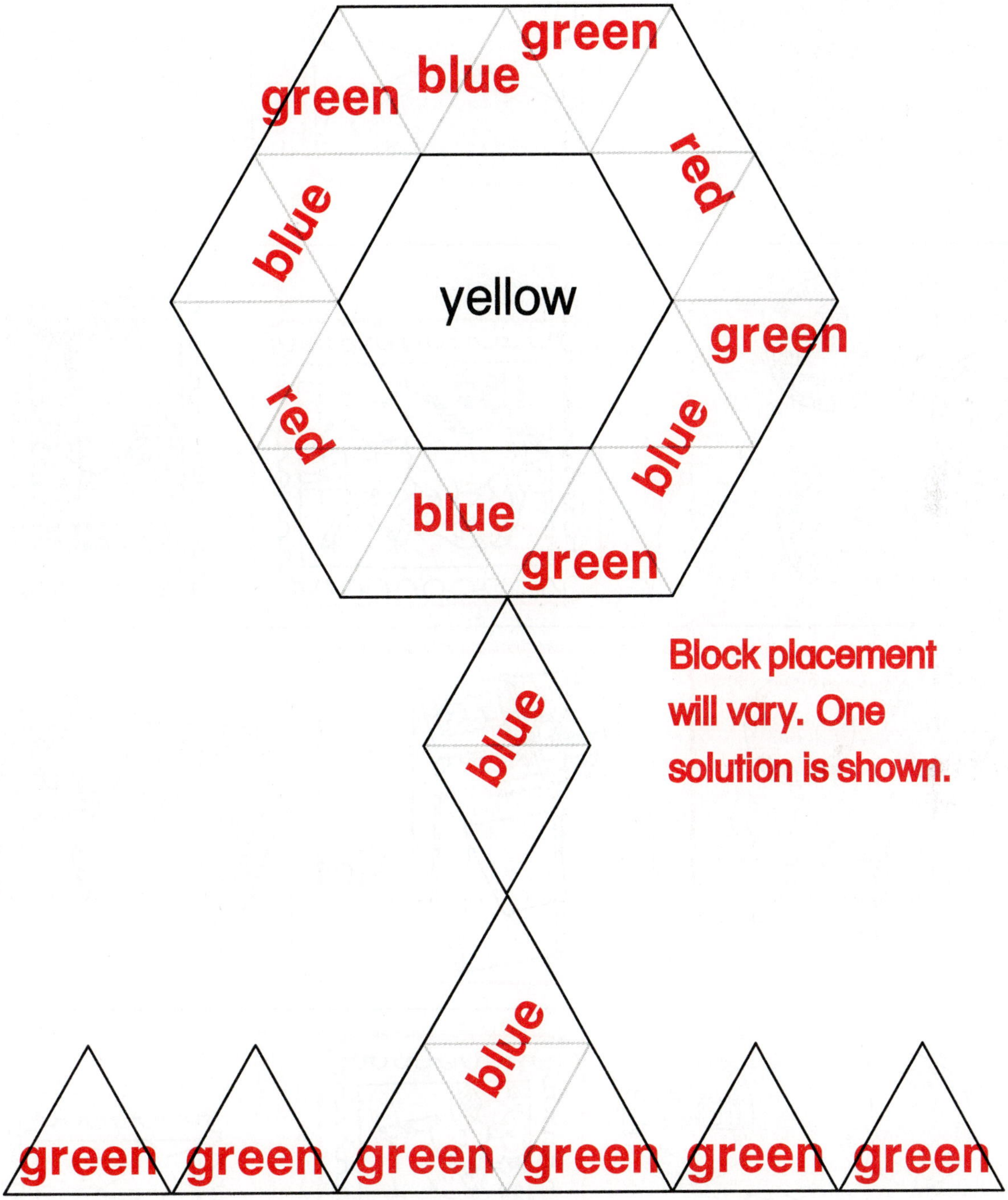

Block placement will vary. One solution is shown.

Children place a yellow pattern block on the shape where shown. They must use red, green, and blue pattern blocks to cover the rest of the picture. Children use matching-color crayons to record their complete pattern on the page. Then they share the different ways the shape was colored.

May/June: Use when children are familiar with *Cover Up*.

What Can You Buy?

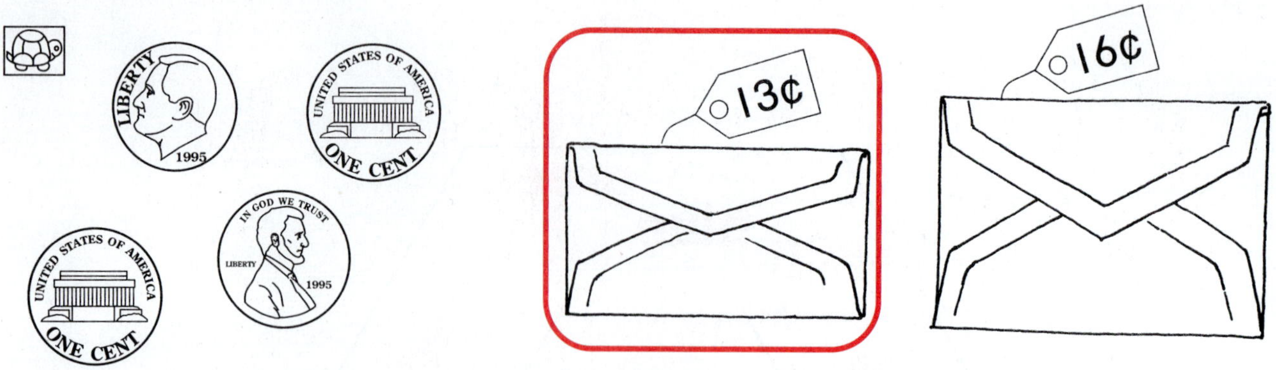

In each row, children circle the item that they can buy or mail with the money shown.

Name ______________________

Equal Parts

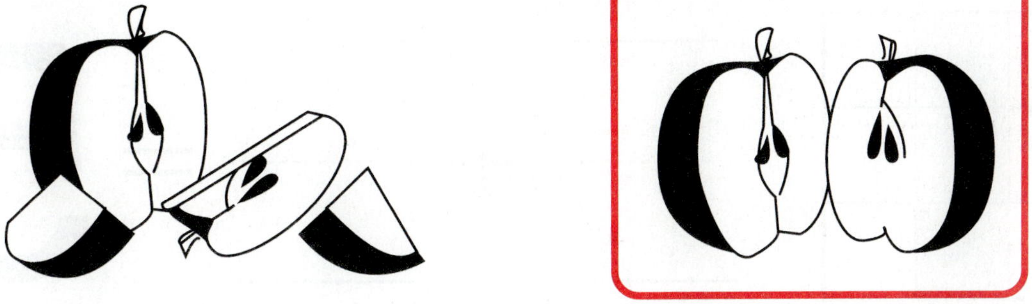

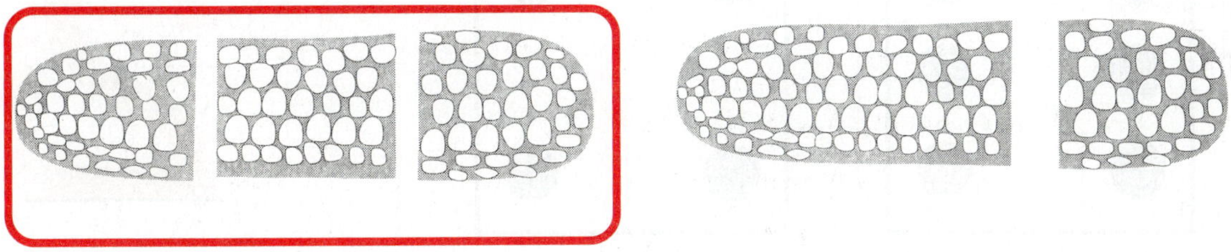

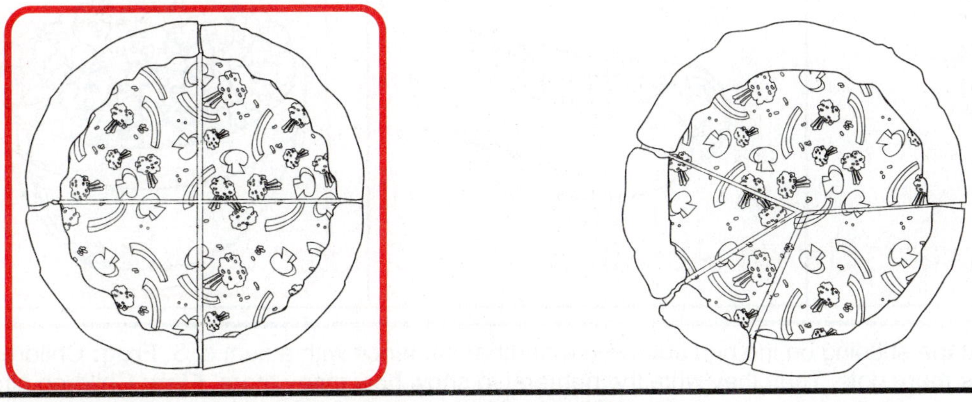

Children circle the item in each row that shows equal parts.

May/June: Use when children are familiar with *Literature Corner, Eating Fractions.*

Review/Test

Possible answers are: 5 + 0, 1 + 4, 2 + 3, 3 + 2, 4 + 1, and 0 + 5.

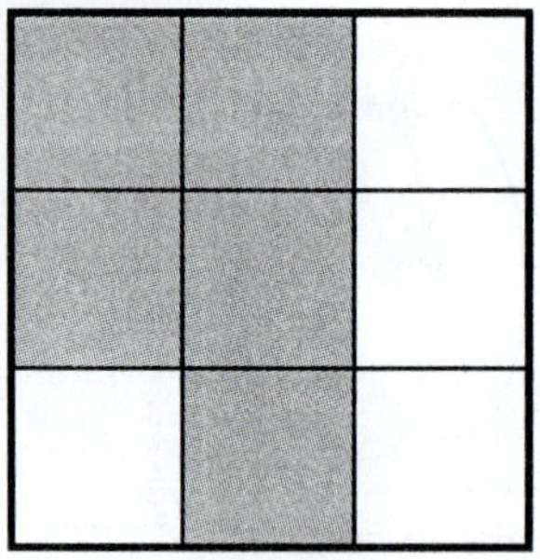

____ + ____ = 5

2

Spot Check

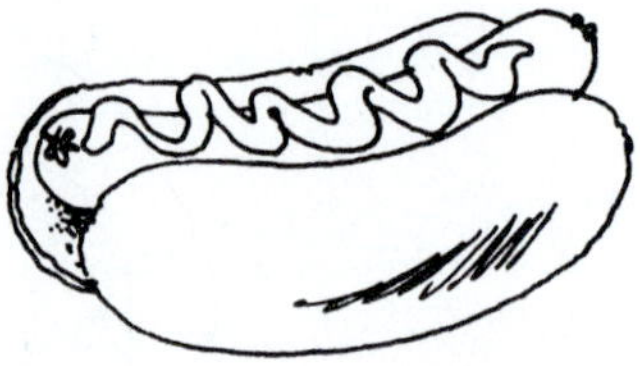

Possible answer is shown. Accept any that children can justify.

Turtle: Children look at the shading on the grid and write a number sentence with a sum of 5. **Frog:** Children circle the domino that has more dots. Then they write the numeral to show how many more. **Fish:** Children circle the item that they can buy with the coins shown. **Spot Check:** Children circle the food that takes the most time to eat and draw an X on the food that takes the least time to eat.

Name ______________________________

Numeral Writing

Children color in the dot in the domino half and write the numbers.

Numeral Writing

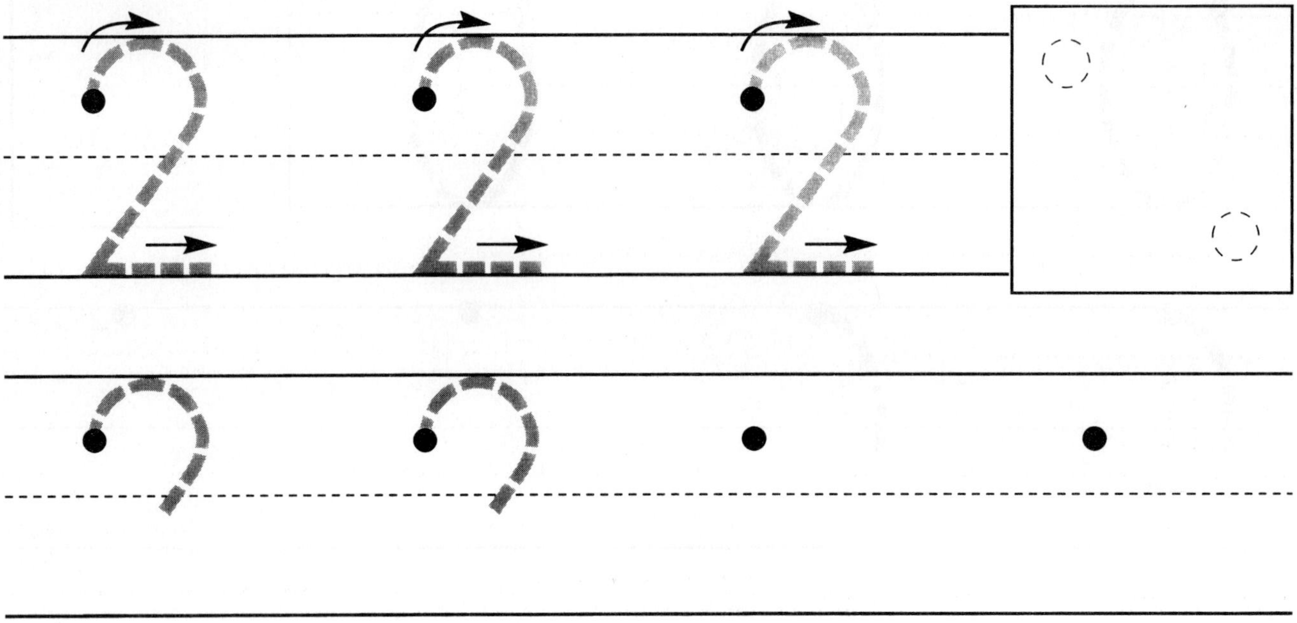

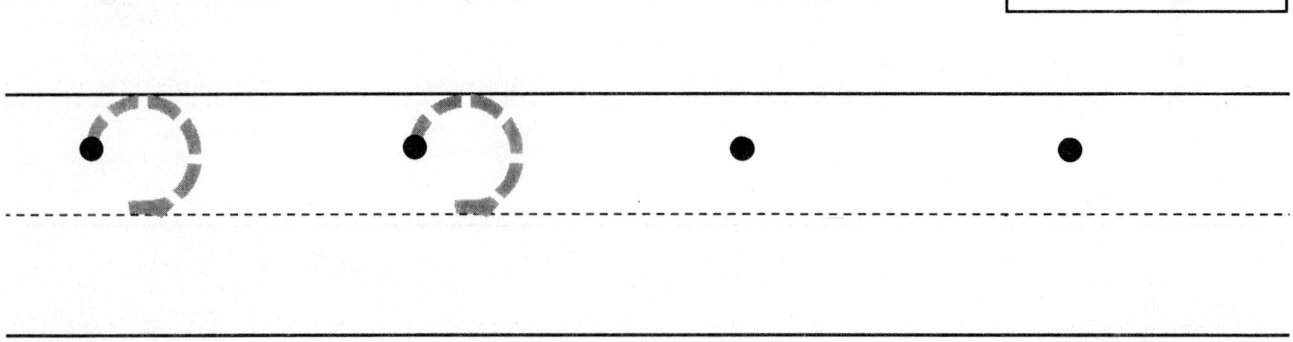

Children color in the dots in the domino halves and write the numbers.

Name ______________________________

Numeral Writing

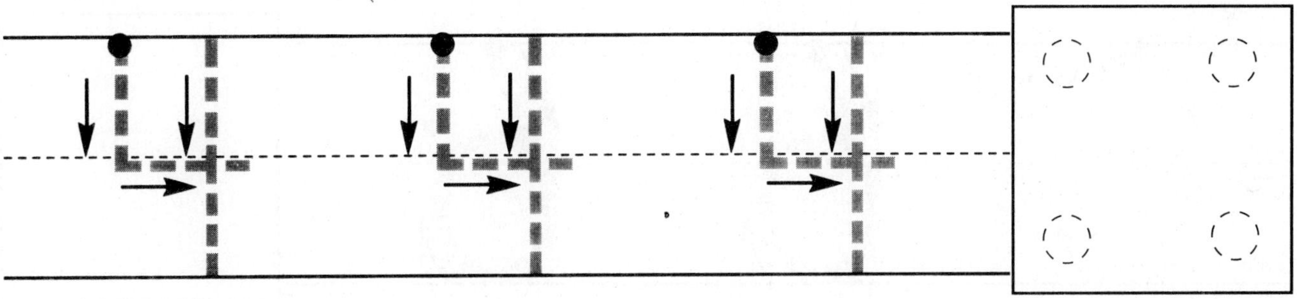

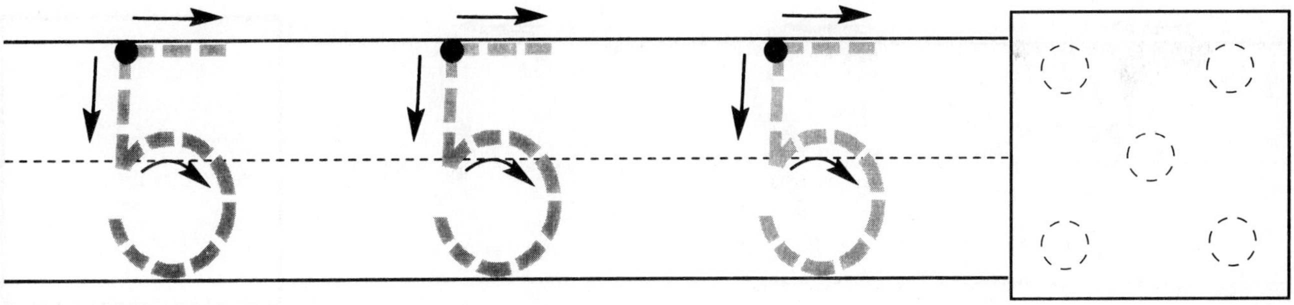

Children color in the dots in the domino halves and write the numbers.

Numeral Writing

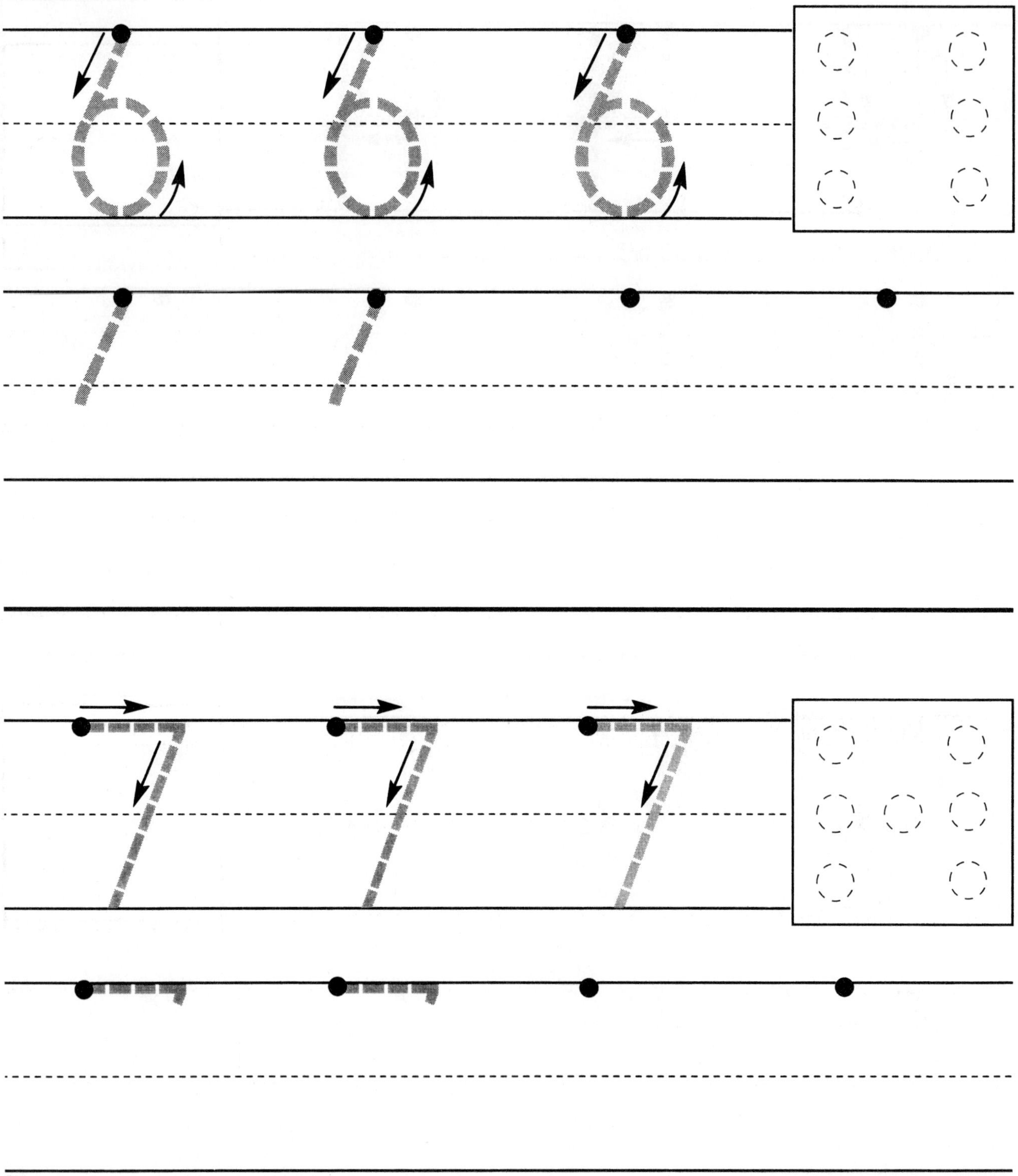

Children color in the dots in the domino halves and write the numbers.

Name ________________________________

Numeral Writing

8 8 8

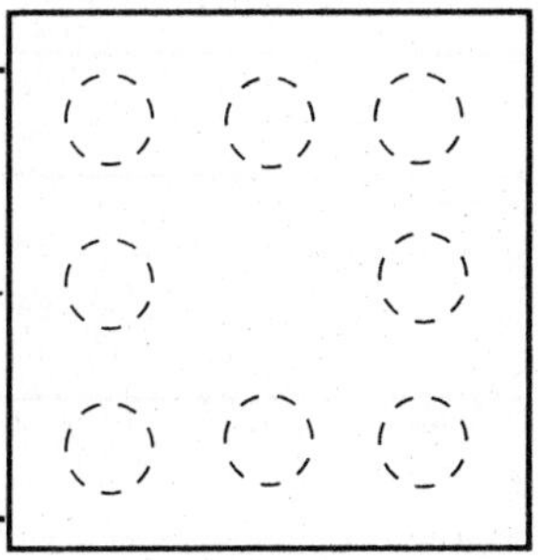

9 9 9

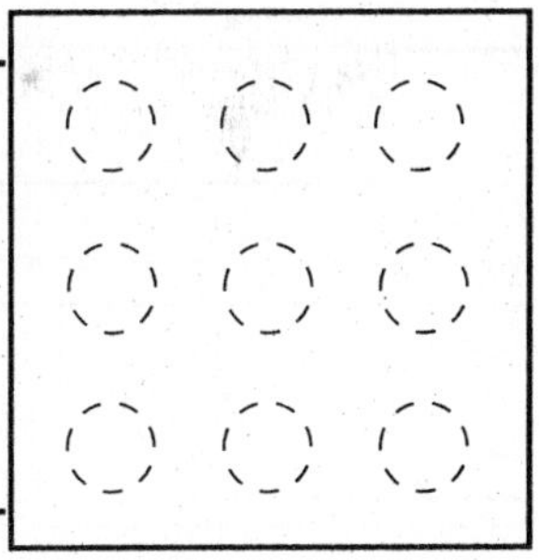

Children color in the dots in the domino halves and write the numbers.